Sovereign States
in an Age of
Uncertainty

Edited by RONALD HOFFMAN
and PETER J. ALBERT

Published for the

UNITED STATES CAPITOL HISTORICAL SOCIETY

BY THE UNIVERSITY PRESS OF VIRGINIA

Charlottesville

THE UNIVERSITY PRESS OF VIRGINIA

Copyright © 1981 by the Rector and Visitors

of the University of Virginia

First published 1981

Library of Congress Cataloging in Publication Data
Main entry under title:

Sovereign states in an age of uncertainty.

   (Perspectives on the American Revolution)
   Includes index
   1. United States—Politics and government—Revolution, 1775–1783—Addresses, essays, lectures. 2. United States—Politics and government—1783–1789—Addresses, essays, lectures.
I. Hoffman, Ronald, 1941–. II. Albert, Peter J. III. Series. E210.S75 973. 3
81–19660 ISBN 0–8139–0926–0 AACR2

Printed in the United States of America

MERRILL JENSEN (1905–1980)
Do not go gentle into that good night

Contents

SOVEREIGN STATES

Preface

THE EXPERIENCES OF the sovereign states during the years of the Revolutionary War and its immediate aftermath form the central focus of this volume. It is a subject about which our knowledge is limited. There are only two comprehensive treatments of the states during this period. Allen Nevins's *The American States during and after the American Revolution,* while now outdated by subsequent research and largely devoted to political developments after 1783, still remains the only broadly conceived study of the entire era from the perspective of the states. Jackson Turner Main's *The Sovereign States* ambitiously seeks to reconstruct the political, social, and economic history of the states for the war years, 1775–83. Soon after commencing his research for this volume, Main discovered that the task he had set for himself was more formidable than he had anticipated. While the number of state studies for the years immediately preceding the Constitutional Convention of 1787 were few, those for the war years were even scarcer. Most of the scholarly work on the war years had invariably centered on national history, primarily on the clash of contending armies or on the operation of the Continental Congress, and had paid only slight attention to the states. Similarly, most of the specialized investigations of the period—many of them in dissertation form—had provided only a partial understanding wherein the gaps in knowledge loomed far larger than the accumulated information. "I have tried," Main wrote with admirable candor, "to plug with temporary fillings," but he cautioned that "anyone trying to develop a general understanding of the period must read the original sources. These are voluminous enough to occupy teams of scholars, and I have only rifled their pages."

Two factors account for this lack of attention to the states between 1775 and 1787. The first one is obvious—most historians, because of their interest in determining the relationship between causes and consequences, have focused on the Revolution as the consequence for which the events of the years 1763–76 provide a precise and attractive problem of causality. The second factor, which is somewhat less apparent, speaks directly to our relatively substantial knowledge of what happened during the pre-Revolutionary years within the colonies. As of the 1760s, the thirteen mainland colonies were a mosaic of commonality and diversity. Pre-Revolutionary Americans shared a common language, heritage, and many general cultural values, but at the same time they were distinctively shaped by the nature of their particular provincial existences. The coming of the Revolution amidst this sort of diversity provided important reference points for establishing a common framework through the progressive unfolding of events. The litany of these years is familiar—the Sugar Act, the Currency Act, the Stamp Act, the Townshend Acts, the Boston Massacre, the Tea Party, the Intolerable Acts, and so on. But if the sequence is well known and has been depicted by historians literally hundreds of times, this has always been done on the tacit assumption that its dimensions could be properly understood only through direct reference to a specific colony and through the accumulation of detailed information about that particular locality. A thorough understanding of the Stamp Act, for example, requires imposing a comparative developmental order that traces the influence of the tax in each of the affected colonies. The same process is necessary for comprehending virtually all of the events before 1774, if not 1776.

In contrast, the prevalent assumption among historians has been that the provincial differences that played important causal roles before the Revolution became either marginal or less significant after the calling of the First and Second Continental congresses. The history of the Revolution after 1776 is portrayed, in most historical accounts, as national in character—a test of wills, first between national institutions, Congress and Parliament, and, later, between national armies. Some aspects of the states' particular experiences during this period—such as the writing of the state constitutions and the influence of various provincial legislative bodies on Congress in the years immediately preceeding

Independence—have been studied systematically, but even here only the beginning of a comprehensive synthesis has been made. More attention has been directed toward developments within the states as they affected the convening of the Constitutional Convention and the struggle over ratification. But here again the focus has been primarily outward toward the interaction between state and national politics rather than on the interior experiences of the states.

This volume begins appropriately with an essay by Jackson Turner Main that studies the Revolution from a state or local perspective, rather than from a national one. He focuses on the important accomplishments of the American people acting through the sovereign states during the Revolutionary period, and explores the impact of these accomplishments in such areas as military affairs, economic activity, social change, cultural development, and political innovation. His study effectively challenges the assumption that the contributions of the people and the local governments to the Revolutionary effort diminished significantly after 1776, leaving the burden to be carried primarily by national leaders and national institutions.

The next three essays deal with dimensions of the struggle for political control in Massachusetts, South Carolina, and Pennsylvania during the Revolutionary era. Stephen E. Patterson explores the changing character of Massachusetts politics after Independence, analyzing the roots and the development of partisan divisions, and the emergence of new leaders who were less committed than their predecessors to a tradition of political consensus. He contrasts the members of the nascent Federalist party, men united by class, interest, and education, political pragmatists who advocated toleration of diversity within a pluralistic community, with their opponents who espoused a traditional, corporate, homogeneous democracy. Their program during the 1780s, he argues, demonstrated the use of untraditional, modern means to achieve conservative ends. Jerome J. Nadelhaft studies the redistribution of political power that occurred in South Carolina. There the dominance exercised during the pre-Revolutionary period by a small, wealthy, geographically concentrated lowcountry elite was gradually eroded during and after the Revolution by the political awakening of underrepresented groups, such as Charleston dissidents, backcountry settlers, and inhabitants of lowcountry parishes outside the Charleston District. The culmination of this shift came with the new constitution of 1790, which increased the representation in the assembly of the backcountry and the lowcountry outside Charleston and provided for the movement of the state's capital to a more central location. Richard Alan Ryerson analyzes the membership, ideology, program, and accomplishments of Pennsylvania's Constitutionalist party. He maintains that in the decades before the Revolution the Constitutionalists had been outsiders, politically, economically, and socially. This background distorted their perception of the nature of their society and the role of government within it. Consequently, despite the fact that the Pennsylvania Constitution of 1776 provided for a durable, workable government and enjoyed widespread support in the state, the Constitutionalists were doomed by their inability to deal effectively with conflicting interests and factional disputes.

The essays of Edward C. Papenfuse and Edward Countryman explore political factionalism during the Revolution, particularly in the context of the state legislatures. Papenfuse discusses the problem of dealing with the economic impact of the Revolution in Maryland in an assembly dominated by shifting coalitions and temporary alliances among numerous factions. His perspective is twofold. First he examines the career of Daniel of St. Thomas Jenifer as the state's intendant of revenue, a man who represented the vanguard of nationalist sentiment in Maryland; then he focuses on Charles Ridgely, a factional leader in the assembly who stood for parochial interests, reduced spending, and less government, arguing that Jenifer's efforts to pursue a sound financial policy were undercut by the factional nature of the state's political system. Countryman discusses the exercise of power in the lower house of the New York legislature during the Revolutionary era. Like Papenfuse, he finds no evidence of a polarization into majority and minority parties but, rather, a fragmentation into shifting coalitions that reflected little continuity from issue to issue. Indeed, legislators sought to prevent the concentration of power among themselves and to forestall the creation of an internal elite. Although some members were more influential than others, this was not signified by tenure within a stable committee system. Countryman focuses on one influential member, Egbert Benson, who had a hand in shaping much of the legislation passed between 1777 and 1781; he demonstrates that Benson's involvement in the passage of radical legislation stood in sharp contrast to his conservative personal views.

In contrast to Papenfuse and Countryman, Emory G. Evans deals with the executive branch of a state government in the Revolutionary period—that of Virginia. Specifically, he studies the executive's role in such matters as shaping military strategy and directing military operations, raising troops for the Continental army, obtaining supplies such as foodstuffs, equipment, and clothing, and dealing with discontent and disaffection within the state. Virginia's executive was constitutionally weak, adequate for peacetime but not for a wartime situation. Evans concludes, however, that despite their limited powers Virginia's three wartime governors, Patrick Henry, Thomas Jefferson, and Thomas Nelson, did a commendable job.

In the volume's concluding essay Merrill Jensen examines the rivalries among the states and regions of the new nation and evaluates their impact on the Constitutional Convention of 1787. Conflicting sectional interests were of fundamental importance, he maintains, and transcended state loyalties and local stereotypes. Rivalry between northern and southern states underlay conflicts at the Convention over such major issues as representation, the regulation of commerce, the slave trade, and the settlement and eventual absorption of new states into the union.

Shortly after completing his contribution to this volume, Merrill Jensen died. As it was the distinct privilege of both of the editors to have been his students, they feel highly honored to have edited his last essay. The conception of the conference that produced this collection was his, for throughout his monumental academic career, Jensen maintained that the history of the years 1763–89 could be properly understood only through a comprehension of the experiences of the "sovereign states." Thus, it is especially fitting that, in grateful acknowledgment of the debt that all of us who seek to interpret the American past owe to his scholarship, we dedicate this book to Merrill Jensen.

SOVEREIGN STATES

in an Age of Uncertainty

JACKSON TURNER MAIN

The American States in the Revolutionary Era

THE AMERICAN STATES during the Revolutionary era have suffered from a bad press. Some calamity seems to have struck them down about the time of the First Continental Congress. Before, the gallant assemblies fought governors to a standstill, challenged the Crown, and boldly demanded liberty. Afterwards, so it appears, the legislatures frustrated Congress and argued with one another, the war governors proved inefficient mediocrities, and the militia ran away. In their stead we enshrine Congress and the Continental army. Fortunately for our cause and despite the states' abysmal failure to provide money, supplies, and men, Congress and its army won the war. In this second American Revolution, power and glory shifted from the sovereign states to the United States. Or so they say.[1]

So too our attention turns from the common folk and their spokesmen to the great men. Before 1776 the citizens of Lexington, Newport, Annapolis, and Greenwich defied the British army, navy, stamp collectors, and laws. From their ranks arose such folk heroes as Samuel Adams, Patrick Henry, Samuel Chase, and Alexander McDougall. After Independence, a new pantheon of heroes dominated while the older men shrank and became mere obstructionists. George Washington, John Jay, Robert Morris, and Alexander Hamilton

[1] The best scholarly treatment of the new central government is Edmund Cody Burnett's *The Continental Congress* (New York, 1941). E. James Ferguson, *The American Revolution* (Homewood, Ill., 1974), surveys the whole period 1763–90, as does Edmund S. Morgan's *The Birth of the Republic, 1763–1789* (Chicago, 1956).

1

became the prime movers, the saviors of their new nation. Or so they say.[2]

Why did this interpretation arise and dominate? There are a number of reasons. First, people tend to attribute historical causation to particular individuals, whether talented, powerful, blessed, or lucky. One focuses on the most conspicuous heroes and villains, the prominent men, sometimes without investigating whether they or less visible persons actually moved earth and heaven or whether indeed they moved anything at all. These leaders appear of course not in the villages and farms, not in state legislatures or their militia units, but in Congress and its army. We are no longer concerned with George Clinton, Jonathan Trumbull, or William Livingston, and we never were concerned with a Nathan Beeman or an Obadiah Horsford.[3]

Second, historians celebrate the creation of a strong central government with its accompanying national economy, a single great society molded in the melting pot, an American civilization, all ratified by wars and the welfare state. The whole course of our history seems to approve such a transformation and to condemn any opposition to it. Most writers side with the Federalists on this interpretation no matter what their own politics, while they disapprove of all contrary

[2] This point of view is reflected in Allan Nevins, *The American States during and after the Revolution, 1775–1789* (New York, 1924), Richard B. Morris, *The American Revolution Reconsidered* (New York, 1967), and Forrest McDonald, *E Pluribus Unum: The Formation of the American Republic. 1776–1790* (Boston, 1965).

[3] Trumbull, who died in 1785, had little influence outside Connecticut. He still lacks a full-scale biography, for Glenn Weaver's *Jonathan Trumbull, Connecticut's Merchant Magistrate, 1710–1785* (Hartford, 1956), focuses on his economic activities. Clinton became vice-president but his opposition to the Constitution turned most of the state's influential upper class against him; he has remained a minor figure, his only biography brief and now dated (E. Wilder Spaulding, *His Excellency, George Clinton* [New York, 1938]). William Livingston, New Jersey's capable war governor, deserves a modern, full-scale biography.

Nathan Beeman was the boy who piloted Ethan Allan into Fort Ticonderoga. He died in Malone, New York. Col. Obadiah Horsford (1725–83) lived in Hebron, Connecticut.

acts, such as the Hartford Convention. A majority vote goes to Jackson on the Nullification controversy, to Lincoln on the Civil War, and, without venturing much farther, to the advocates of federal regulation of railroads and the authority of the Supreme Court. Opponents of this trend appear in the literature as men of little faith, petty minded, at best provincial, at worst faintly traitorous.[4]

Third, the nature of the historical source material thrusts the researcher strongly in the same direction. Among public records, until recently our libraries rarely contained the proceedings of state legislatures, and even now one can trace only with difficulty the activities of the governors and their officials.[5] Newspapers were scattered, and broadsides, legislative petitions, and other local records existed only in particular archives. In contrast the journals of Congress have long been available in lovely, big, published volumes.[6] Similarly, almost all printed writings are those of the principal generals and politicians, men operating on the national, not the local scene. George Clinton's papers and those of Patrick Henry and Samuel Adams are the major exceptions, but the two last thin out after 1776. The first volumes of the Trumbull and Livingston papers have yet to appear. On the other hand we have long possessed the works of George Washington, Thomas Jefferson, John Adams, Alexander Hamilton, James Madison, and John Jay, to mention only the principal figures, supplemented by the magnificent Burnett's *Letters* which made available the correspondence of the members of

[4]The phrase "men of little faith" comes from an influential article by Cecelia Kenyon in the *William and Mary Quarterly*, 3d ser. 20 (1963): 223–45.

[5]Many state archives end in 1776 or remain unpublished. Even the legislative proceedings of such important states as Massachusetts and South Carolina are in manuscript. Until after World War II only a few newspapers had been microfilmed, and those which reflected a popular point of view were unavailable until very recently.

[6]Worthington C. Ford, ed., *Journals of the Continental Congress, 1774–1789*, 34 vols. (Washington, D.C., 1904–37); Edmund Cody Burnett, ed., *Letters of Members of the Continental Congress*, 8 vols. (Washington, D.C., 1921–36).

Congress.[7] From these we learn vividly of the struggles to achieve Independence and to overcome endless obstacles, a courageous enterprise in which the state governments and the people at large seem recalcitrant, even hostile. The points of view of Congress and the army finally become our own. This same bias pervades the sources through the entire period of the Confederation both because the principal leaders are usually literate and because their writings are preserved. They help to create and confirm the dominant interpretation which we have outlined.

This interpretation has not gone without critics, and in recent years enough historians have challenged it to make possible, not a refutation, but an extensive modification.[8] Specifically, we are reassessing the contribution of the state governments and the people as opposed to Congress and the great men, together with the significance of the Revolution for ordinary folk. This new approach reflects both the nature of our own bias, the current climate of opinion, and changes in sources and methods.

We are not so sure, nowadays, that centralization is a blessing. The rise of the nation-states, which once seemed so advantageous, now threatens human survival. When those men of the 1770s and 1780s warned that standing armies and taxes, even their very own armies and taxes, were dangerous to liberty, we say "Amen." It is not just a matter of foreign tyrannies, the number of which seems to increase as fast as the creation of new countries, but a reexamination of our own past and present. We are less inclined to celebrate victories over the Indians and Mexicans, we deplore the use of force to maintain slavery and great class distinctions, we wonder whether the forcible preservation of the Union was an unmixed blessing, we doubt the ethics of our military interventions overseas. Moreover, we question whether the trend

---

[7] Typically, Burnett omitted passages that did not pertain to Congressional affairs. A new, greatly enlarged collection edited by Paul Smith will include everything.

[8] Writers of the Progressive school had begun before 1900 to stress the significance of social, economic, and environmental forces upon politics, and they also tended to sympathize with the "common man."

toward centralization in other forms—economic, social, cultural, or ethnic—should be encouraged or reversed. Perhaps the people who loved the locality more than the nation were at least partly right.

At the same time many historians are expressing an affection and admiration for the common people. This influences our interpretation of history in several ways. We become interested in the events that affected people's lives, including not only wars and other political calamities but also many economic, social, ideological, and cultural forces. From this point of view the American Revolution becomes not just a war for home rule and for who would rule at home but an epoch, and in estimating the accomplishments of the states and their people we must pursue a wide range of topics, many of which never came before Congress.[9]

With the people now the center of attention, the historian is inclined to reevaluate the contribution of the great men and the institutions they controlled—Congress and the Continental army. This shift reflects in part the old familiar debate over the relative influence of men versus socioeconomic forces, but it is more than that. We ask, to what extent did victory flow from the generals or the people? Did Independence and Revolution occur solely because of certain leaders? Or should we consider the leaders more as the agents of the majority than as a prior and independent force? What were the consequences of the Revolution for ordinary folk? Did the ideas and the values and the wealth and the principal changes of the era come from the top or swell up from the commonalty? One need not deny or disparage the Founding Fathers, but neither may we forget that many thousands of fathers—and mothers—helped with the founding.

In studying these thousands, historians can now use

[9]The passage about home rule comes from Carl Lotus Becker's *The History of Political Parties in the Province of New York, 1760–1776* (Madison, 1909). Interest in the lower class is best represented by Jesse Lemisch, "The American Revolution Seen from the Bottom Up," in Barton J. Bernstein, ed., *Towards a New Past* (New York, 1968). Articles on practically everybody except the leaders are printed in Alfred F. Young, ed., *The American Revolution: Explorations in the History of American Radicalism* (DeKalb, Ill., 1976).

sources and methods unavailable to their predecessors. If we wish to discover the activities of state governments and private citizens, any good library contains or can secure a variety of documents in microform.[10] It remains more difficult to trace the ideas of a Concord farmer or a Boston partisan than those of a Thomas Hutchinson or a John Adams, but newspapers, manuscript collections, and local records make it possible.[11] The problems of research for that kind of enterprise remain immense, despite or perhaps because of a technological revolution, but historians have been tackling them vigorously. The first results are now at hand, and we can sketch a new story. Without denying the influence of the Continental Congress, its officials, army, or officers, let us outline by way of corrective the contributions of the people acting through their sovereign states in the new nation.[12] These are evident in many ways, among them military affairs, economic activities, social changes, cultural developments, and political innovations.

[10] Anything other than periodicals published during the period is now available on microprint in the American Antiquarian Society's series *Early American Imprints, 1639–1800*; the legislative journals and the laws are contained in the microfilm *Records of the States of the United States of America* (Washington, D.C., 1949). The records contained in this edition are listed in William Sumner Jenkins and Lillian A. Hamrick, eds., *A Guide to the Microfilm Collection of Early State Records* (Washington, D.C., 1950). Any library can obtain these.

[11] See Robert A. Gross, *The Minutemen and Their World* (New York, 1976). Some sources useful for research on the ordinary folk are in microform, an old guide to which is now being replaced (Richard W. Hale, Jr., ed., *Guide to Photocopied Historical Materials in the United States and Canada* [Ithaca, N.Y., 1961]). The Library of Congress catalog *Newspapers in Microform* is periodically reprinted to include revisions. Virtually all the periodicals of the Revolutionary era, and most of those to 1820, are in microform. Microfilms of the papers of prominent men often contain letters from a great variety of citizens. For example, completed or in process are the papers of the Adamses, Henry Knox, Rufus King, Jonathan Trumbull, Robert Morris, Tench Coxe, the Virginia Lees, Washington, Madison, Jefferson, Franklin, Charles Carroll of Carrollton, Henry Laurens, and William Livingston.

[12] The final phrases come from my *Sovereign States, 1775–1783* (New York, 1973) and Merrill Jensen, *The New Nation: A History of the United States during the Confederation, 1781–1789* (New York, 1950).

Men who led the Continental army ended with a widely shared though not quite unanimous conviction that the army won the war and that the militia units could not defend the country.[13] There existed, however, a contrary view, popular among most civilians and heard occasionally since, that the people had defeated the British regulars and that the best defense of liberty rested with an armed and virtuous citizenry. The debate depended upon one's prejudices, because it involved the insoluble question "what if?" The observation that without the Continental Line the rebels would have failed, is on a par with the assertion that French aid was necessary, or that victory depended upon British blunders, or the Marblehead mariners, and so on down to the proverbial nail for the last horseshoe. Of course they all helped. Each state inherited a militia system, in which the able-bodied men of the communities, under officers from their own neighborhoods, sometimes even chosen by the men themselves, fought when danger threatened. The militia consisted primarily of the respectable—married men, farmers, and craftsmen—whom the community could not spare for any length of time and whose lives had particular value. It provided a large reservoir of part-time soldiers whose training and armaments varied greatly, better in the recently settled areas where they still had to prepare for fighting, worse where danger had ended. They were available in emergencies and they could fight well if they chose. They possessed certain qualities that did not endear them to the officers, who especially in the South came from the upper class. They preferred independence to discipline and they resented taking orders, even New Englanders, who apparently kept forgetting that they belonged to a deferential society in peaceable kingdoms.[14] They liked to fire from a safe place, or if they

---

[13] Richard Kohn, *Eagle and Sword: The Federalists and the Creation of the Military Establishment in America, 1783–1802* (New York, 1975), contains a discussion of this point of view.

[14] The reference is to Michael Zuckerman's *Peaceable Kingdoms: New England Towns in the Eighteenth Century* (New York, 1970). Many historians find New Englanders cooperative and deferential during the seventeenth century; such men make obedient soldiers. Zuckerman has them remaining so, where other scholars perceive a change toward individualism and

had to start close to the enemy they would fire and run to safety where they could reload without being bayonetted. And they wanted to return home as soon as the battle ended.

By contrast, the soldiers of the Continental army were the community's expendables—young, single, poor, unskilled, often undesired. They had to be whipped into shape and disciplined strictly, but once trained they furnished a comparatively permanent and reliable fighting force. Washington and his generals complained of the militia at once, and tried to incorporate them into the regular army. Most military historians agree with Washington that they made inferior soldiers. Yet they provided the essential numbers. The new nation contained about 400,000 potential soldiers. If we subtract one-third for neutrals, one-sixth for loyalists, and one-sixth for maintaining order at home against the loyalists and slaves, or for other purposes, and add those who came of age between Lexington and Yorktown, the total was about 170,000—a sizable force. Remember that over 10,000 had gathered before Boston within a few days after the first shots, and there were half again as many by the time Washington arrived. The militia drove the British out of Boston; one can argue that they sealed Burgoyne's fate at Bennington and Cornwallis's at King's Mountain. To these one might add a very large number of engagements conducted under officers of the state governments, supported by the state legislatures, and fought by the states' citizenry, beginning with the capture of Ticonderoga. Privateers, the maritime equivalent of a militia, inflicted three times as much damage as did the United States Navy. Surely the war could not have been won without the Continentals, but surely it could not have

---

hostility toward authority, best presented in Richard L. Bushman, *From Puritan to Yankee: Character and the Social Order in Connecticut, 1690–1765* (Cambridge, Mass., 1967). There seems to have been considerable individualism even in the earlier period, especially in the trading towns and in areas geographically removed from the centers of Puritan strength. See Darrett Rutman, *Winthrop's Boston: Portrait of a Puritan Town, 1630–1649* (Chapel Hill, 1965), and Charles E. Clark, *The Eastern Frontier: The Settlement of Northern New England, 1610–1763* (New York, 1970). Probably Bushman's interpretation will stand up if we acknowledge more of the Yankee at first, and an uneven rate of change.

been won without the militia either. Events of our own times confirm the idea that a people numerous and armed can win wars.[15]

Winning wars requires not only men but food, clothing, blankets, transportation, weapons, and pay. We think of this as demanding a great deal of money, but in fact it might need none at all. The Indians got by without it. A people determined to fight can raise their own food, make clothing, haul supplies, even produce weapons though with increasing difficulty as technology advances, and reward the fighters in various ways, for example by granting land; medieval rulers did this and so had the colonials. Matters were not so simple in 1776. The people did produce the needed food, clothing, shelter, and transportation, but except for militia operating locally, all cost money. Guns required repair and replacement, and the governments had to buy powder, shot, and artillery. Soldiers and civilian officials wanted pay. Some states could and eventually did discharge this obligation by means of land grants, but nowhere could that be done at once, and often it could not be done at all.[16] From the first we find the local committees of observation requiring money, and throughout the war the governments had to buy most of the goods and services. The exceptions occurred in purely local militia engagements, as at King's Mountain.

One might think that in theory the governments could levy taxes equal to their expenditures, recovering at the end of each year the amount spent for the campaign. Several circumstances prevented them from even attempting to balance their budgets in this way. First, some purchases had to be

[15] See John Shy, *A People Numerous and Armed* (New York, 1976), and the essay by Don Higginbotham in the collection he edited, *Reconsiderations on the Revolutionary War: Selected Essays* (Westport, Conn., 1978), pp. 83–103. Biographies of the generals often defend their particular subjects at the expense of all the others, and one might easily conclude that the rebel soldiers won despite the blunders of their leaders.

[16] The states did not pay their men directly in land but instead handed out IOUs that the governments accepted after 1783 in payment for vacant land. Georgia, North Carolina, Virginia, Pennsylvania, and New York possessed large tracts. Other states could not anticipate such a resource though some of them later obtained sections in the West.

made overseas. Second, a considerable proportion of the population opposed the war or were indifferent toward it and easily might have been alienated. The governments did not dare to impose taxes much beyond the customary level, if at all.[17] Third, even the patriots resisted any exceptional economic burden. Among the liberties they fought for was that of property, and they certainly did not want to replace the British government with another of the same sort. Hard money had always been scarce and was generally concentrated in the hands of a few men, many of whom had now fled. State treasuries rarely contained a surplus of any kinds of monies. For example, Virginia's leaders had the political power to collect taxes but little hard money because the principal currency before 1775 consisted of paper certificates entitling the possessor to tobacco ready for export, together with IOUs issued by the government. Therefore deficit financing was unavoidable. Finally, most of the colonies underwent a transition period during which extralegal governments lacked the administrative machinery to collect money in the usual way, so that by the time an effective legislature met, it already confronted quite a debt, originating both from provincial expenditures and the Continental Congress's requisitions. Starting in this way with a deficit, forced to spend large sums before any taxes could be collected, prevented even from attempting to impose taxes equal to the expenditures, and then unable to collect what they did impose without unthinkable compulsion, the states had no choice but to borrow.

Borrowing did include loans of specie, but for the most part the states paid the costs of war by promissory notes, presumably to be redeemed when taxes brought in coin. The people were familiar with this policy, having adopted it dur-

---

[17] Loyalists included one-sixth to one-fifth of the people. See Paul H. Smith, "The American Loyalists: Notes on Their Organization and Numerical Strength," *William and Mary Quarterly*, 3d ser. 25 (1968): 259–77. In a few states the people were enthusiastic enough about the war that the governments could levy taxes without fear of alienating a significant number. That was true in New England. As a rule, however, the rebels scarcely formed a majority, and in Delaware they were outnumbered by those indifferent to the whole business.

ing past wars and even in times of peace. Confronted with a sudden need for large sums, without banks from which to borrow, with little money of any sort anywhere and certainly none in the "treasury" (generally a solid wooden chest), the government would print "tax anticipation warrants," paper notes of various denominations, and use them to buy supplies, pay wages, and meet other costs. At the same time the legislature would levy a tax of the same amount, to be collected presently. The holders of the notes would eventually take them to the treasury and receive payment in gold and silver coin. The prospect of such payment persuaded people to accept the notes as though they were indeed coins.

The solution worked well so long as the government could collect the promised taxes and did not print more notes than the colony's credit would support. Otherwise people refused to accept the notes except at a discount. In colonial South Carolina the paper certificates fell to one-seventh of their value before the government limited the quantity. In New England the legislatures ran into debt beginning with Queen Anne's War early in the eighteenth century and continued to finance military and other expenditures with paper issues until the money sank to one-tenth its original value or even less. At that point the British government abruptly prohibited the practice. During the French and Indian War the colonies borrowed in the same way, and the royal governors pragmatically consented. The Currency Act of 1764 forbade any colony from requiring people to accept such money, which effectively limited the quantity.[18]

The practice had already come under attack by hard money advocates, and their point of view came to dominate historical writing until recently. The depreciation of Revolutionary paper issues and such later events as the collapse of the Confederate dollar and of the German mark after the First World War seemed to demonstrate the evil consequences of paper money, while the inflationary demands of the Populists, Bryan Democrats, and some New Deal sup-

---

[18] The best account is in E. James Ferguson, *The Power of the Purse: A History of American Public Finance, 1776–1790* (Chapel Hill, 1961).

porters appeared to prove the evil intent of its advocates. Historians accordingly attacked the Revolutionary state governments for inefficiency, ignorance of economics, and moral turpitude. These attacks are entirely unjust. The policy had worked before 1776 and would have succeeded despite the difficulties already noted had the war lasted five years instead of more than six. The Second World War and later events showed that deficit financing actually works well and even has its advantages.

Probably a majority of people continued to support that policy even after a runaway inflation began in 1779. They did not want to pay high taxes but hoped to spread the cost of the war over a long period of years. They advocated strict price controls, government regulation of monopolistic activities, laws requiring everyone to accept the paper money, and the confiscation of loyalist and British-owned property to help pay for the war. Most of the leaders, however, and almost all men of property recommended a contrary course. They would abandon paper money. Congress and the states would attract loans from individuals by offering good rates of interest, obtaining money for the interest by substantial taxes paid in gold and silver. The return to a specie basis would at once reduce prices to their prewar level, thus lowering the cost of war proportionately. Prices would continue to float freely. A free market system would replace price regulation. The policy favored entrepreneurs and people with specie to lend, and it also tended to transfer fiscal authority to Congress, whereas the alternative continued economic control in the states. The debate thus involved not only the question of who would benefit or suffer financially but the location of power—the familiar power of the purse. Since the previous policy was failing, the advocates of change won during the winter of 1780–81, less than a year before Yorktown. The rest of the war was paid for by a combination of taxes contributed by the people generally, loans received from those with money, additional promissory notes, and timely specie from France.[19]

[19] Ferguson provides the details about the federal debt in *The Power of the Purse*. For state activities see my *Sovereign States*, ch. 7. Most books on

The Continental Congress paid more than half the cost of the war, mostly derived from loans. But the state governments spent ten million pounds collected in taxes and another ten million acquired by borrowing. After the war, most legislatures began to retire their own debts and started in on the federal debt as well, so that with the return of prosperity the whole sum might have been discharged by the states themselves had the federal government not assumed it. The record was not a failure. Contemporaries complained quite properly of inefficiency, dishonesty, and a general reluctance to pay the price of liberty. These are qualities not unknown today, which members of the Continental Congress and their agents shared equally with state legislatures and the citizenry. But together they financed an immensely expensive war and ended with a debt amply secured by the value of land.[20]

The abnormal character of the period prevents any simple statement about other economic accomplishments or failures. For our purposes the important point is that we must look less at nationwide and more to local activities. A century would pass before a truly national economy emerged. Robert Morris's Bank of North America, after all, served little outside Philadelphia and very few business concerns extended much beyond state lines.[21] An occasional entrepreneur operated extensively and these large enterprises are striking, but that had always been true: Richard Lord of Hartford, when he died in 1662, had debtors in Newfoundland, Massachusetts, New York, the Delaware region, Virginia, Barba-

---

finance concentrate on Congress's problems and adopt the Congressional, hard-money view. An exception is James R. Morrill, *The Practice and Politics of Fiat Finance: North Carolina in the Confederation, 1783–1789* (Chapel Hill, 1969).

[20] Ohio alone contained over 26 million acres which at 6 shillings an acre would bring in over £7 million. Georgia, North Carolina, Virginia, New York, and Pennsylvania had enough vacant land to take care of their own obligations and their share of the federal debt as well.

[21] Clarence L. Ver Steeg, *Robert Morris, Revolutionary Financier* (Philadelphia, 1954); Robert A. East, *Business Enterprise in the American Revolutionary Era* (New York, 1938). Curtis P. Nettels stresses the wide range of entrepreneurial activities in *The Emergence of a National Economy, 1775–1815* (New York, 1962).

dos, and England.[22] That remained unusual, and even the Continental quartermasters operated through a network of individuals, each responsible for a limited area. The inter-colonial postal service had originated before the Revolution, and Congress did not improve upon it nor upon transportation facilities, which still depended upon local initiative. Congress did encourage manufacturing, but there, too, state governments provided most of the public aid, such as it was. Control over monetary policy remained decentralized since no restrictions replaced England's Currency Act; even the later Bank of the United States did not succeed in nationalizing the banking system. Business companies of all sorts were almost as local as the coopers' shops and the farms. In short, the Revolution transferred control over economic affairs not from one central government to another, but from London to thirteen state capitols. It brought the triumph not of a national economy but of laissez-faire capitalism.[23]

The economic circumstances of the years between 1775 and 1789 remain unclear, primarily due to the lack of hard evidence. Without data on agricultural production, manufacturing output, internal trade, or financial profits, and with only scattered figures on overseas trade, we cannot derive a GNP or more than a vague notion of trends. Estate inventories, another major source, provide a great deal of information, but nobody has used them systematically.[24] Literary

[22] For Lord, Hartford district probate records, 2:162, Connecticut State Library, Hartford. The best study of an exceptional merchant is Stuart W. Bruchey, *Robert Oliver, Merchant of Baltimore, 1783–1819* (Baltimore, 1956). See also Robert C. Alberts, *The Golden Voyage: The Life and Times of William Bingham, 1752–1804* (Boston, 1969); James B. Hedges, *The Browns of Providence Plantations*, 2 vols. (Cambridge, Mass., 1968); Benjamin W. Labaree, *Patriots and Partisans: The Merchants of Newburyport, 1764–1815* (Cambridge, Mass., 1962); Philip L. White, *The Beekmans of New York in Politics and Commerce, 1647–1877* (New York, 1956); and Edward C. Papenfuse, *In Pursuit of Profit: The Annapolis Merchants in the Era of the American Revolution, 1763–1805* (Baltimore, 1975).

[23] Arguing for a national economy is Nettels, cited above. See also Louis M. Hacker, *The Triumph of American Capitalism* (New York, 1940).

[24] These records, for example, supply information about the price of land, private debts, and standards of living, all important for a study of economic trends.

evidence is unreliable for two reasons. Business men, whose letters have survived in considerable numbers, invariably complained no matter how much money they were making. One would think every ship that sailed was wrecked or captured. Anyone wanting to demonstrate economic doldrums can do so easily—for almost any year. Second, political bias influenced writing just as it does today: Some view with alarm as others are pointing with pride. When Benjamin Franklin bragged about Philadelphia's prosperity in the mid-1780s, he combined local patriotism with a defense, to an English friend, of the new republic; as evidence it is weak.[25] Others in the city were arguing in print that the nation faced disaster without political reform, while still others insisted that only minor changes were needed for full prosperity.

Everyone agrees that beginning in the mid-eighties the country experienced a primary postwar depression, lasting for several years, and that an economic boom did not occur until war began in Europe. Most historians have been quick to blame the form of government and the various sins of state legislatures. But if the causes for the business cycle lie in politics, nobody else has discovered it. We would have to attribute the depression of the mid-1760s to the government of George III and that of 1819 to Monroe, to proceed no farther. As variables, the type of government and the party in power seem worthless, though they may affect the timing and particular circumstances. The depression began and ended because of factors beyond the control of anyone in the United States, and the Constitution had nothing fundamental to do with the matter.

Historians identify three primary causes for the economic difficulties. First, the governments followed a deflationary fiscal policy beginning about 1780. As the war ended, the legislatures ceased spending and began to withdraw money from circulation. Meanwhile the people bought heavily from foreign countries, creating a severe currency shortage. One solution called for the governments to create more money instead of less, but most of the economic upper class opposed

[25] See Jensen, *New Nation*, pp. 248–49.

this until, a decade later, Hamilton acted to increase the money supply in such a way as to benefit them.[26]

Another solution was connected with the second factor in the depression: the decline in exports. Reversing this so as to obtain a favorable balance of trade would bring in money, help everyone producing for market, and stimulate business in the towns. The governments could do little about this situation. By the late 1780s energetic entrepreneurs were beginning to open new markets in Spanish America and the Far East, but full recovery had to wait for war in Europe.[27]

Neither the states nor Congress could combat the third cause: a depression in manufacturing. American craftsmen could not meet foreign competition because they lacked capital and cheap labor. They called for taxes on imports that would assure them a market despite their difficulties, and supported the Constitution of 1787 in the hope of getting a protective tariff; but no legislature, state or federal, regardless of constitutions, could pass an effective law because nobody else wanted it. The state legislatures could and did subsidize certain industries during wartime, but the fate of American manufacturing in general depended upon basic economic and political circumstances beyond the control of the states.

Most Americans were farmers, so the harvests and prices decided their yearly income. Neither they nor their representatives could do much about either. During the war most of them prospered unless, like producers of tobacco, rice, and indigo, they depended upon exports. Prices then declined in the mid-1780s and remained low for several years. Deflation contributed and also made it hard for the farmers to pay debts and taxes. Farmers on good land, who engaged in diversified agriculture and who had avoided debts, survived reasonably well. Those who suffered favored lower taxes, postponement of debts, and inflation, some of which

[26] Bray Hammond presents the hard-money view in *Banks and Politics in America, from the Revolution to the Civil War* (Princeton, 1957).

[27] See Gary M. Walton and James F. Shepherd, *The Economic Rise of Early America* (Cambridge, England, 1979). They show that by 1790–92, exports exceeded prewar levels but had not recovered per capita.

they obtained; but essentially they had to await a better market.

The major advance economically, which partly counteracted the depression, was the growth of population on the frontier, a remarkable migration conducted almost entirely under state auspices. It continued a movement that had speeded up after 1764 but had been restricted by the Indians and British policy.[28] Certainly over half a million people migrated, accounting for the entire increase between 1775 and 1790, and they must have improved ten million acres, thus raising the value of that land from almost nothing to ten million pounds, to which must be added the value of mills, smithies and the like, livestock, and grains. The states almost gave this land away, retiring in the process a significant part of their debt and minimizing the effects of the depression.[29]

Despite this substantial addition to the national wealth, the per capita value of the people may have diminished slightly between 1773 and 1789. If we define personal wealth as including debts receivable, the average worth did not decline because of the public debt, but we ought not so to define it. We may, however, legitimately anticipate the boom of the 1790s and consider the economy over a complete cycle of prosperity and depression. In that case the GNP seems close to normal, and the actions of the states and the people successful in preparing for the advances of the next two hundred years.[30]

[28] Jack Sosin, *The Revolutionary Frontier, 1763–1783* (New York, 1967).

[29] Reginald Horsman, *The Frontier in the Formative Years, 1783–1815* (New York, 1970); Dale Van Every, *Ark of Empire: The American Frontier, 1784–1803* (New York, 1963).

[30] Studies that find a decline compare an economy in prosperity just before the Revolution with one in depression during the mid-1780s, and are therefore invalid. Moreover they focus on the towns, where the business cycle was the most severe. Estate inventories do not seem to reveal any secular trend. It is possible that after the war the inventories became less representative, containing proportionately more large estates than earlier. My *Social Structure of Revolutionary America* (Princeton, 1965) found no change, much to everyone's surprise including mine, but it did not test for biases. Research for my *Connecticut Society in the Era of the American Revolution* (Hartford, 1977) included about 2,000 inventories, 1765–74,

Whether the state legislatures, Congress, or the people generally might have improved this record seems doubtful, especially since we today perform no better and with no more agreement over the correct policies. Most of the strong influences came from long-range trends. The new nation financed the war without disaster, and by the end of the period a vigorous western expansion combined with signs of growth in trade and agriculture heralded renewed prosperity. The new national government under the Federalists gained the credit, but at least equal praise belongs to the state legislatures and the citizenry.

The record of the states and the people with respect to social change is similarly mixed. Such movements occur gradually, often imperceptibly, seldom intentionally, and we know too little about them to distribute praise or blame. We need to establish, as an essential preliminary, the direction and degree of trends before the war. The most common current hypothesis argues for a gradually rising inequality of wealth, greater poverty, and less mobility.[31] There are some problems with this view. First, it underestimates the degree of inequality at the very beginning, for the early colonies contained some men of large property and a great number of poor settlers. Second, it concentrates on the cities and the coastal area while ignoring the interior despite the large population back from the coast. Finally, it mistakes fluctuations in the business cycle for secular trends. We are only beginning to obtain precise data, but it looks as though the distribution of wealth was not very different in 1776 from what it had been at the time of settlement, with the exception of the areas most affected by slavery, and even there the major shift took place in the early 1700s. Probably after a brief period of high mobility immediately following colonization, and again after the expansion of slavery, little change oc-

and another 2,000 during 1781–89. These showed no per capita change unless one eliminated debts, especially certificates of the public debt, in which case there was a slight decline in personal, though not in real, wealth.

[31] James A. Henretta, *The Evolution of American Society, 1700–1815* (Lexington, Mass., 1973).

curred until the very end of the colonial period. At that time the continual formation of new settlements, which had counteracted the adverse trends in the older areas (insofar as these really did occur), began to slow down especially in the North, because of the Indian presence and British policy. It is also arguable that British economic policy threatened, if it did not yet seriously impede, social and economic progress. As we have noted, restrictions on trade and the money supply limited expansion, American manufacturers could not win protection for themselves, and the granting of large tracts of land endangered the yeomanry, perhaps even the colonial-born speculators.[32]

If this interpretation is correct, then the Revolution may have saved the people from declining into a social state characteristic of England, if not Ireland, with an entrenched social and economic aristocracy created and maintained by royal authority. As to what actually did occur, rather than what might have been, a series of developments, some quite important, impelled the people in opposite directions. For these the states bore a responsibility equal to that of Congress.

First, the level, distribution, and inequality of wealth changed very little, if we allow for the business cycle. Second, two circumstances partly counteracted each other. The renewed western movement served as a safety valve, especially after the postwar depression began. Without this the other development might have been more important, namely, the creation and concentration of the public debt. This raised the mean personal (not the real) property of the country by 5 or 10 percent, and since a relatively few persons owned most of it, the share of the top wealth-holders increased significantly in certain areas. Most of the state legislatures, however, reduced the debt either by paying it off or limiting the value of the certificates; it was the Federalists and the new Congress that maximized the debt, not the majority of the people or their assemblies.

[32] No modern book discusses satisfactorily the economic aspects and probable effects of British policy upon society. Joseph Ernst, *Money and Politics in America, 1755–1775* (Chapel Hill, 1973), traces currency policy before Independence but not its social implications for a longer period.

Third, the sale of loyalist land, if it did not democratize landholding, at least halted the growth of large landed estates. When the process resumed it would take place under American rather than British auspices.[33] Fourth, the victorious citizenry resumed the expulsion of the Indians, a process which was perhaps inevitable but now took place more rapidly. Until after 1790 we must look to the states, rather than to Congress, for a history of Indian policy.[34]

Fifth, the slavery issue was primarily a state question. Congress's decision to prohibit slavery in the Northwest Territory and its encouragement of black enlistments during the war entitle it to some credit, especially since the southern states refused to consider any modifications of the system. Indeed one consequence of the Revolution was the triumph of the southern slave owners. On the other hand northern blacks either gained their freedom at once, with or without legislative action, or began the process.[35] This represents a clear

[33] Studies of the sale of loyalist property have appeared in scattered articles. Apparently these confiscated estates were purchased not by small-property owners but by men with money or access to credit, which is hardly surprising. These assets were therefore transferred from one upper class to another. However in certain cases large tracts of land held by Britishers now belonged to Americans; some ordinary folk did buy farms; and—what nobody has studied—the speculators who picked up these estates on credit sometimes had to resell, which may very well have democratized ownership.

To settle the effect of the Revolution on the distribution of land we would have to project for some years the degree of inequality under British rule and then compare the result with what actually happened. Since the new governments did not hesitate to sell large tracts to speculators, encouraged by the acquisitive instinct of Americans, we are quite unable to predict the result of such a research project.

[34] Several good books trace our Indian policy, including Francis Paul Prucha, *American Indian Policy in the Formative Years: The Indian Trade and Intercourse Acts, 1780–1834* (Cambridge, Mass., 1962) and Bernard W. Sheehan, *Seeds of Extinction: Jeffersonian Philanthropy and the American Indian* (Chapel Hill, 1973). Pro-Indian advocates such as Francis Jennings are now assaulting vigorously, sometimes viciously, the white actions. The best general survey is Wilcomb Washburn's *The Indian in America* (New York, 1975).

[35] Arthur Zilversmit, *The First Emancipation* (Chicago, 1967); Duncan J. MacLeod, *Slavery, Race, and the American Revolution* (London, 1975).

gain, for despite some abolitionist sentiment and occasional emancipations, the number of slaves in the North had been increasing before the war. While liberty did not bring equality, it was certainly an improvement on slavery.

Sixth, the increase in black mobility that came with emancipation may have paralleled a greater social opportunity among whites. Since we have little precise information about this, either before or after the Revolution, such a statement remains tentative. During the war years a number of individuals earned money and prestige through business enterprise, sometimes moving into positions vacated by upper-class loyalists. This shows up particularly on the city tax lists. Most manufacturing enterprises boomed, and farmers producing for the armies prospered. The depression wiped out many of these gains, but a new group of entrepreneurs survived to grow rich during the 1790s, and the boom out west must have aided the farm boys. Other men rose as army officers or in the new governments. On balance, society became a little more open after 1775.[36]

Finally, the Revolution is supposed to have completed the decline of deference, a process certainly not attributable to the likes of Washington or to Congress but to the ordinary people. Now there is some doubt about the reality of the change, since the colonists had never been notably deferential, and if whatever existed was diminishing, one might trace its demise as easily to the Great Awakening or the Glorious Revolution; arguably, Independence merely ratified it. Certainly there is no doubt that the general thrust of the period was toward individualism rather than subordination, liberty instead of authority, equality and the cult of the common man rather than aristocracy. Even the rise of successful entrepreneurs contradicted the old assumptions. The people themselves ended the deferential system, but various state laws expressed associated ideas, such as those repealing primogeniture and entail, defending debtors, equalizing taxes, revising the criminal code, and protecting the rights of prisoners.[37]

[36] Or so I argue in *Social Structure*, ch. 5. I would not bet on it.

[37] Jensen, *New Nation*, ch. 6.

The governments had only limited influence on cultural change.[38] Economic, military, and political affairs required their full attention during the war years, and indeed Congress lacked authority to consider anything else. Many religious groups, particularly the pacifists and northern Anglicans, suffered. Formal education declined. Theaters closed, literature became disputatious and splenetic. After the peace, however, the people and the legislatures returned to cultural matters. This was no renaissance or even a reformation, but some activity did follow even if we consider only the proceedings of governments.

The legislatures did not try to assist or regulate art except in the case of the theater, which they were asked to license.[39] This request caused much dispute in the North, where middle-class values condemned plays—one might say that liberty did not encourage license. The theaters did finally open despite opposition that continued for many decades. Religious liberty on the other hand seemed inevitable, and actually the English had moved more rapidly toward it than had the colonists. Once the animus against pacifists and Anglicans faded, the people began to heed their own political slogans. Most of the southern state constitutions guaranteed the right to worship. New York, New Jersey, and Pennsylvania continued to maintain some bias against non-Protestants engaging in politics but otherwise tolerated dissent, and even the New England states permitted greater religious freedom.[40]

[38] Russel B. Nye, *Cultural Life in the New Nation: 1776–1840* (New York, 1960), only partly replaces Evarts B. Greene, *The Revolutionary Generation, 1763–1790* (New York, 1943).

[39] Some changes did occur in the arts, but these cannot be attributed to the ordinary folk. Thus the Classic Revival in architecture, clearly a result of the Revolution, was upper class in origin.

[40] As usual, when referring to New England, one must except Rhode Island, in this case bowing to its traditional religious freedom. On the subject in general see Sydney E. Ahlstrom, *A Religious History of the American People* (New Haven, 1972). The refusal of the Anglican church to support the Revolution damaged its successor, the Episcopalian. Quakers and other pacifists opposed the use of force. The most enthusiastic rebels were usually Congregationalists and Presbyterians, who did derive some pres-

Yankees had led the way in formal education, and with four colleges and numerous schools they could simply repair wartime damages. Elsewhere, college education had almost disappeared and public instruction lagged. With peace, people began to talk and write about the need for major improvement. This pressure came partly from men who hoped to improve their economic position through education and from men who believed that a republican form of government required an enlightened electorate. Arguments such as these led logically to a system of universal state-supported education, even at the college level. Five of the state constitutions said as much, three state legislatures created universities by law, and several other states contributed land or money to colleges. Such efforts proved premature. Money was tight and other needs more pressing. Too many wealthy people opposed donating, and too many farmers refused to pay taxes for a cause which, as it seemed, would benefit only the well-to-do city folk. Half a century or more would pass before a new effort succeeded, but the states had meanwhile established the principle of a democratic system of education.

Democratic political principles also won a partial victory. Even before Congress resolved for Independence, the people and local conventions were debating the proper form of government. The states then became the laboratories for testing theories, trying the institutions in the various forms that presently appeared in constitutions of the United States and other countries.[41]

---

tige from their position. The greatest growth, however, occurred among the Methodists and Baptists and had nothing to do with the Revolution except perhaps through an increased toleration and stronger democratic impulse. The two might have flourished anyway.

[41] The fullest presentation of whig ideology in Britain is Caroline Robbins, *The Eighteenth-Century Commonwealthman: Studies in the Transmission, Development, and Circumstance of English Liberal Thought from the Restoration of Charles II until the War with the Thirteen Colonies* (Cambridge, Mass., 1959). Bernard Bailyn in his *Ideological Origins of the American Revolution* (Cambridge, Mass., 1967) and *The Origins of American Politics* (New York, 1968) explains the American version as one accepted by all colonials. Gordon S. Wood accepts this original uniformity and traces an emergence of demo-

In the debate a division appeared at once between those who wanted a popular government and those who did not. The latter advocated a system of checks and balances among the executive branch and a two-house legislature, reflecting the then familiar monarchical, aristocratic, and democratic principles, classic whig ideology through which the English form would be purged of its imperfections.[42] Most of the men agreed that liberty required limiting the power of the executive and the senate and restricting also that of the popular branch, believing that the people did not yet possess the ability to judge correctly. While granting the majority the ultimate right to combat tyranny, they would normally entrust the conduct of government to the most capable—the natural aristocracy. This approach did not necessarily require a strong central government, since these ideas could be fulfilled by state constitutions, but almost all of its adherents supported a central authority if it conformed to their basic principles. This group included nearly all of the educated, upper-class leaders of the Revolutionary movement including most members of Congress, and they had behind them the whole weight of political theory.

Other men preferred a government that located power in the majority of voters, with few or no checks. Democratic ideas arose from several interrelated sources. The British people had always retained an influence in local government, varying from place to place but substantial in some towns. The earliest settlers expressed this tradition, which one also finds in non-British immigrants such as the Dutch and French Huguenots. Second, a broad European trend toward

---

cratic views out of left-wing whiggism (*The Creation of the American Republic, 1776–1787* [Chapel Hill, 1969]).

[42] Curiously, we lack a full-scale treatment of colonial democratic ideas, no doubt because the sources are difficult to assess. Most articulate colonists preferred rule by some sort of aristocracy (though they resented external control) so that we must look for evidence of popular ideology more in actions than in words. Such actions would include the preference for local autonomy in religious government (the Congregational form), resistance by the lower order of society to social control, and the speedy overthrow of or rebellion against authoritarian regimes and actions, instances of which occurred nearly everywhere.

individualism, though very gradual, reinforced the older tradition. Third, the Reformation challenged religious authority in the most fundamental way. Men of these convictions formed a large proportion of the early immigrants to this country.[43]

They differed from even the left-wing whigs in several critical respects. Fundamentally, because they were themselves ordinary folk, they possessed a respect for and trust in public judgment that their leaders lacked. They had considerably less trust in the monarchy and the aristocracy. They therefore questioned the need for monarchical and aristocratic elements in government and would minimize or even abolish these, concentrating all power in the people without any checks. Even government officials, instead of acting independently of public opinion, should be its instruments.

The geographical circumstances of the colonies promoted the extension of democratic thought. Even if we deny any magic to the American forest, sheer distance from the centers of power encouraged local independence, and a conviction of self-sufficiency also developed out of economic circumstances, from the absence of clerical authority, and from the lack of a hereditary aristocracy. Evidences of resis-

[43] Until recently most books on particular colonies from 1763 to 1776 concentrated on the relations between the colonials and the British government and the differences among the colonists about resistance. The reader of Lawrence Henry Gipson's magnificent volumes *The British Empire before the American Revolution*, 17 vols. (New York, 1936–70) would not learn of the intense internal conflicts, for example, between the Charleston artisans and the merchant-lawyer upper class. The new point of view alluded to earlier is reflected in the following representative books: Richard Walsh, *Charleston's Sons of Liberty: A Study of the Artisans, 1763–1789* (Columbia, S.C., 1959); Ronald Hoffman, *A Spirit of Dissension: Economics, Politics, and the Revolution in Maryland* (Baltimore, 1973); Charles S. Olton, *Artisans for Independence: Philadelphia Mechanics and the American Revolution* (Syracuse, 1975); Larry Gerlach, *Prologue to Independence: New Jersey in the Coming of the American Revolution* (New Brunswick, N.J., 1976); Stephen E. Patterson, *Political Parties in Revolutionary Massachusetts* (Madison, 1973); David Skaggs, *The Roots of Maryland Democracy, 1753–1776* (Westport, Conn.), 1973, and Dirk Hoerder, *Crowd Action in Revolutionary Massachusetts, 1765–1780* (New York, 1977). The best general survey is Merrill Jensen, *The Founding of a Nation: A History of the American Revolution, 1763–1776* (New York, 1968).

tance to authority appeared sporadically through the colonial period, climaxed by the Revolutionary movement itself.[44]

In that movement the left-wing whigs also participated, and because they possessed appropriate ideas and the skills to express them, they spoke and wrote for all. But even before Independence a basic rift appeared among the rebels. The leaders were attacking primarily the monarchy, rather than the aristocracy—namely, themselves, and they did not want an unchecked democracy, whereas a majority of the voters sought precisely that. The contest took place primarily within the states, and only at the end of the period did the national debate become critical. By that time the various issues had already been thoroughly examined, so the arguments over the ratification of the Constitution followed familiar lines.[45]

To illustrate briefly: At first both groups agreed in severely limiting the power of the executive, the democrats from principle, the whigs because they had been trying for over a century to check the king and royal governors. The whigs quickly shifted, partly to balance the government but primarily because of events. The wartime governors found their lack of power a serious handicap, and even the democrats recognized the problem, especially since they learned that they could trust an executive if he responded to them. The movement to restore efficiency to the office was therefore gaining ground even before the Philadelphia Convention met.

More controversial was the role of the upper house, for the whig leaders considered it the stronghold of the natural aristocracy, the wisest and best men. In order to make it so, they introduced high property qualifications believing that wealth reflected ability, raised the age requirement, length-

[44] The division of opinion here described is outlined in my *Sovereign States*, pp. 99–221. For later disputes see my *Political Parties before the Constitution* (Chapel Hill, 1973).

[45] Jackson Turner Main, *The Upper House in the Revolutionary Era* (Madison, 1967). For general discussions of the debate over the state constitutions see Elisha P. Douglass, *Rebels and Democrats: The Struggle for Equal Political Rights and Majority Rule during the American Revolution* (Chapel Hill, 1955), and Wood, *Creation*.

ened the term of office to obtain stability and independence, limited the number of members to give it prestige, tried to broaden the area that the senator would represent so as to restrict the office to widely known men, and finally hit upon the electoral college as a means of "refining" the vulgar preference for demagogues. Maryland's constitution proved especially successful. There, the voters chose electors who owned property worth £500, probably $50,000 today, and these then convened to select senators owning twice as much for five-year terms. The senators themselves filled vacancies. The process effectively ensured that the state's wealthiest and best educated men could veto undesired legislation. More democratically inclined people tried to abolish the upper house entirely, as in the constitutions of Georgia, Pennsylvania, and Vermont. They discovered, however, that a senate popularly elected for short terms—democratized—had its advantages, and by the end of the 1780s they were prepared to accept a second house if purged of any aristocratic taint.[46]

Disputes about the proper form of government, which extended into other areas as well, should not distract our attention from the extensive accomplishments which did not arouse debate but which contributed greatly to American government. The people in the states expanded court systems, creating a much more effective judicial process than that existing before 1776, one under the control of the state governments rather than the Crown. Many states adopted bills of rights to protect newly won liberties, and these were often quite elaborate. Advisory councils aided the governors and guarded against executive usurpation. The principle of representation by population, though not universally approved, gained ground.[47] Democratic ideas found expression in the secret ballot to protect the voter against pressure, reduced property requirements for voting, the idea of recall, the abolition of plural officeholding, and the great increase

[46] J. R. Pole, *Political Representation in England and the Origins of the American Republic* (New York, 1966).

[47] David S. Lovejoy, *Rhode Island Politics and the American Revolution, 1760–1776* (Providence, 1958); Theodore Thayer, *Pennsylvania Politics and the Growth of Democracy, 1740–1776* (Harrisburg, 1953).

of roll calls on significant votes, which then became publicized in the newspapers or the official proceedings. These roll calls revealed another significant development in the states: the beginning of political parties.

Organized and consistent opposition within the legislatures had appeared before 1776, notably in Rhode Island and in Pennsylvania.[48] In most of the colonies, however, political power rested in an upper class that might contend internally for office but agreed upon basic policies. With the Revolution, however, a major shift of power occurred, in most states incomplete but everywhere evident, that brought into the legislatures men who reflected the ideas and objectives of the majority of the people. These men then pressed for laws and policies desired by their constituencies. The legislatures came to be divided into factions, legislative blocs, or parties, depending upon one's definition.[49]

---

[48] Van Beck Hall, *Politics without Parties: Massachusetts, 1780–1791* (Pittsburgh, 1972), examines divisions in the legislature but defines parties out of existence. See also Irwin Polishook, *Rhode Island and the Union* (Evanston, 1969); E. Wilder Spaulding, *New York in the Critical Period, 1783–1789* (New York, 1932); Alfred F. Young, *The Democratic Republicans of New York: The Origins, 1763–1797* (Chapel Hill, 1967); Robert L. Brunhouse, *The Counter-Revolution in Pennsylvania, 1776–1790* (Harrisburg, 1942); Patricia Watlington, *The Partisan Spirit: Kentucky Politics, 1779–1792* (New York, 1972); and Norman K. Risjord, *Chesapeake Politics, 1781–1800* (New York, 1978). Much research along the same lines is still in article form.

[49] Recent biographers of the principal leaders almost invariably accept without question the Federalist argument that major reforms were necessary and that the Constitution was virtually flawless. For example, Irving Brant, *James Madison*, 6 vols. (Indianapolis, 1941–61); Robert Ernst, *Rufus King: American Federalist* (Chapel Hill, 1968); James Thomas Flexner, *George Washington and the New Nation, 1783–1793* (Boston, 1970); Broadus Mitchell, *Alexander Hamilton*, 2 vols. (New York, 1957–62); Page Smith, *John Adams*, 2 vols. (New York, 1963). History's major defect lies in the impossibility of testing such assumptions. The counterfactual argument would postulate a defeat for ratification, a second convention influenced strongly by Antifederalists, and the adoption of amendments either to the Articles or to the proposed constitution so as to reduce the power of the central government relative to that of the states and to increase popular influence. Would this have resulted in disaster? Since we cannot test the question, perhaps we should write a little less confidently about the subject.

This political revolution meant that men who held power in the government, instead of receiving the deference and obedience of the people, faced opposition. Most significantly it meant that the upper class did not rule unchallenged but confronted active and often successful resistance. Revolution in the states promoted democracy. The established leaders hated it because, aside from the insult, it put them on the defensive to justify their policies and made them submit to laws they detested. Therefore their letters—those sources that mold our responses—are filled with attacks on the "vile" state governments and on their principal opponents. Since the authority of the leaders faced continual challenges at the local level, they turned instead to a strong national government as their only salvation. Historians have turned with them.

The state governments were certainly not all good; no government ever is. It is even possible that we have improved upon them. Nor must we deprive the leaders of their rightful place of honor in order to elevate the people. Congress and the principal leaders deserve much of the credit for the successes of the new nation; the states and the people share the blame for its failures. We must remember too that the distribution of functions under the Articles of Confederation limited Congress's activities, notably in economic affairs. We must not replace an old bias with a new one.

Still, we need to stress the positive accomplishments of the states and the people. Most of the ablest men of the period served in the state legislatures and some became governors, such as James Bowdoin, Thomas Burke, George Clinton, John Dickinson, Benjamin Franklin, John Hancock, Patrick Henry, Thomas Jefferson, Thomas Johnson, John Langdon, Jonathan Trumbull, William Livingston, Thomas Nelson, John Rutledge, and Mesech Weare. The militia contributed to many minor and some major victories. The economic record of the legislatures, like that of Congress, is much better than is sometimes depicted, especially considering the circumstances; they financed the war and laid the foundation for future growth. The resumption of the westward movement, the freeing of northern slaves, and the replacement of deferential attitudes by egalitarian ideas came more from the people and local action than from Congress, as did religious toleration and the beginnings of state universities. Political democracy gained because ordinary folk wanted it. Finally, political parties, which in their origin served as vehicles for popular influence in government, grew despite the opposition of almost all the leaders of the Revolutionary years. The resistance to a recreation of a strong national system came from the people acting through their state legislatures. Not everyone would agree about the merits of the changes we have been considering. But to understand and to appreciate them, we must look primarily to the people of the sovereign states.

STEPHEN E. PATTERSON

The Roots of Massachusetts Federalism

Conservative Politics and

Political Culture before 1787

ONE OF THE most striking changes that occurred in the Massachusetts legislature after Independence was the almost complete withdrawal of the early Revolutionary leadership. Samuel Adams, John Hancock, John Adams, James Otis, and several others—the men who had shaped political history in the province for the previous fifteen years—went on to Congress, the foreign service, executive rather than legislative politics, or into retirement. Without them, politics acquired a new character and style based on partisan divisions that the early leaders neither understood nor approved. They belonged, it now seemed, to a different generation of political thought, a generation that had sought political harmony and public consensus on the great issues debated with Great Britain, a generation attached to what we now call the republican principles of virtue, industry, frugality, social harmony, and nonpartisanship. Samuel Adams was in many ways archetypal. While his role in the Revolution has over time been the subject of much distortion and unsubstantiated interpretation, he has recently been fairly understood as a man deeply committed to traditional values, motivated by his republican vision of American society, and frustrated by the modern clash of economic interests that characterized much of the politics of the post-Independence era.[1] His principles simply left him out of step with the direction of the 1780s.

[1] For a useful discussion of the literature on Samuel Adams, see James M. O'Toole, "The Historical Interpretations of Samuel Adams," *New En-*

While the modernizing trend of legislative politics in Massachusetts tended to leave the old leaders behind, there were other men who were not so deeply committed to traditional ideals, who infrequently used republican rhetoric, and who took a more self-consciously interested and even partisan approach to politics. These men accepted, and in fact were part of, the changes taking place. They saw nothing wrong with diversity in society, they saw clearly their own interests and how they conflicted with other interests, and some of them, at least, actively sought ways of changing the political system so that it might accommodate these modern forces at work in their everyday lives.

The Federalists were the most significant group of such men in Massachusetts. While they did not call themselves Federalists until 1786,[2] these men constituted an organized body of political opinion whose emergence can be traced from the beginning of the Revolutionary War. Their consolidation as a group was certainly complete by 1780, their experimentation with ideas that were distinctly nonrepublican can be observed in their writings of the late 1770s and throughout the 1780s, and they became, ultimately, the nucleus of the Federalist party that emerged in the 1790s. In Massachusetts it is thus possible to speak of a Federalist movement from roughly the time of Independence until the 1820s. The men themselves provide the strongest evidence of continuity since, for this state at least, the correlation between creditor politics during the war, support of the Federal Constitution, and membership in the Federalist party is high.[3] One can also identify a consistent commitment to such

---

gland Quarterly 49 (1976): 82–96. Among recent reinterpretations of Adams, see Richard D. Brown, *Revolutionary Politics in Massachusetts* (Cambridge, Mass., 1970); Pauline Maier, *From Resistance to Revolution* (New York, 1972); Stephen E. Patterson, *Political Parties in Revolutionary Massachusetts* (Madison, 1973); and Pauline Maier, "Coming to Terms with Samuel Adams," *American Historical Review* 81 (1976): 12–37.

[2] A writer in the *Boston Gazette* of Dec. 4, 1786, stated: "There are two parties in the state—jealous of each other; federal men and anti federal."

[3] Biographical sketches of leading supporters of the Constitution appear in Jackson Turner Main, *Political Parties before the Constitution* (Chapel

conservative goals as the preservation of order and property. Beyond these most general principles, however, Federalism was shaped by the historical context in which it developed. Their search for order and self-preservation forced Federalists to experiment with a rich variety of new ideas, making of their movement a constant interaction between what was desired and what was possible.

Ironically, for Massachusetts as elsewhere, we seem to know more about opponents of early Federalism than we know about the Federalists themselves.[4] Despite their very considerable achievement in promoting the Constitution of 1787, Federalists have generally escaped close scrutiny as a coherent movement until their coming together as a national political party in the 1790s. Even then Federalism has been seen less as a movement than as a static phenomenon: a simple fixed idea rather than a process constantly responding to shifting historical circumstance. The result has been the formulation of a shallow, stereotyped Federalism, found in college textbooks and scholarly monographs alike. Simply put, this Federalism seems to have been a reflection of the order and stability of a traditional New England town, its primary values those of family, church, and community.[5] The

Hill, 1973), pp. 409–13, and of Federalist party leaders in David Hackett Fischer, *The Revolution of American Conservatism* (New York, 1965), pp. 245–62.

[4] There is no work on the Federalists equivalent to Jackson Turner Main's *The Antifederalists: Critics of the Constitution, 1781–1788* (Chapel Hill, 1961). A useful discussion of the Massachusetts conservatives in the context of state politics during the 1780s is Robert A. East, "The Massachusetts Conservatives in the Critical Period," in Richard B. Morris, ed., *The Era of the American Revolution* (1939; reprint ed., New York, 1965), pp. 349–91.

[5] Such a link between Federalist politics and the traditional, organic New England town is found in Samuel Eliot Morison and Henry Steele Commager, *The Growth of the American Republic*, 4th ed. (New York, 1950), pp. 306–9 and 335–36; Stephan Thernstrom, *Poverty and Progress: Social Mobility in a Nineteenth-Century City* (Cambridge, Mass., 1964), pp. 34–42; Oscar Handlin, *Boston's Immigrants, 1790–1865* (Cambridge, Mass., 1941), pp. 18 and 24–47; and Roger Lane, *Policing the City: Boston, 1822–1885* (Cambridge, Mass., 1967). Lane sees a Federalist-like Josiah Quincy, mayor of Boston in the 1820s, as a "maverick" because he was both an

immediate trouble with this formulation is that New England town scholarship of the last ten years has completely under- mined the concept of the traditional town as an ideal type. We now know about momentous changes, beginning roughly in the last quarter of the seventeenth century, brought about by land shortages, population growth, social differentiation, and growing commercialization. In many ways, rival value systems had already developed by the time of the American Revolution.[6] Some rigidly defended the old ways, and others more easily adjusted to the new; unquestionably, there were also many torn ambiguously between the two. In Massachu- setts, as it turned out, conservative men who became Feder- alists also led in the modernization of politics. Perhaps it may seem contradictory to call agents of change conservatives, but, in fact, it was to preserve their own social and political preeminence that these men began to experiment with the new ways of doing things and to fashion new political theo- ries to suit the altered conditions of their times. Necessity, once again, became mother to invention.

The summer of 1780 represented a first plateau for Massa- chusetts conservatism. After several years of sometimes bit- ter struggle between contending political forces, conservatives won approval of a state constitution that seemed to ensure their legislative preeminence. Only shortly thereafter, three conservative-minded men, chosen by the Massachusetts Gen-

---

aristocrat and reformer (pp. 14–15). It could be, however, that Quincy was less a maverick than a representative of a more complex and ambiguous Federalism than we have hitherto understood.

[6] Among the many such studies are Richard L. Bushman, *From Puritan to Yankee: Character and the Social Order in Connecticut, 1690–1765* (Cam- bridge, Mass., 1967); Kenneth Lockridge, *A New England Town: The First Hundred Years, Dedham, Massachusetts* (New York, 1970); Philip J. Greven, Jr., *Four Generations: Population, Land, and Family in Colonial Andover, Mas- sachusetts* (Ithaca, 1970); Michael Zuckerman, *Peaceable Kingdoms: New En- gland Towns in the Eighteenth Century* (New York, 1970); and Robert A. Gross, *The Minutemen and Their World* (New York, 1976). Zuckerman is more impressed than the others with the persistence of traditional com- munity values, despite social pressures and change. He is supported in this view by James A. Henretta, "The Morphology of New England Society in the Colonial Period," *Journal of Interdisciplinary History* 2 (1971): 379–98.

eral Court, set off for Hartford, Connecticut, to meet with the legislative appointees of other New England states to talk about war problems. This first Hartford convention suggests not only an interesting symmetry to the history of New England Federalism but also provides a useful introduction to the leaders and their ideas. There were only five delegates, three from Massachusetts and one each from Connecticut and New Hampshire. The expected Rhode Islander never joined them. Thomas Cushing, Nathaniel Gorham, and John Lowell represented Massachusetts; Jesse Root, Connecticut; and John Langdon, New Hampshire. They chose Cushing chairman. They sought answers to three questions: What should the states do to comply with the requisitions of Congress, to render effectual the operations of the present military campaign, and to support public credit? Their answers diverged from matters of state, however, and they turned their report into a statement of what was becoming the conservative position on a number of related social and economic issues. It was necessary that farmers provide both the army and civilian markets with provisions at fair prices. Regulations governing interstate commerce by land should be dropped by the several states. The old Continental currency should be sunk as requested by Congress while every state should have a sinking fund and a taxation system for supporting the public credit. The states should cease emitting bills of credit. The report brought nods of approval from merchants and public creditors everywhere, along with the hope that more such meetings would be held.[7]

That Cushing, Gorham, and Lowell should have agreed to recommendations for free trade among the states and an end to paper money would have surprised none of their friends or colleagues back in Massachusetts. In fact, they were ideal spokesmen for the two leading groups that had constituted the conservative legislative faction since the be-

[7] Report of the Committee from Massachusetts, Connecticut, and New Hampshire, sent to Matthew Griswold, E. Dyer, and William Pitkin, Aug. 3 and 9, 1780, Jonathan Trumbull, Sr., Papers, Connecticut Historical Society, Hartford; Jeremiah Wadsworth to Gen. [Nathanael] Greene, Sept. 3, 1780, Wadsworth Correspondence, Connecticut State Library, Hartford.

ginning of the war, one group centered in Boston, the other
in Essex County. Thomas Cushing was probably the leading
figure among Boston conservatives. Born into a prospering
merchant family, educated at Harvard, Cushing had established himself in trade before entering town and then provincial politics. By the early 1770s he was seen by Gov.
Thomas Hutchinson as a leader of the revolutionary party,
but of far more moderate principles than the incendiary
Samuel Adams. Hutchinson's impression seems supported
by almost everything Cushing said or did at that time. Like
most Boston merchants, he openly adhered to the Revolutionary movement lest it get out of hand, but he resisted economic boycotts that thrust the burden of antiparliamentary
protest on merchants, he clung to the hope that Parliament
would let the issue of its supremacy die so that "Great Britain
would regain the affections of the people in America," he
resisted the arming and training of Massachusetts militiamen
because he feared it would trigger an unwanted military conflict with Britain, and he longed for reconciliation right down
to the time of the Declaration of Independence. In all of his
moderate positions he collided with Samuel and John Adams
and he finally split openly with them at the Second Continental Congress. Back in Massachusetts, he was elected to the
Council, or upper house of the legislature, where he quickly
became its leader and the champion of merchant and other
conservative interests on almost every issue that came before
the legislature from 1776 to 1780.[8]

Nathaniel Gorham and John Lowell were Cushing's political allies in the legislature. Though somewhat younger than
Cushing, they shared many of his values, took similar posi-

[8] Thomas Hutchinson to Lord Dartmouth, Oct. 9, 1773, Massachusetts
Archives (microfilm in State House, Boston), 27: 549–51; Thomas Cushing to Arthur Lee, Sept.-Oct. 1773, "Letters of Thomas Cushing from
1767 to 1775," Massachusetts Historical Society *Collections*, 4th ser. 4
(1858): 360 and 363; [Thomas Cushing] to Joseph Hawley, Feb. 27, 1775,
Hawley Papers, New York Public Library (microfilm copy, Massachusetts
Historical Society, Boston); Clifford K. Shipton, *Biographical Sketches of
Those Who Attended Harvard College in the Classes 1741–1745*, Sibley's Harvard Graduates, vol. 11 (Boston, 1960), pp. 377–95; Patterson, pp. 130–
36, 142, 168, and 174.

tions throughout the Revolution, and spoke for a conservative elite. Gorham was a merchant of Charlestown and Boston who as early as 1770 had antagonized and embarrassed the popular wing of the revolutionary party by importing from Great Britain contrary to the nonimportation agreement. He would eventually become one of the Massachusetts delegates to the Philadelphia convention of 1787 and an ardent Federalist.[9] John Lowell was a lawyer and a son of a minister in Newburyport. Harvard educated and socially prominent, he mixed easily with the merchants and their lawyer friends in Essex County. With little thought of what the popular reaction might be, he joined other "gentlemen" of the province in paying "dutiful respects" to Thomas Hutchinson upon his replacement as governor in 1774 and in a similar loyal greeting to the new military governor, Thomas Gage. While he had to repent of his indiscretion in order to satisfy popular sentiment in Newburyport, he seems to have lost no political favor, was sent as one of its representatives to the legislature in 1776, and played a leading role in the Essex convention that drew together leading conservatives on the eve of Independence.[10] In fact it was this convention which met in May 1776 that represented the first steps in organizing conservative forces in Essex County into what eventually became known as the Essex Junto, certainly the most powerful wing of the conservative party that emerged in the new state legislature and a political force whose mythical importance long outlived its real influence upon the Federalist party of the 1790s. Among its early members were Lowell's fellow lawyers Theophilus Parsons and Timothy Pickering and numerous merchants, such as

[9] *Boston Chronicle*, Jan. 22, 1770; Robert A. East, *Business Enterprise in the American Revolutionary Era* (New York, 1938), p. 57; Van Beck Hall, *Politics without Parties: Massachusetts, 1780–1791* (Pittsburgh, 1972), pp. 263–64; *Massachusetts Historical Society Proceedings* 48 (1914–15): 430; and ibid., 55 (1921–22): 186.

[10] Benjamin W. Labaree, *Patriots and Partisans: The Merchants of Newburyport, 1764–1815* (Cambridge, Mass., 1962), pp. 11, 38; Fischer, p. 268; *A Journal of the Honorable House of Representatives of the Colony of the Massachusetts-Bay . . . Begun . . . on . . . the Nineteenth of July . . . 1775*, May 2, 1776 (Watertown, 1776), pp. 235–36.

Tristram Dalton, Jonathan Greenleaf, Jonathan Jackson, Azor Orne, William Pynchon, George Williams, and later George Cabot.[11]

The occupation and the siege of Boston during 1775 and early 1776 temporarily threw the leadership of Massachusetts commercial interests to Essex County, but by 1777 Boston was beginning to resume its traditional role, aided now by an influx of merchants, lawyers, and others eager to fill the places left vacant by departing tories. John Lowell was one of these; his friend Jonathan Jackson, another. Thus strengthened, Boston's commercial interests immediately reasserted their control over Boston's town politics, filling almost all offices of any importance and regaining a level of power and influence that they had not enjoyed since the days before Samuel Adams's ascendancy. In the town meeting merchants had at times been publicly humiliated in their confrontations with more popular forces between 1765 and 1774; after 1776 they rarely lost a vote, and such spokesmen as Cushing and Lowell, along with other merchants like Ellis Gray and Joseph Henshaw, regularly were chosen to represent the town in the legislature.[12]

While Boston and Essex County provided the leadership of the new conservative movement within the state, the alliance extended to most of the coastal towns and to many of the inland commercial centers. Even in areas where the prevailing sentiments of the voters were unfriendly, some leading conservatives maintained contact with like-minded men elsewhere so their isolation was only geographical. Including men who entered politics in the early 1780s, the conservative network embraced Theodore Sedgwick of Berkshire, Caleb

[11] Patterson, pp. 143–44; Labaree, pp. 43, 210–11, 213, 214, and 215–16; David Hackett Fischer, "The Myth of the Essex Junto," *William and Mary Quarterly*, 3d ser. 21 (1964): 191–235.

[12] [Twenty-Sixth] *Report of the Records Commissioners of the City of Boston Containing the Boston Town Records, 1778–1783* (Boston, 1895), pp. 18, 21, 98, and 101. Compare the names of those elected with the list of Boston merchants of the Revolutionary period in Stephen E. Patterson, "Boston Merchants and the American Revolution," Master's thesis, University of Wisconsin, 1961, pp. 154–71.

Strong of Hampshire, Artemas Ward of Worcester, Fisher Ames of Suffolk, and David Cobb of Bristol, among others.[13]

All of these conservative leaders were united by class, interest, and education, and most of them by geography, but it was the events and issues of the Revolution that brought them together as a political party within the legislature and forced them to organize in support of their party outside it. By others they were designated the eastern party or the commercial interest; they referred to themselves as the "friends of order" or the "men of property." In all the issues in which they saw principles of order or of property at stake, they had a clear and fairly uniform opinion, they voted together, and they politicked both within the legislature and without to fashion continuing majorities. They were therefore more than an aggregate of like-minded men, even in the earliest years of the new state; they were a nascent political party, rather primitive in organization, which survived in a relatively coherent form from the 1770s to the fragmented ending of the Federalist party in the 1820s. The issues of the 1770s not only brought them together but, for the student who would understand them, these issues provide a primer on conservative principles and outlook.

The overriding issue of the 1770s was the question of a state constitution. From the very moment the reins of government were taken up by a provincial congress in the fall of 1774, conservatives feared the unchecked democracy it seemed to represent, eagerly sought the reinstatement of the constitution of 1691 which gave coequal powers to a council and a house of representatives, and denounced the various reformist demands for a unicameral legislature and no governor. Lexington and Concord provided the perfect rationalization for resuming the old charter without the royal governor, in defiance of Britain, and when the Continental Congress itself lent support to this tactic, the provincial congress agreed. But conservatives still had to beat off demands

[13] Patterson, *Political Parties*, pp. 122, 137, 151, and 205–7; Hall, pp. 66, 263–64, and 312; Fischer, *Revolution of American Conservatism*, pp. 12–14, 20–21, and 257.

for reform embodied in a new constitution and, after Pennsylvania adopted its radically democratic model in 1776, conservatives in Massachusetts became even more convinced that wartime was not a proper time for Americans to concern themselves with such matters. For four more years they succeeded in putting off a constitutional settlement, fearing it would generate, and perhaps even consolidate, social and political revolution. As they held off the constitutionalists, the conservatives sought to strengthen the institutions of order. Through Thomas Cushing they sought more power for the Council; following a total disruption of the courts of law in 1774 and 1775, they gradually and carefully restored the judicial system; they pressed for caution in the issuing of paper money, and, once its inflationary problems were encountered, they maneuvered the legislature into what turned out to be the most conservative financial management of any of the new states. They succeeded legislatively in all of these matters by altering the system of representation to favor the larger seaport and commercial towns of the state and, by careful house management, drawing on legislative experience when committed conservatives were outnumbered.[14]

Conservative organization, however, was more than a legislative phenomenon. Beginning with the Essex County convention of May 1776, conservatives met to develop and unify their position on the issues and to organize the votes they would need in the General Court. With their control of towns like Boston and Salem, merchants and their allies saw to it that the instructions of representatives became statements of conservative principle. The Essex convention of 1778, called to coordinate the reply of county towns on what proved to be an abortive constitution for the state, produced one of the longest expositions of conservative principles during the war years—the "Essex Result." Also reinforcing the conservative position were the statements issued by numerous merchant meetings and conventions held periodically in Boston and Essex County to discuss the need for price regulation, controlled markets, and limits on paper currency emissions. In Boston a revived association of merchants was active by 1779,

[14] Patterson, *Political Parties*, chs. 5–8.

while in that same summer, a convention of merchants from all over New England met at Concord to discuss price fixing.[15] When Thomas Cushing and the others went to Hartford in 1780, therefore, they spoke for more than a conservative faction in the General Court; they represented the well-developed sentiments of an active conservative movement.

Fundamental to all conservative positions, of course, was the belief that order, good government, and property were threatened by what some called a "rage for innovation" but what others recognized as an increasingly coherent political force aiming at democratization. Evidence of a growing class-consciousness among farmers and urban workers had appeared sporadically at election times and in occasional crowd actions stretching back into the 1740s and 1750s. In the early years of controversy with Great Britain, such popular leaders as James Otis articulated and encouraged the sense of class grievance by claiming that those who governed Massachusetts "have no natural or divine right to be above me, and entirely owe their grandeur and honor to grinding the faces of the poor." Beginning in August 1765, the Boston crowd emerged as a significant revolutionary force that constantly strove to press reform beyond the constitutional question of the relationship between colonies and mother country. Otis and the other Revolutionary leaders quickly ceased fanning the embers of social discontent, while many merchants actively sought to extinguish them.[16] Ironically, many British officials and tory leaders took up where Otis left off by insist-

---

[15] Theophilus Parsons, *Memoir of Theophilus Parsons* (1859; reprint ed., New York, 1970), pp. 49–50 and 370–88; "Diary of John Rowe," *Massachusetts Historical Society Proceedings*, 2d ser. 10 (1895–96): 108; George Williams to Timothy Pickering, Aug. 15, 1779, "Revolutionary Letters Written to Colonel Timothy Pickering by George Williams of Salem," *Essex Institute Historical Collections* 43 (1907): 313; Rev. Manasseh Cutler to Rev. Enos Hitchcock, Sept. 20, 1779, ibid. 76 (1940): 375.

[16] Gary B. Nash, "Social Change and the Growth of Prerevolutionary Urban Radicalism," and Dirk Hoerder, "Boston Leaders and Boston Crowds, 1765–1776," both in Alfred F. Young, ed., *The American Revolution: Explorations in the History of American Radicalism* (DeKalb, Ill., 1976), pp. 26, 235–41, and 245–46.

ing that the real cause of revolution was economic—smuggling merchants and men without property were pursuing their personal interests—and while they condemned what they saw, they continuously reinforced the notion that the object of Revolutionary crowds was class war and a general leveling.[17] Whatever the limitations of such statements as guides to our understanding the Revolution, they were statements nevertheless which were heard by common people, confirming any who may have been predisposed in their belief that revolution could change Massachusetts society fundamentally.

By the summer of 1774 the populist movement in the Revolution had spread to every corner of the province. Once it had begun to organize in numerous county conventions, it went on to express itself in ways very similar to those of the conservatives: in instructions of representatives, in bloc voting in provincial congresses and the legislature, and in written statements on state constitutional matters. In the legislature the movement was referred to by contemporaries as the western party or the inland towns. Within the context of the times, however, it may rightly be viewed as a democratic party. It shared the same objectives as the rather widely scattered groups of late eighteenth- and early nineteenth-century democrats: annual elections, broadened suffrage (if not always universal manhood suffrage), payment of representatives' expenses, and adequate representation. In addition, many of these democrats wanted the popular election of all county officials, such as sheriffs and registrars of probate, a unicameral legislature or a lower house with most of the powers of government, and a reformed court system in which the activities and especially the fees of lawyers were strictly curtailed. On numerous issues they stood as polar op-

---

[17]Gov. Francis Bernard to the Earl of Halifax, Aug. 31, 1765, C.O. 5/755, Public Record Office, reproduced in Merrill Jensen, ed., *American Colonial Documents to 1776*, English Historical Documents, vol. 9 (London, 1955), pp. 675–80; *Letters to the Ministry from Governor Bernard . . .* (Boston, 1769); *Peter Oliver's Origin & Progress of the American Revolution*, ed. Douglass Adair and John A. Schutz (Stanford, 1961), pp. 4, 52–54, 61, 65, and 72; [Daniel Leonard], "Massachusettensis," in *Novanglus and Massachusettensis* (Boston, 1819), pp. 145, 149, 159–60, 165, 215, and 219.

posites to the conservatives. They generally favored inflationary paper money emissions and a legal-tender provision
forcing creditors to accept paper at a fixed value. From 1775
to 1780, when farm produce was in great demand, they opposed regulated markets and price fixing. Above all else,
they wanted a fixed constitution for the state in which their
reform ideals would be embedded: a goal many of the westernmost democrats in Berkshire and Hampshire counties
agitated for constantly until 1780.[18]

All of these positions challenged—in fact, frightened—
Massachusetts friends of order and men of property. But if
we are to understand fully the depths of their fear of the
democratic movement, we must recognize in it an additional
dimension that has received little attention from historians.
The democracy the conservatives saw emerging was not democracy as we know it. Democracy then, as now, took on the
attributes of the culture in which it developed. Like an unstable chemical element, democracy is never found in a pure
state—something men of the eighteenth century recognized
and frequently acknowledged. In the case of Revolutionary
Massachusetts, a remarkable number of the towns which
made up the democratic movement were small farming communities that had never before played any part whatever in
the legislative politics of the province. They were, in addition, remarkably homogeneous. Almost all of their inhabitants were small farmers, most of them had only one church
to which practically everyone in town adhered, and almost
none had experienced the land shortages that had trans-
formed such older towns as Dedham and Norton.[19] In many
ways these towns were almost an anachronism; they almost

[18] Massachusetts Archives, 156: 329–89; Robert J. Taylor, ed., *Massachusetts, Colony to Commonwealth: Documents on the Formation of Its Constitution,
1775–1780* (Chapel Hill, 1961), pp. 95–97; Patterson, *Political Parties*,
ch. 8.

[19] Compare the list of democratic towns found in Patterson, *Political Parties*, appendix B, pp. 269–80, with the typology of towns developed by
Hall. For other discussions of the constraints on the practice of democracy
in colonial and Revolutionary times, see Richard Buel, Jr., "Democracy
and the American Revolution: A Frame of Reference," *William and Mary
Quarterly*, 3d ser. 21 (1964): 165–90; and Michael Zuckerman, "The Social

always voted unanimously on issues before their town meetings, and their interests were introverted and localistic. They demanded conformity of their inhabitants, which is another way of saying that they placed a higher value on community than on the individual personality; and they resisted the intrusion of outsiders. For example, well into the 1760s, numerous towns in Worcester County maintained the old New England practice of "warning out" unwanted indigents, if anything on a greater scale than they had in the past.[20] While they were not, strictly speaking, closed corporate peasant communities, especially during the war when military service and the commercial demand for agricultural surpluses drew them into the mainstream, traditional corporate forms were still a powerful constraint on their behavior. Their revolutionary objective was, therefore, not a modern, liberal democracy as we know it but, rather, a kind of corporate democracy: radical in substance, traditional in form.[21] They wanted fair and equal treatment for ordinary people, but they thought of those people in groups, in organized communities, rather than as individuals.

Conservatives reacted to the democratic movement from a very different cultural perspective. They came from Boston, the coastal communities of Essex, Plymouth, and Barnstable counties, the river towns of the Connecticut Valley, and larger commercial towns elsewhere. Such towns were socially and economically diverse. Their inhabitants identified themselves by profession—they were merchants, traders, shopkeepers, shipwrights, carpenters, fishermen, and so on— and social institutions like the taverns catered to different

---

Context of Democracy in Massachusetts," *William and Mary Quarterly*, 3d ser. 25 (1968): 523–44. See also Patterson, *Political Parties*, p. 249.

[20] David Grayson Allen, "The Zuckerman Thesis and the Process of Legal Rationalization in Provincial Massachusetts," *William and Mary Quarterly*, 3d ser. 29 (1972): 454. For the unanimity of these towns, see votes on the 1780 constitution in Massachusetts Archives, vols. 276 and 277.

[21] Among the many historians who have wrongly read back into the eighteenth century their rigid twentieth-century understanding of democracy as "liberal democracy" is John J. Waters, "The Massachusetts Commonwealth: Family versus Party in the Eighteenth Century," *Reviews in American History* 3 (1975): 192–95.

groups, reinforcing their sense of identity. What religious diversity there was in New England was found in such towns— here were the Anglicans and the Quakers—while even many of the smaller towns had experienced the split into New Lights and Old Lights during the Great Awakening of the 1740s. These were the most cosmopolitan towns in Massachusetts. They gathered news from the far corners of the Atlantic world; sailors who had seen the Guinea coast, the Rock of Gibraltar, and the coral reefs of the Caribbean swaggered through the streets of Salem, Newburyport, and Boston. In a word, these were plural communities, modern in their social mix and increasingly modern in their ability to accommodate individual differences.[22] While they were not perfectly so, these townsmen were more open, individualistic, and tolerant than their rural counterparts. The cultural assumptions of conservatives led them therefore to see danger not only in the democrats' demand for greater social and economic equality but in what conservatives perceived to be the intolerant and thus oppressive way in which those demands were made. They feared democracy precisely because its proponents were simultaneously attached to uncompromising, traditional values.[23]

Three issues illustrate how in Revolutionary Massachusetts it was the conservatives who argued for pluralism in the face of what they believed to be an intolerant, unitary democracy. The first had to do with the treatment of tories. Early in 1778 the Massachusetts General Court proscribed the state's most notorious tories. By summer, however, conservatives in Boston were actively seeking pardons for tories and advocated allowing their return. They supported a motion to this effect in the legislature and dragged their heels when that body took up a bill to confiscate tory estates. "It labours very hard,"

---

[22] The commercial-cosmopolitan character of these towns is developed in Hall. Jackson Turner Main also breaks down the parties of the preconstitution period into "localists" and "cosmopolitans," terms that are suggestive if not perfectly comprehensive (*Political Parties*, pp. 83–119).

[23] Valuable insights into the dual attraction of traditional and modern values in late eighteenth-century communities are found in Thomas Bender, *Community and Social Change in America* (New Brunswick, N.J., 1978).

wrote one observer, "and if it passes at all will not be very comprehensive." He believed that "some people of influence are against the principle and consequently every part of it" and there was thus no probability of the act's passing—"so far from it that even some members on the B[oston] seat have without reserve expressed their sentiments that they [the tories] should be suffered to return. *Tempora Mutantur.*" In April 1779, however, when western representation in the legislature was at a much higher level, confiscation was reintroduced and passed very quickly. The comment of one eastern conservative was fairly typical: "To confiscate the estates of all such absentees without distinction or exception, I must deem, till I have more light, cruel—cruel, superlative cruel."[24]

There the matter rested until the end of the war when the state split along similar lines over whether or not the tories should be permitted to return. In 1783 attitudes were still harsh, but in 1784 a new law permitted the governor to issue licenses to all but the worst offenders and allowed returnees to reclaim confiscated estates not already sold by the state. By 1785 all antitory legislation had been rescinded.[25]

There can be no question but that the sympathy of conservatives for the tories rested on social and economic motives. In their battle against the democrats, they needed all the help they could get, and they saw among the tories former men of property who would be natural allies. Timothy Pickering went so far as to suggest that there were patriots he would be glad to see shipped out in exchange for some tories.[26] But the question also involved the principle of toleration of different opinions, and in this respect it was simply

[24] James Warren to Samuel Adams, Sept. 30, 1778, Worthington C. Ford, ed., *Warren-Adams Letters*, 2 vols. (Boston, 1917–25), 2:47–48; Warren to John Adams, Oct. 7, 1778, ibid., 51–52; *The Acts and Resolves, Public and Private, of the Province of the Massachusetts Bay*, 21 vols. (Boston, 1869–1922), 5:966–68; William Gordon to John Adams, May 8, 1779, "Letters of the Reverend William Gordon," *Massachusetts Historical Society Proceedings* 63 (1929–30): 410.

[25] Merrill Jensen, *The New Nation: A History of the United States during the Confederation, 1781–1789* (New York, 1950), pp. 269–70; Hall, pp. 138–42; Main, *Political Parties*, pp. 90–95.

[26] Jensen, *New Nation*, p. 267.

part of the larger struggle between opposing political cultures. Theodore Sedgwick was one of several conservatives who saw the issue in this light. "I wish my country happy, great, and flourishing," he wrote. "I wish her independent; but that she may be happy under the last, it is necessary that she become wise, virtuous, and tolerant." Of all "human follies" and prejudices, he believed none was surer "evidence of the weakness of head and depravity of heart, than that narrow and confined policy, which has for its end a uniformity of opinions, whether political or religious." If the happiness of even one person were "sported with" in order to please "popular, malignant malice," then "not only the flame" but also "every spark of liberty is extinct." Perhaps relying on John Locke, he asserted that of the two sides in the Revolution, whig and tory, "all the assurance that we can obtain that we are right is an opinion that we are so." Political questions were relative, it now appeared, shaped by "a vast variety of circumstances," not the clear-cut absolutes of early Revolutionary leaders or of corporate democrats. Sedgwick realized that most ordinary people did not think as he did. "Minds the most enlarged, possess a degree of liberality from which little ones are excluded," he wrote, but one would find among these men of enlarged views "charity, softness, and mutual forbearance, even with those who most essentially differ."[27] What Sedgwick and other conservatives were coming to understand was that the toleration of differing views and the security of private property belonged together. They both represented an elevation of the rights of the individual far beyond the level they had attained in the traditional value system of New England society, and they were more in tune with the changing values of their own plural communities.

A second example of how political cultures clashed had to do with how the parties organized themselves. Althoug'

[27]Sedgwick to Peter Van Schaack, Aug. 12, 1778, Henry Cruger Van Schaack, *The Life of Peter Van Schaack, LL.D., Embracing Selections from H. Correspondence* . . . (New York, 1842), pp. 116–17; Sedgwick to Henry Van Schaack, Mar. 24, 1783, Henry Cruger Van Schaack, *Memoirs of the Life of Henry Van Schaack Embracing Selections from His Correspondence* . . . (Chicago, 1892), pp. 91–92. See also Rufus King to Dr. Dan. Kilham, Feb. 18, 1784, Rufus King Papers, Library of Congress.

their message seemed constantly to have class overtones, the western democrats never attempted to organize all the small farmers in the state nor to link up with urban artisans or laborers. Their organization was severely constrained by their corporate ways of thinking. Their towns represented the basic unit of organization where, by whatever means, they sought and maintained unanimity. From the town they moved on to the next level, the county, where in county conventions they hoped to establish similar corporate uniformity. County conventions were an innovation of the Revolution that preserved intact the sense of community that prevailed in rural towns. They provided in the first instance for face-to-face interaction among the delegates, they were open, and they were frequently attended by hundreds of curious townsmen whose simple presence lent to the proceedings a kind of popular sanction and moral weight. The object in all such meetings was consensus, and where that was difficult to achieve, exclusion of differing opinions seems to have been preferred to accommodation. To suggest a meaningful comparison, the committees of correspondence that originated in Boston in the early 1770s provided a functional means of exchanging political ideas among a widely scattered and often socially diverse group of towns, a method of communication that invited political action on a narrow basis of shared concerns.[28] The county convention, in sharp contrast, perpetuated traditional methods and complicated political union by its attachment to the values of localism.

Conventions were held in just about every inland Massachusetts county at various intervals over the period from the summer of 1774 to 1787. At first they were the creatures of crisis; the Massachusetts Government Act had reduced society, so it was believed, to a state of nature. Worcester County probably enjoyed the greatest success in reconciling the various sentiments of the inhabitants and preserving the unanimity of the county, the professed goal of a convention that met in November 1776. But the corporate form worked best in Worcester because there was already considerable eco-

[28] For a full discussion of the committees of correspondence, see Brown, *Revolutionary Politics*.

nomic and cultural uniformity. In Hampshire, with its prosperous river towns mixed with rocky-soiled, subsistence farming communities, unity was harder to come by; this was also true in Bristol, Middlesex, and Suffolk counties. To get the unity they wanted, many of the so-called county conventions were in fact representative of only some towns, and on a number of occasions there were rival conventions, the one standing for reform and the other for order. Others were like the Hampshire convention of 1783, where the reformers could achieve their united purpose only after they got rid of the Northampton and Southampton gentlemen Jonathan Judd and Joseph Hawley. "They want to get rid of Major Hawley and myself," wrote Judd in his diary. "Near night we set off, leaving all the rest." Once free of contrary opinion, the reformers quickly agreed to stop paying taxes to the state. A simple majority decision, apparently, would not have been good enough. Corporate solidarity was expressed in other ways. When a legislative committee came into the west to investigate growing disaffection in 1782, the town of Conway in Hampshire replied "that the town had no grievances distinct from that of the county." Thirteen other towns said essentially the same thing.[29]

By 1784–85 the connection between what happened in county conventions and how democrats voted in the legislature was clear. The issues were various, but at the bottom of them all was the fact that the agricultural prosperity of the early war years had given way in the 1780s to an agricultural depression. Economics united the democrats on the tender provision in paper money acts, on the questions of an impost for Congress and pensions for former army officers, on how the courts should treat debtors, and on the level of taxation and the unequal treatment of public creditors. All of these questions were discussed in county conventions, and the towns that were represented in such discussions almost in-

[29] Patterson, *Political Parties*, pp. 95–98, 289; *Massachusetts Spy*, Dec. 4, 1776, and Mar. 25, 1784; Robert H. Taylor, *Western Massachusetts in the Revolution* (Providence, 1954), p. 107; "Jonathan Judd's Diary," in James Russell Trumbull, *History of Northampton Massachusetts*, 2 vols. (Northampton, 1902), 2:468–69; Charles Martyn, *The Life of Artemas Ward* (1921; reprint ed., Port Washington, N.Y., 1970), p. 265.

variably voted together in the General Court. Moreover, by 1786 several of the counties were caucusing in the General Court, laying plans for the next elections and determining who among them would return for the following sessions.[30] In other words, far from being an ephemeral legislative faction, the western party was persistent and structured, and county conventions, corporately organized, constituted the grass-roots organization of the party.

The conservative reaction against conventions was both intense and massive. Although such men as those constituting the Essex Junto had organized political sentiment through conventions before 1780, once Massachusetts had a constitution they thought acceptable, they rejected this form of organization and denounced anyone who resorted to it. Peaking in 1784–86, their criticism labeled the democrats partisan, anticonstitutional agents of Britain. One writer to the *Massachusetts Spy*, calling himself "a friend to order and the interests of America," warned that it was "folly and madness" to resort "to private party Conventions." Another reported that in Worcester County conventions "they recommended one another of their members for Senators, and the President of the Convention, publicly on election day read off his own recommendation to that office." Yet another claimed that a Worcester convention debated "who should be promoted to the principal offices in government." The town of Cambridge rejected a call to a convention from a fellow Middlesex town, claiming that the town was attached "to the present constitution and administration of government" and was expressly opposed to "any irregular means for compassing an end which the constitution has already provided for."

[30] Ralph V. Harlow, "Economic Conditions in Massachusetts during the American Revolution," *Publications of the Colonial Society of Massachusetts* 20 (1920): 182; William A. Benedict and Hiram A. Tracy, *History of the Town of Sutton, Massachusetts* (Worcester, 1878), p. 119; East, "Massachusetts Conservatives in the Critical Period," pp. 359–60; *Massachusetts Spy*, Apr. 18 and May 23, 1782; *Boston Gazette*, Mar. 27, 1786. See the vote on the Tender Act in the "Journal of the House of Representatives of the Commonwealth of Massachusetts . . . 30 May 1781 . . . 10 May 1782," June 13, 1781, pp. 67–68, in William Sumner Jenkins, ed., microfilm *Records of the States of the United States of America* (Washington, D.C., 1949).

By the summer of 1786 practically every convention that met felt obliged to assert its constitutional right to do so while their conservative critics, sounding more and more like the tories of a decade or so earlier, charged treason. The leaders, they said, were "destitute of property, without reputation, hardy and factious in their tempers, and eminent only for their vices and depravity." Another critic resorted to the language of class by calling for "men of principle, who love their country and regard the happiness of society, [to] unite with men of property, of wisdom and influence, to counteract the nefarious conduct of the desperate and unprincipled."[31]

This call for men of property to unite goes to the heart of their difference with democrats in the matter of partisan organization. Democrats tried to organize towns and counties; conservatives appealed to class and interest. In this respect it was the conservatives who were the modernizers. It was they who perceived society in its segments and who preferred a strictly defined functionalism, or instrumentalism, in institutions as opposed to an all-embracing organic unity. In such towns as Boston there was a history to this outlook, as well as some resistance. For example, in 1751 merchants and others of their class formed a Merchants Club that met fairly regularly at the British Coffee House in King Street. Chiefly a social club, it encountered no hostility, at least so far as the records show. In 1763, however, the club reorganized itself into an exclusive Society to Encourage Trade and Commerce and began to devote itself to the specific task of promoting the merchants' interest. A major clash with communitarian principles followed in the late 1760s when merchants proved reluctant to adopt and enforce an economic boycott of British manufactures. It was at this point that nonmerchants began coming to merchant meetings in ever larger numbers, transforming the club from an instrument of class into a modified town meeting. Adopting the name of the general assembly of merchants, "the Body" revived traditional New England political practice: face-to-face encounter and an in-

---

[31] *Massachusetts Spy*, Mar. 28, 1782, Feb. 26, Mar. 25, and Apr. 22, 1784; *Independent Chronicle*, Apr. 5, 1784, July 27, Aug. 3, 10, and 17, 1786; *Hampshire Herald*, Aug. 29, 1786.

sistence upon the principle of commonwealth, or community, consensus. The moral economy of the crowd linked a kind of incipient democracy with community tradition in much the same way that later rural conventions were to do. Merchants were enormously relieved when, in the summer and fall of 1770, the enthusiasm of the crowd dwindled and merchants' meetings once again became exclusively their own; they voted overwhelmingly to renew trade with Britain.[32]

As one might expect, these clashing views of how Boston as a community should function had other manifestations. Beginning before 1760 and continuing periodically over the years, a movement existed to modernize town government, to throw out the traditional town meeting and to replace it with a mayor and representative council. Such a system would have been more in line with the growing diversity of the town and would have eliminated the hazards of demagoguery and the crowd. The idea was elitist, but it was also pluralist innovation, the stuff of what we have here identified as the new conservatism. Not surprisingly, as conservatives attacked county conventions in 1784, in Boston they mounted a new attack on their own town meeting, again without success.[33] The hold of pluralist conservatives upon Boston clearly was not absolute.

Despite the perpetuation of the traditional town meeting, voluntary organizations based on common social and economic interests were springing up in Boston and within a very short time were to play a political role of much greater significance than the defeat of incorporation. By 1787 vari-

[32]Samuel Adams Drake, *Old Boston Taverns and Tavern Clubs* (Boston, 1917), pp. 38–39; G. B. Warden, *Boston, 1689–1776* (Boston, 1970), pp. 141, 145, 156, 157, and 261; the manuscript copy of the constitution and subscription list of the Society for Encouraging Trade and Commerce is in the Ezekial Price Manuscripts, Mass. Hist. Soc., Boston. The best treatment of nonimportation in Boston remains Charles M. Andrews, "The Boston Merchants and the Non-Importation Movement," *Publications of the Colonial Society of Massachusetts* 19 (1918): 159–259. For some modifications of Andrews's view, see Patterson, *Political Parties*, pp. 65–70.

[33]*Massachusetts Centinel*, Apr. 28, May 1, 12, 15, 19, and 26, 1784; *Boston Gazette*, Feb. 7 and Nov. 28, 1785.

ous trades of skilled artisans began organizing and analyzing their place in the economy. They were immediately susceptible to arguments from conservatives that the Articles of Confederation posed definite problems for their future economic well-being. Initially they favored revision of the Articles and ultimately the drafting of a new constitution as the best means of promoting American manufacturing and advancing their own interests.[34]

The example of Boston, therefore, furnishes evidence of both a new functional politics of class and economic interest and a persistence of traditional communitarian practices. In matters of greatest moment, however, the pluralists seemed to have had the upper hand.

By contrast, the continued reliance on corporate methods of partisan organization proved to be the most serious obstacle to the success of the western democrats. In the first instance the failure of the western party to transcend geographical boundaries may be directly attributed to this commitment. County conventions did not try to establish a link among all like-minded people in the state. The Hampshire convention of August 1786 sought to correspond with conventions in neighboring Berkshire and Worcester known to be sympathetic. But no attempt was made to contact the Middlesex convention where a large number of towns adopted resolutions identifying similar grievances.[35] Localists invariably distrusted those who were distant, while proximity to Boston and the existence in Middlesex of significant anticonvention sentiment also posed barriers. Reformers in Maine also remained isolated. Here in September 1786 rural towns assembled in a convention came to the conclusion that only separation from Massachusetts would free them from the

---

[34] *Boston Gazette*, Jan. 14, 1788; *Massachusetts Centinel*, Feb. 9, 1788; Jonathan Elliot, ed., *The Debates in the Several State Conventions on the Adoption of the Federal Constitution*, 5 vols. (n.d.; reprint ed., New York, 1974), 2:59; Samuel Bannister Harding, *The Contest over the Ratification of the Federal Constitution in the State of Massachusetts* (1896; reprint ed., New York, 1970), pp. 96–97.

[35] *Independent Chronicle*, Sept. 14, 1786. The Worcester County convention corresponded only with other counties that were meeting in convention (*Boston Gazette*, Aug. 28, 1786).

heavy burdens of taxation, discrimination against debtors, and the shortage of money. Separatism, so common a phenomenon in colonial New England churches and towns, was the classic solution of those seeking to tighten the traditional bonds of community. Significantly, the larger coastal town of Portland, where the traditional concept of community was weakest, refused to support the separatist move.[36] In a word, the democratic movement throughout Massachusetts suffered from the same tendency. Organization was vertical, through towns and counties, rather than horizontal, along class or economic lines. As a result, the western party tended to exaggerate its strength in the three western counties of Berkshire, Hampshire, and Worcester (virtually ignoring the presence of active conservatives like Theodore Sedgwick) and to exaggerate its weakness in other areas of the state, where democrats were perhaps the minority, but a very significant one.

This same organizational deficiency also contributed to the failure of Shays's Rebellion. By any measure Daniel Shays and his fellow insurgents in rural, western Massachusetts should have been able to count on widespread support when they openly challenged the operation of the courts of law in December 1786 and January 1787. By the fall of 1786, in fact, the accumulation of grievances among the rural population of Massachusetts had expressed itself in angry conventions in all but the coastal counties and in armed demonstrations against the courts in Worcester, Berkshire, Hampshire, Middlesex, and Bristol. Sympathetic support even came from isolated pockets of Essex County, the stronghold of conservatism. Everywhere there were bitter complaints about the lack of circulating cash, about the disproportionate weight of taxation upon rural areas, and about the harsh laws against debtors, particularly touching the role of the courts of common pleas in the recovery of debts. The sense of class grievance was inflamed by the state's determination to pay off the present holders of state securities at par, when thousands of ordinary people had surrendered them years before at depreciated rates. The language

[36] *Boston Gazette*, Sept. 18, 1786.

of class colored the rhetoric on both sides. The protestors identified themselves as "the yeomanry of the country" and claimed that, of their number, "almost every individual . . . derives his living from the labour of his hands or an income of a farm." Securities which they had surrendered for a quarter or a third of their nominal value, they said, had "been purchased up by the wealthy part of the community, mostly in the sea ports." The contest from their point of view was between the poor and the wealthy; from the conservative viewpoint, between "ignorant men" of desperate fortune and the propertied, thinking men of the community.[37]

But while the Shaysites and the government men both used the language of class, here the similarities ended. There was no effort to draw the dissidents together on the basis of class solidarity. Shays attempted to consolidate his hold on the three westernmost counties and believed that he had their near-unanimous support, "except about 50 men, in Northampton and Hadley." In fact, he believed it a proof of his strength that the insurgency "is not confined to a factious few, but extended to towns and counties." A state recruiting officer venturing into the west, however, discovered that there were whole towns that were anti-Shays (the larger, more commercial towns as it turns out), while Henry Knox, the commander of government forces, discovered that he could muster about nine hundred in Springfield as against the two thousand insurrectionists, who never did manage to come together as a single force.[38] In other words, the attempt to organize by counties laid Shays open to serious challenge from within, while supporters off in Essex County could do no more than cheer for him ineffectually from the distance.

[37] *Independent Chronicle*, Aug. 31 and Sept. 14, 1786; *Boston Gazette*, Aug. 28, Sept. 4 and 11, and Nov. 13, 1786; *Hampshire Herald*, Sept. 26, 1786; John Pickering to Timothy Pickering, Oct. 27, 1786, Pickering Papers, 19:85, Mass. Hist. Soc., Boston; Nicholas Pike to James Bowdoin, Feb. 12, 1787, Bowdoin-Temple Papers, 4, Mass. Hist. Soc., Boston; Theodore Sedgwick to Nathan Dane, July 5, 1787, Sedgwick Papers, 2(1774–1800), Mass. Hist. Soc., Boston.

[38] [Insurgents' Petition], *Boston Gazette*, Dec. 18, 1786; "Extracts of a letter from an officer," *Boston Gazette*, Jan. 22, 1787; Henry Knox to John Jay, Oct. 3, 1786, Henry Knox Papers, box 19: 23, Mass. Hist. Soc., Boston.

Conservatives everywhere, by contrast, came together not only in language but in fact as "men of property" and defenders of a constitution that guaranteed to them the private rights of person and of property. Shays failed, but the rebellion revealed how divergent political thinking and organization had become.

Beyond the matter of how the parties organized themselves, there was a third issue which divided the parties of Revolutionary Massachusetts and which, more than any other, forced conservatives to articulate their concern about uniformity. The issue was representation. From the very moment that Massachusetts resumed its charter government in the summer of 1775, the issue of representation became pressing. The western party developed a simple, consistent position that clearly reflected its corporate way of thinking. Every town, no matter how small, should be represented in the legislature. Some concession could be given the largest towns in terms of increased representation, but fundamentally it was the integrity of the town that needed to be recognized, not its size. The town's interests could be represented by one voice as well as by several. Ironically, it was the conservative towns of Essex County who thought otherwise. They insisted in 1776 that representation should be based on property and population. While at this stage they were not certain how both of these principles could be implemented, they came closest of all the towns of Massachusetts to arguing the principle of "one man, one vote." [39]

It was Theophilus Parsons who took this idea and gave it theoretical elaboration in the "Essex Result" in 1778. The representation of property was simply disposed of by the unoriginal proposal to create a two-house legislature with the senate designed to represent property. But his handling of representation in the lower house is revealing. He argued that all interests among the people must be represented in actual proportion to their weight in the community. He began, in other words, with the assumption that the community

[39] Patterson, *Political Parties*, ch. 8; *Acts and Resolves*, 5:502–3, 542–43; *Boston Gazette*, May 6, 1776; James Warren to John Adams, May 8, 1776, Ford, ed., *Warren-Adams Letters*, 1:239.

had a plural rather than a corporate character and that pluralism must in some fashion be brought into the legislature. The secret, he believed, was to mirror society, with all its classes and interests, so that the legislature would be in effect a "miniature" of society as a whole. "The laws will be made with the greatest wisdom, and best intentions, when men, of all the several classes in the state concur in the enacting of them." The system of representation in Massachusetts, therefore, must be changed. It was not the towns that should be represented, but the people, and "all the members of the State ought to be equally represented."[40]

What Parsons said of the state, his conservative ally Jonathan Jackson said later of the central government. He argued that the system of representation under the Articles of Confederation failed to represent the diverse interests of the American people. The Congress was "only a jumble of communities too discordant, and which contain a constant tendency to separation." The error was in supposing that "states, as such, may have an interest distinct from the interest which individuals have, to be free, and to defend their property against the attacks of robbers and conquerors." The interests of the state, ultimately, are the interests of the individuals in it compounded. If a state has a commercial interest, it is identical with the interests of its merchants; its agricultural interest must be the combined interest of its farmers. Government must therefore represent the people directly if it is to represent their interests. Jackson thereupon proposed a system whereby representatives would be chosen pyramid fashion. Ten men would choose one, ten of these, one, and so on until one man representing perhaps 100,000 should be chosen as a federal legislator. In any event, representation must be based on numbers.[41]

In Massachusetts, therefore, the modern concept of representation by population was a proposition of conservative defenders of property. It emerged in theory and remained as such through the Revolution even while conservatives

[40]Parsons, *Memoir*, pp. 360, 375, 376–77, and 391.

[41][Jonathan Jackson], *Thoughts upon the Political Situation of the United States of America* (Worcester, Mass., 1788), pp. 36, 37–40, and 109–10.

struggled for control under the system of representation by towns. It also influenced the move there for a federal constitution. The same basic premises underlay the concept, whether applied at the state or federal level. In the state representation controversy, propertied easterners saw representation by towns as a block to representation of interests. The towns served as homogenizing agents, destroying the distinctions among classes and reducing conflicting opinions to a single "general will." In like manner, the Articles of Confederation, in providing for congressional representation by states, erected an intermediary block between people and government to prevent the representation of interest. Representation by population would change this. At least in the minds of Massachusetts "men of property," representation by population was equated with interest politics, an innovation that challenged some of the basic precepts of eighteenth-century political thought.

To conclude, the men who became New England's Federalists responded creatively and imaginatively to the social and economic pressures placed upon them by the American Revolution. While their ends, the preservation of their own property, status, and power, remained conservative, their means shifted to reflect the pluralistic cultural environment in which most of them lived and to counter a rising democracy which most of them found intolerant and stifling. In place of the corporate, conformist mold of traditional theory and frequently of practice, they proposed a new science of politics: one in which society would recognize the fragments of which it was composed, tolerate all viewpoints, govern itself by representing the people and their diverse interests directly, and permit the organization of classes and interests along partisan lines.

None of the Massachusetts leaders of this creative phase in the history of New England Federalism ever put it as succinctly as James Madison did, but it is clear from what they said and did during and after the Revolution that they came to the same conclusions he did in *Federalist No. 10*. Politics was a clash of interests, the regulation of which "forms the principal task of modern Legislation, and involves the spirit of party and faction in the necessary and ordinary operations of Government."[42]

In the end, the Federalists did not seek to destroy democracy, but rather to transform it. Left in its corporate form, it was unacceptable: masses of the unpropertied or the small-propertied would exercise unlimited control over men with larger holdings by defining the consensus. The alternative, Federalists came to believe, was the restructuring of political theory on the basis of individualism, toleration, and "separate interest." The people would emerge in politics, not as a unitary force, not as a "mob," but as an aggregation of interests, competing and cooperating among themselves in an accommodative political order. In that kind of system, property would have a chance.

Must we therefore dispose of the notion that New England Federalism derived from an organic, corporate sense of community supposedly inherent in the New England town? The evidence presented so far suggests as much, but it is important that we not replace one distortion with another. Federalism had a long and flourishing history after the ratification of the Constitution. Moreover, what happened after 1790 seems not to follow logically upon the trend towards openness, functionalism, and cosmopolitanism evident in the Federalist movement of the 1780s. One could perhaps argue that what we have are two separate movements, with no connection between them. The facts, however, suggest otherwise. Federalist leadership remained the same through both decades, and its conservative goals did not change. Its methods did, however, and some suggestion as to why they did is in order.

The very fact that Federalists organized themselves as a national political party must partly explain changes in political style. Modern parties cast their nets widely: winning votes is primary. Federalism, as an organized political force at the

[42] James Madison, *Federalist No. 10*, in Jacob E. Cooke, ed., *The Federalist* (Middletown, Conn., 1961), p. 59. For a Massachusetts argument in favor of political parties, see "Atticus" in the *Independent Chronicle*, Oct. 18, 1787.

turn of the century, appealed to many of the areas in western Massachusetts that had supported Shays and Antifederalism, while in many towns the consensual support of a single political movement gave way to competitively balanced adherence to two political parties. While the Federalists may not have become all things to all people, clearly they succeeded in meeting many voters on the voters' own terms. This led at some times to ideological ambiguity, at others to factionalism, not only among the rank and file but among the leadership. John Adams could attach himself to a Federalism with a substantial traditional component, but he could never reconcile himself to Alexander Hamilton's appeal to self-interest nor with that group in Massachusetts he associated with Hamiltonianism, the Essex Junto.[43]

Several historical developments are also suggestive. Among them Hamilton's policy of assumption looms large. By relieving Massachusetts of the indebtedness that generated the most bitter political controversy of the decade, assumption defused the explosive and disintegrative tendencies represented by Shays. Simultaneously, the Federal Constitution itself became popular as the machinery of the new government began turning. More broadly, two countertendencies brought rural New England towns and Federalist politics closer together by breaking down whatever cultural rigidities might have separated them. On the one hand, the towns themselves experienced a rapid growth of voluntary social and cultural societies that in effect represented an increase in modern urban behavior and values. Extralocal contacts were thereby increased and a broader sense of regionalism and even nationalism began to vie with traditional commitments to family, church, and town.[44] The sense of community was al-

[43] Fischer, *Revolution of American Conservatism*, pp. 17–19; Stephen G. Kurtz, *The Presidency of John Adams* (Philadelphia, 1957), pp. 98–99, 192, 194, 371–73, and 374–75; Fischer, "Myth of the Essex Junto," pp. 192 and 226; Winfred E. A. Bernhard, *Fisher Ames: Federalist and Statesman, 1758–1808* (Chapel Hill, 1965), 204–5 and 325; Manning J. Dauer, *The Adams Federalists* (Baltimore, 1953).

[44] Hall, pp. 341–50; Richard D. Brown, "The Emergence of Urban Society in Rural Massachusetts, 1790–1820," *Journal of American History* 61 (1974–75): 29–51.

tered, although not necessarily reduced. While the cultural milieu of rural towns changed in the direction of urbanism, community leaders who espoused the open, tolerant values of pre-Constitution Federalism began to fall back on the rhetoric of their grandfathers, celebrating consensus, harmony, and peace. Whether they did so to regain their lost local influence or simply to expand the popular base of their party, they succeeded in both. Theodore Sedgwick, so isolated politically in 1778, was by 1795 the Federalist master of a Federalist town.[45] No longer challenged by an intolerant democracy, Federalists relaxed their innovative faculties while their vision of a new pluralistic society blurred. As a conservative movement embracing both the Federalism of the 1780s and the national political party that followed, Federalism had a period of creative, innovative origin, followed by a period of consolidation and, in many ways, reaction.

In the end, the early history of Federalism shows that political ideology responded not so much to separate and discrete social and cultural modes as to a continuing and continually changing tension between two ideals: the early traditional values of the closed community and the broadening, rationalist functionalism of modern society. The Massachusetts experience evidences a perceptible shift, however incomplete, toward the latter. Yet while the American Revolution was a modernizing experience, the period of constitutional experiment and theorizing produced sharper visions of America's pluralistic future than would be realized in the short run. Modern liberal democracy would come later. Still, the very fact that crisis forced such a creative leap into the future ensured that the Constitution of 1787 would contain the elements upon which a modern nation could be sustained.

[45] Fischer, *Revolution of American Conservatism*, pp. 12–14.

JEROME J. NADELHAFT

"The Snarls of Invidious Animals"

The Democratization of
Revolutionary South Carolina

I AM NOW by the will of God brought into a new world, and God only knows what sort of a world it will be; what may be your particular opinion of this change I know not." So wrote Henry Laurens, slave trader, merchant, plantation owner, and a committed rebel, to his son in 1776. The answer of John Laurens, studying law in England, was unequivocal: If his country submitted to British oppression, he would forget he was an American; if it was steadfast and triumphant, he would "glory in the name which will thenceforth raise the associate Ideas of brave and free." Father and son, however, foresaw serious problems. The elder Laurens worried that "horrible butcheries" would result from British-encouraged Indian attacks and slave insurrections, and "fraud, perjury & assasination" would be the consequences of divisions within the white community.[1] After witnessing the growing political activity of "the Country people," he denounced the idea that "no Man is now supposed to be unequal to a share in Government." His son returned home to fight despite concern that the conflict was overturning established rules of political behavior. He "most heartily lament[ed]" that people

---

[1] Henry Laurens to John Laurens, Aug. 14, 1776, Frank Moore, ed., *Materials for History Printed from Original Manuscripts* (New York, 1861), p. 31; John Laurens to Francis Kinloch, Mar. 10, 1775, *Charleston Yearbook* (Charleston, 1882), p. 347; Henry Laurens to John Laurens, July 30, 1775, Henry and John Laurens Papers, Library of Congress.

"illy calculated to move in the most limited ministerial spheres, [were] unfortunately suffered to have a voice in matters of the greatest Intricacy and Importance."[2] But the political disruption that worried the Laurens family and others of similar minds was welcomed by people who had reason to hope and expect that a new political world would emerge from the crisis in Anglo-American affairs.

Independence did lead to dramatic political change in South Carolina, but there was no violent internal revolution. Because the colony's elite were in the forefront of resistance to Great Britain, working first through the colonial legislature and then in newly created representative bodies, there was no abrupt end to established institutions, no purge of leadership, no radical innovation in government. At no time would a Carolinian who returned home after six months or a year abroad have had difficulty placing himself or recognizing the political world around him. Nonetheless, anyone who had left before 1774 and returned after the state adopted its second constitution in 1778 would have been startled by the differences. Between the 1760s and 1790, the change was overwhelming. The comfortable, familiar state of South Carolina's elite was gradually eroded by dissident groups. Although the elite were by no means rendered powerless by the Revolutionary struggles and were often still in control, the changes were significant. The nature of the differences, of the accumulated changes, was apparent to contemporaries, but it has eluded historians since.

South Carolina's colonial government is easily described. By the 1760s the royal governor and the English placemen on the royal council were dominated by a forty-eight-man Commons House of Assembly. The assemblymen were intimately acquainted, related, and intermarried. Between 1762 and 1768, seventy-five men served as representatives; at least forty-seven were related to others by blood or marriage (first

[2] Henry Laurens to John Laurens, Jan. 4, 1775, "Letters from Hon. Henry Laurens to His Son John, 1773–1776," *South Carolina Historical and Genealogical Magazine* 4 (1903): 271; John Laurens to Francis Kinloch, Mar. 10, 1775, *Charleston Yearbook*, pp. 345–47.

cousin or closer). In wealth they were Commoners who were anything but common. Over two-thirds of the representatives in 1765 had property worth at least five thousand pounds, while the others owned property worth more than two thousand. Not all had inherited wealth. Probably between 20 and 40 percent of the members of the assembly were self-made men. Two of the twelve most active representatives between 1762 and 1765 were immigrants; four or five, the sons of immigrants.[3] Few quarrels erupted among these Carolina representatives; they and their constituents were generally united by a threat from the slaves who surrounded them. Fear of an uprising by blacks thought to be "barbarous [and] wild" led whites to avoid lasting controversy among themselves lest they appear divided and weak.[4]

But despite the apparent unanimity among Carolina leaders in their dealings with slaves, there were divisions among Carolinians. In simple but inadequate terms, the most significant was between east and west, lowcountry and backcountry; in addition the lowcountry parishes in the immediate vicinity of Charleston sometimes stood against the rest of the colony. Nor was the city of Charleston free of dissension.

Although the members of the Commons governed in the name of all the people, they were chosen by the relative few who lived within a small area and were themselves, as planters, lawyers, and merchants, among the wealthiest people in America. Descriptions of South Carolina divide the colony into two regions: the lowcountry and the backcountry. The former consisted of the sea islands and a strip of coastal land about sixty miles wide. After 1769 this area was divided into three circuit court districts: Georgetown, bordering North Carolina; Beaufort, bordering Georgia in the south; and Charleston District in the middle. Long before the Revolu-

[3] Jackson Turner Main, "Government by the People: The American Revolution and the Democratization of the Legislatures," *William and Mary Quarterly*, 3d ser. 23 (1966): 396; Robert M. Weir, "'Liberty and Property, and No Stamps': South Carolina and the Stamp Act Crisis," Ph.D. diss., Western Reserve University, 1966, pp. 37 and 60.

[4] Robert M. Weir, "'The Harmony We Were Famous For': An Interpretation of Pre-Revolutionary South Carolina Politics," *William and Mary Quarterly*, 3d ser. 26 (1969): 473–501.

tion, much of the lowcountry, and especially Charleston District, was settled by colonists attracted by the proprietors' promotional campaign and the promise of religious toleration. The Church of England, however, became the established church. Many Dissenters converted and families intermarried. The area came to be dominated by plantations, a slave labor force that worked the rice and indigo crops, and wealthy individuals who controlled the legislature.[5]

Settlement in the backcountry did not begin until the 1730s and 1740s. Another wave of settlers began to arrive in the 1760s, after the Cherokee War. In 1775 the population of the backcountry numbered 50,000; most of them were German, Swiss, Dutch, Irish, Scotch-Irish, or Welsh rather than English. Most were Presbyterian rather than Anglican, but there were also Baptists, Quakers, and other Dissenters. Almost all settled small farms where they produced provision crops of corn, wheat, and, in some areas, tobacco and indigo.[6]

Georgetown District, usually considered part of the lowcountry, had much in common with the interior. Large numbers of settlers, many of them Welsh and French, arrived in the 1740s and 1750s. Though parts of Georgetown were like Charleston-area parishes, with slaves and plantations, other sections of the large district contained small farms.[7]

The backcountry and Georgetown shared political weakness. South Carolina's government was dominated not by the people of the entire lowcountry but by Charleston District. In 1771 that district, which ten years earlier probably contained no more than five thousand adult white males, elected thirty-six members of the lower house. St. John Berkeley, one of its parishes, sent three men to the legislature; a road census of 1762 had listed seventy-six adult white males in the

[5] M. Eugene Sirmans, *Colonial South Carolina: A Political History, 1663–1763* (Chapel Hill, 1966), pp. 36–37, 61–62, 77, and 96–100.

[6] Backcountry settlement is best described in Robert L. Meriwether, *The Expansion of South Carolina, 1729–1765* (Kingsport, Tenn., 1940), and Richard Maxwell Brown, *The South Carolina Regulators* (Cambridge, Mass., 1963), chs. 1 and 2.

[7] Brown, *South Carolina Regulators*, pp. 40 and 54–55.

parish.[8] With roughly the same area as Charleston District and far more whites, Georgetown elected only four representatives. Beaufort, too, was politically weak; with perhaps half Georgetown's white population, it elected five representatives. The backcountry elected three. Few politically important people came from non-Charleston areas. During the 1760s, for example, only one of the twelve most important members of the lower house came from a parish outside Charleston District. In the Revolutionary Council of Safety, eight of the thirteen members came from the port of Charleston, and the remaining five from parishes close to the city.[9]

Because of their wealth, and probably because domination of slaves enhanced their sense of superiority, the elite politicians assumed that they could govern the colony alone. The Massachusetts traveler Josiah Quincy exaggerated only a little in commenting that the "Planting interest" alone was represented. And planters, he continued, have "but little solicitude about the interest or concerns of the *many*."[10] Western Carolinians and Georgetown settlers certainly agreed. Rising in protest in the 1760s after their repeated complaints about criminals, oppression by lawyers, and inadequate representation had failed to impress lowcountry leaders, these Regulators observed that legislators had heard their "Cries" with their ears, but had not allowed them to penetrate their hearts. No wonder that one English official thought the Commoners men whom "no King can govern nor no God . . . please."[11]

[8]David Morton Knepper, "The Political Structure of Colonial South Carolina, 1743–1776," Ph.D. diss., University of Virginia, 1971, p. 36; Weir, "'Liberty and Property,'" pp. 37–38.

[9]Weir, "'Liberty and Property,'" p. 95n; Jack P. Greene, *The Quest for Power: The Lower Houses of Assembly in the Southern Royal Colonies, 1689–1776* (Chapel Hill, 1963), appendix, pp. 475–88; Edward McCrady, *The History of South Carolina under the Royal Government, 1719–1776* (New York, 1899), p. 797.

[10]*Memoir of the Life of Josiah Quincy, Junior, of Massachusetts Bay: 1774–1775* (Boston, 1875), p. 87.

[11]The Regulators' "Remonstrance" (1767), in Richard J. Hooker, ed., *The Carolina Backcountry on the Eve of the Revolution: The Journal and Other*

The controversy with England produced quick and inevitable changes. Artisans and mechanics, without voice in running the unincorporated port of Charleston since it was governed by the legislature, seized the opportunity to assume a public importance. The changing times were indicated by their success in pushing through a nonimportation plan in 1769 with planter support but in the face of merchant opposition. They highlighted that success, and the very legitimacy of their participation, by joining with others to create a committee of enforcement that included equal numbers of planters, merchants, and mechanics. By the early 1760s the Commons' concern for harmony had required recognition of only three major interests—planters, merchants, and lawyers. But by 1774 both "the Gentlemen & Mechanic, those of high and low life, the learned & illiterate," were discussing politics and "American affairs" and influencing policy.[12]

Since no war could be fought without the support of westerners, a political system to include them and city workers began to take form. In July 1774, 104 Carolinians, drawn to Charleston by letters sent to every parish and section of South Carolina, met until midnight on three consecutive days to consider American rights and the election of delegates to the First Continental Congress in Philadelphia. Then they set up a General Committee to run the colony. The meetings, said Peter Timothy, editor of the *South Carolina Gazette*, were "such an example of pure democracy as has rarely been seen since the days of the Ancient city republics."[13]

Writings of Charles Woodmason, Anglican Itinerant (Chapel Hill, 1953), p. 214; William Knox to Gov. William Henry Lyttelton, Mar. 5, 1760, quoted in Sirmans, *Colonial South Carolina*, p. 320.

[12] Richard Walsh, *Charleston's Sons of Liberty: A Study of the Artisans, 1763–1789* (Columbia, S.C., 1959), p. 31; Weir, "'Liberty and Property,'" p. 95n. John Pringle commented on the people discussing politics, but he did not indicate who was influencing decisions (Pringle to William Tilghman, July 30, 1774, Preston Davie Collection, University of North Carolina Library, Chapel Hill).

[13] *South Carolina Gazette*, July 11, 1774, quoted in George Edward Frakes, *Laboratory for Liberty: The South Carolina Legislative Committee System, 1719–1776* (Lexington, Ky., 1970), p. 122.

Timothy exaggerated, but contemporaries sensed the meaning of the political developments. Merchant Benjamin Smith wrote that lower-class people had become "men of consequence" by rioting against the Stamp Act; he welcomed the act's repeal because it had sunk those upstarts "into nothing." The "Mobility," as another upper-class gentleman referred to the people, had become active.[14] Francis Kinloch found it "dreadful" to be mixed up with "butchers, bakers, [and] blacksmiths," and Henry Laurens denounced inexperienced and unqualified representatives: They thought business could be "completed with no more words than are necessary in the bargain and sale of a cow."[15]

But there was no going back. The alterations of government were incorporated into two state constitutions. The first, adopted in 1776 before Independence was declared, dramatically altered the apportionment of representation in the House of Commons. Charleston District had elected 75 percent of the colonial Commons; it chose 48 percent of the new representatives (96 of 202). The backcountry, which had elected 6 percent of the old Commons, chose 38 percent of the new lower house (76 representatives). Representation for Georgetown and Beaufort districts declined from 19 percent of the old Commons to 15 percent of the new (30 representatives).[16]

Despite the change in apportionment, dissatisfaction with the constitution quickly surfaced, and the legislature responded in 1778 with a plan of government more to the liking of the new political forces and more in line with

[14] Smith to Rev. William Smith, May 16, 1766, quoted in George C. Rogers, Jr., *Evolution of a Federalist: William Loughton Smith of Charleston (1758–1812)* (Columbia, S.C., 1962), pp. 46–47; John Pringle to William Tilghman, Sept. 15, 1774, Preston Davie Collection.

[15] Kinloch to John Laurens, Apr. 28, 1776, quoted in Rogers, *Evolution of a Federalist*, p. 79; Laurens to John Laurens, Jan. 22, 1775, quoted in William Edwin Hemphill and Wylma Anne Wates, eds., *Extracts from the Journals of the Provincial Congresses of South Carolina, 1775–1776* (Columbia, S.C., 1960), p. xxiii.

[16] For a more detailed account of South Carolina's constitutions and of historians' inaccurate summaries, see chapter 2 of my book, *The Disorders of War: The Revolution in South Carolina, 1775–1790* (Orono, Me., 1981).

philosophies expressed in the constitutions adopted by other states. Amendments attacked not only the "capitol and adjacent Parishes," whose political advantage one legislator feared would cause the government to "degenerate into an oligarchy," but also the governor, whose power allowed him to overturn the wishes of the people.[17] The danger of the oligarchy came from the upper house, members of which were elected by the lower house from its own membership. The first two elections demonstrated what could be expected. Because several men resigned to fill other positions or declined to serve, seventeen men had to be chosen to fill the thirteen positions on the first Legislative Council. Eleven were from parishes in or close to Charleston, four from the backcountry, and only two from the coastal parishes near Georgia; none at all were from Georgetown District. Of the fourteen elected to the second council, six were from the parishes surrounding Charleston, and five from the city of Charleston. The constitution of 1778 made the upper house more representative of the entire state. The backcountry filled eleven of twenty-nine Senate seats, and Georgetown and Beaufort five. (The apportionment of representation in the lower house was not changed, but the constitution provided for reapportionment in 1785 and every fourteen years thereafter on the basis of white population and taxable property.)

Other states writing constitutions in 1776 and 1777 had been so fearful of executive power, "ever restless, ambitious, and ever grasping" for more, that they stripped their governors of most "badges of domination." Seven states limited the number of successive years governors could serve. All denied them the power to veto legislation.[18] South Carolina had

[17] William Tennent, "Historic remarks on the session of Assembly began to be holden Tuesday, September 17th, 1776," Newton B. Jones, ed., "Writings of the Reverend William Tennent, 1740–1777," *South Carolina Historical Magazine* 61 (1960): 189; William Edwin Hemphill et al., eds., *Journals of the General Assembly and House of Representatives, 1776–1780*, Oct. 12 and 14, 1776 (Columbia, S.C., 1970), pp. 143 and 148–49.

[18] The quotations and the provisions of other state constitutions are found in Gordon S. Wood, *The Creation of the American Republic, 1776–1787* (Chapel Hill, 1969), pp. 132–43.

taken no such steps in 1776, but in 1778 it turned the governor into a figurehead. He was denied a fixed salary, turned out of office after a two-year term, and removed from the legislative process by being denied the right to veto legislation.

John Rutledge, governor of the state in 1778, acknowledged the significance of these changes when he vetoed the proposed constitution. Rutledge reasoned that he had taken an oath to govern the state according to the constitution of 1776 and that he could not in good conscience agree to its alteration even though, according to one representative, the assembly had been elected to change the constitution. But Rutledge objected to more than what he considered the unconstitutional nature of the new plan; he regarded it as too democratic. "The people," he said, "preferred a compounded or mixed government to a simple democracy, or one verging toward it," because the effects of democratic power are "arbitrary, severe, and destructive." He specifically repudiated the new method of choosing the upper house, asserting that Carolinians preferred the old way because it was "more likely" that representatives would choose men of "integrity, learning and abilities" from their own membership than the people would elect in their local districts. He did not add that the old way had kept the upper house in the control of a few who, one observer thought, were "in the interest of the Rutledge family."[19] Rutledge also objected to the loss of the veto.[20] After vetoing the constitution, Rutledge resigned. Arthur Middleton (a brother-in-law of John Rutledge's brother, Edward) declined the office because he,

[19] John Lewis Gervais to Henry Laurens, Mar. 16, 1778, Raymond Starr, ed., "Letters from John Lewis Gervais to Henry Laurens, 1777–1778," *South Carolina Historical Magazine* 66 (1965): 29; Rutledge's veto, quoted in David Ramsay, *The History of the Revolution of South-Carolina from a British Province to an Independent State*, 2 vols. (Trenton, N.J., 1785), 1:136; Rutledge to Henry Laurens, Mar. 8, 1778, Moore, ed., *Materials for History*, pp. 103–5; James Cannon to George Bryan, Mar. 14, 1778, Joseph Johnson, *Traditions & Reminiscences Chiefly of the American Revolution in the South* (Charleston, 1851), pp. 156–57.

[20] Rutledge to Henry Laurens, Mar. 8, 1778, Moore, ed., *Materials for History*, p. 103.

too, disapproved of the constitution. Finally, Rawlins Lowndes accepted the post and the constitution.

Rutledge's vision of a South Carolina become too democratic was reiterated by other Carolinians in 1780, shortly after the British took Charleston and established posts inland. On June 5 more than two hundred Charlestonians, many from the respectable and prosperous class, congratulated the British commanders. Independence, they wrote, was a revolting doctrine which "originated in the more northern colonies," and led to a dissolution of the old government. They denounced the creation of "a rank democracy," because it was a kind of "tyrannic domination, only to be found among the uncivilized part of mankind, or in the . . . dark and barbarous ages of antiquity."[21]

Clearly, the end result of the initial changes introduced by the new constitutions was anxiety and uncertainty for the ruling elite, as Rutledge and others recognized. When the Commons sat with 40 to 50 representatives, its members knew what to expect. One could work and anticipate success in a small Commons that contained few unknown men. But how did one behave and predict the turn of debate in a body of 202, even if no more than 100 attended? For example, the Provincial Congress, which had met during the winter of 1775–76, had contained 184 delegates and had witnessed a number of close votes: 51 to 49 on November 8; 49 to 48 six days later; in February 53 to 49; and 49 to 49. The suspense was great; the future, as Henry Laurens had feared, unknown.

Full comprehension came slowly to Laurens and his friends. Laurens himself sailed for Europe on a diplomatic mission in 1780, was captured by the British, and spent more than a year imprisoned in the Tower of London. When South Carolina became a bloody battleground with a shift of the war south, the legislature's concerns, of necessity, became military. And because the British occupation forces spread throughout the state, the legislature did not meet between February 1780 and January 1782.

---

[21] John Almon, *The Remembrancer, or Impartial Repository of Public Events* 10 (1780): 83.

The promise of the new age was seen in 1782. With the British cooped up in Charleston, the legislature met in Jacksonborough, a small village about thirty-five miles from Charleston. The Jacksonborough Assembly has often been described by historians because it confiscated and taxed the estates of loyalists and people deemed too sympathetic to them. Much of the political turmoil of the 1780s in South Carolina, as in other states, was caused by legislation punishing those internal enemies. But despite their frequent descriptions of the legislature, historians have overlooked its real significance.

For the first time, non-Charleston areas controlled the assembly. Only seven of the nineteen senators who appeared represented Charleston District. Much the same alignment existed in the lower house. This was the case partly because the legislature was meeting outside Charleston, and partly because lowcountry residents threw away at the polls their opportunity to continue their usual dominance. The election was sparsely attended, even for a state accustomed to small turnouts. In the election for St. Andrew's members, held in St. John Berkeley, four voters chose six representatives and one senator; St. Peter's thirteen voters selected the same number of representatives and senators. Fifteen Charleston voters elected thirty representatives and two senators. But the visions of the few voters were so narrow and their political society in such turmoil that they did not elect men who could attend. Only sixteen of those elected by Charleston's voters attended the legislature. Henry Laurens was still in England and did not return until 1784. Charles Cotesworth Pinckney, elected by two parishes, was a prisoner on parole in Philadelphia. Thomas Bee was also elected by two parishes but was a delegate to the Confederation Congress and did not serve. All told, the Charleston District was short thirty-nine representatives, the rest of the state only twenty-six.[22]

The election of absentees by the voters of Charleston District demonstrated the elitist nature of lowcountry government. The domination of the legislature by members from

[22] Jerome Nadelhaft, "The 'Havoc of War' and Its Aftermath in Revolutionary South Carolina," *Histoire Sociale* 12 (1979): 108–9.

newly enfranchised areas highlighted the changes precipitated by the Revolution. That shift in power, however temporary, was recognized by Edward Rutledge, a lowcountry representative and brother of John Rutledge. Although he was only thirty-two when the assembly met, he was already an experienced politician. When John Laurens appeared at Jacksonborough with a plan to arm and free slaves, Rutledge feared that he might be the only speaker to oppose the radical scheme. The defeat of the plan by a vote he remembered as about 15 to 100 satisfied him,[23] but his apprehension about his fellow legislators' attitudes toward the institution on which South Carolina lived could not have existed in the 1760s.

The attention of the Jacksonborough Assembly then turned to loyalists. Legislators affected by a civil war that had wreaked havoc in much of the backcountry and Georgetown sought revenge. Some tallied on their guns the men they had slain. Their severest attack was embodied in laws seizing the property of people deemed disaffected with the rebel cause. The legislature confiscated 377 estates and amerced, or fined, 94 others at 12 percent of their appraised value. The only serious disagreements concerned whose property was to be seized. Although in their original drafts the acts had been sweeping in their coverage, as finally passed they mostly affected people from Charleston and the surrounding parishes.[24]

To punish some wartime criminals, the legislature opened the Courts of Oyer and Terminer. Aedanus Burke, a legislator and one of the judges who would be forced into action by the opening of the courts, strongly condemned this because so many people could be prosecuted. More importantly, he feared he was to be "a tool to gratify the fierce revenge of the people." Backcountry people warned him not to let lawyers defend tories; further, he was told to "be cautious how . . . [he] adjudged any point in their favor."[25]

---

[23] Ibid., p. 109.

[24] Ibid., pp. 110–11.

[25] Burke to Arthur Middleton, May 14, 1782, quoted ibid., p. 110.

Domination of the Jacksonborough Assembly by non-Charleston areas did not signify the demise of the old ruling group. Indeed, once the legislature reassembled in 1783, the lowcountry aristocracy used its many weapons to reassert control. Under the terms of the constitution of 1778, Charleston District was still highly overrepresented; its power was automatically increased when the government returned to Charleston. In special sessions that met in 1783 and 1785, its usual advantage of place was increased. On no recorded issue in the summer of 1783 did more than 77 members of the lower house vote. Forty-six of the 60 members who can be identified were from Charleston District. In the special session of 1785 at least 112 representatives were present: Of the 76 whose names are known, 58 sat for the lowcountry, 47 of them from Charleston District, and only 18 for the backcountry. Backcountry representatives simply could not afford the constant travel involved in representing their electors.

Lowcountry residents in the parishes around Charleston continued to be tranquil in their political behavior, as though nothing had changed. Elections continued to be sparsely attended, dull, and uncontested. Throughout the 1780s, for example, voters in St. Thomas and St. Dennis presented a united front. In 1783 seventeen of twenty-two voters cast their ballots for Joseph Atkinson as senator. Two years later nineteen voters elected three representatives, each of whom received seventeen votes while other candidates received five. In 1786 twenty-four voters cast senatorial ballots for John Huger while three supported an opponent. In St. James Goose Creek in 1783, Thomas Middleton won with four votes and the two other candidates together received another four. In 1789, twenty-six men voted in Christ Church and chose seven men for the state's forthcoming constitutional convention. Both Charles Pinckney and John Rutledge received twenty-six votes, the other winners between twenty and twenty-four.[26]

The behavior of lowcountry electors notwithstanding,

[26] Election Returns, Records of the General Assembly, South Carolina Department of Archives and History, Columbia.

there were differences on the political scene. Lowcountry elections no longer represented the only major political activity in the state; backcountry elections were well attended and often highly contested. In 1788, 165 people voted in the backcountry county of Greenville and, in 1792, 677 voted in Chester. That year 201 people participated in Clarendon; the winners received 111 and 103 votes, the losers 97 and 91. In Laurens County, 655 men voted; one loser there received 260 votes.[27]

The new political world was also evident in the legislature. Relative novices, some of them military heroes and all of them less affluent than the colonial legislators, appeared, stayed, gained confidence, and made themselves heard. In the years immediately following the war, according to traveler Johann David Schoepf, the "intelligent and well-informed" merchants and attorneys representing Charleston were usually able to "get the upper hand" of country representatives when it was "a matter of address and a little intrigue." Backcountry members, however, who were without "courage or eloquence enough to oppose matters which might seem to them undesirable or burdensome," occasionally defeated measures. It was understandable that backcountry senators and representatives might have been overimpressed at first by a display of eloquence that would honor "the senate of ancient Rome."[28] But experience gave them courage and confidence, and men like Arthur Simkins, James Knox, and Robert Anderson, backcountry legislators throughout the Confederation period, soon did more than silently oppose the old leadership. In 1788 Arthur Bryan, an unimportant Charleston merchant, sensed the political change. "The great people had an entire sway" before 1784, he wrote, but then "a violent opposition" in the city almost "to-

[27] Ibid.

[28] Johann David Schoepf, *Travels in the Confederation*, trans. and ed. Alfred J. Morrison (Philadelphia, 1911), p. 198; the reference to the Roman senate was made in 1788 by James Lincoln, a backcountry representative (Jonathan Elliot, ed., *The Debates in the Several State Conventions on the Adoption of the Federal Constitution*, 2d ed., 5 vols. [Philadelphia, 1836], 4:312).

tally ruin[ed] the Aristocracy, for if they now carry any thing in the assembly it is by deception."[29]

After the departure of the British troops in 1782, Charleston dissidents, backcountry settlers, and inhabitants of low-country parishes far from Charleston joined to fight the legislature's policies and to denounce some of the legislators as well. They were sufficiently loud, effective, and consistent to be recognized and condemned by the state's "natural" rulers. It was almost unthinkable to John Lloyd, president of the Senate, that in 1784 "gentlemen of property" had to exert themselves to prevent the "Malcontented party" from electing representatives "from the lower class."[30] According to Edward Rutledge, the aristocrats considered the opposition from people they called "worthless" and "foolish" to be so distasteful there was considerable talk of abandoning the field to the malcontented; but a fear of "anarchy and confusion" prevented such surrender. Still, the *Charleston Morning Post and Daily Advertiser* lamented that recent events had caused "many leading members" to withdraw from the next election. The paper tried to counter the trend by arguing that "every man is public property. His time and talents . . . nay more—life, all belong to his country."[31]

Ironically, the idea that men were public property was the very idea causing some people to consider resigning from political life since some argued, in a new departure for South Carolina, that the actions of public officials ought to be dissected and examined for corruption, conspiracy, and intrigue. To Alexander Gillon, who emerged as spokesman for the small merchants, artisans, and mechanics of Charleston, it was "the first feature of a free government" that all officers were "public property," to be watched with an "ever wakeful

[29] Bryan to George Bryan, Apr. 9, 1788, George Bryan Papers, Historical Society of Pennsylvania, Philadelphia.

[30] Lloyd to T. B. Smith, Dec. 7, 1784, John Lloyd Letters, Charleston Library Society.

[31] Rutledge to John Jay, Nov. 12, 1786, Henry P. Johnston, ed., *The Correspondence and Public Papers of John Jay*, 4 vols. (New York, 1890–93), 3:217; *Charleston Morning Post and Daily Advertiser*, July 7, 1786.

vigilance."[32] The simple assertion that the government was run by gentlemen who served "without fee or reward," was answered contemptuously. "Enormous wealth," wrote one commentator, "is seldom the associate of *pure* and *disinterested virtue*."[33] Another writer asked whether calling city councilors men of rank meant that some were *"rank cowards . . .* [and] *rank idiots*."[34]

To attack public servants and make them accountable, the dissidents used the city's presses. Because of newspapers, they wrote, "ladies cannot paint or bare their bosoms," "old virgins cannot marry young batchelors," nor gentlemen "seduce innocence"; more importantly, "magistrates cannot oppress the poor" nor "senators . . . betray their trust."[35] The critics rejected the doctrine of seditious libel that protected incumbents by asserting that constitutionally guaranteed liberty of the press meant only the "liberty to insert any thing that does not tend to disturb the peace of the government." Clearly Blackstone's *Commentaries* did not set the tone of the 1780s. Liberty of the press was of no use if truth, even when unpleasant, could not be printed for all to read. "If truth be a libel," the aristocracy's critics argued, "what must falsehood" be?[36] They printed their versions of the truth in a greatly expanded press. While in the early 1770s two weeklies and a semiweekly had provided Carolinians with information, by the mid-1780s there were four newspapers, and two of them were dailies.

The change in the spirit and nature of politics—and the gradual decline of the aristocracy's power—are evident throughout the 1780s. When the legislature in 1783 allowed

[32] Gillon to Nathanael Greene, Apr. 11, 1783, Naval History Collection, New-York Historical Society, New York City.

[33] *Gazette of the State of South Carolina*, June 2, 1785; *South Carolina Gazette & General Advertiser*, Sept. 16, 1784.

[34] *South Carolina Gazette & Public Advertiser*, Aug. 13, 1785.

[35] *Columbian Herald*, May 2, 1785.

[36] *Charleston Evening Gazette*, Sept. 2, 1785; *Gazette of the State of South Carolina*, Aug. 27, 1783.

British merchants to stay in Charleston and modified the confiscation and amercement acts, its more vehement critics began to use the newspapers and streets of Charleston to mobilize their allies. The intense propaganda was probably designed to bring about an alliance between backcountry settlers and Charleston protestors. Their only recourse, however, was to make life physically and economically unprofitable for British merchants and tories. "The old inhabitants of the town are becoming very uneasy respecting the admission" of British merchants, wrote one Charlestonian. "Riots," he added, had already occurred.[37]

The disorders were taken seriously. David Ramsay noted that the "lower class" was active, and he predicted unhappily that "the licentiousness of the people" would not disappear for half a century.[38] In response, a small number of Charleston-area legislators acted quickly in a special session of the legislature to quiet Charleston, not by considering complaints or redressing grievances, but by incorporating the city, thereby creating the machinery to suppress demonstrators.

Unawed by the disturbances, the legislature touched off more protests in 1784 by further modifying the confiscatory legislation. The government called the July protests "riots," although apparently they were largely vocal and symbolic rather than physical and violent.[39] But, violent or not, the ensuing conflict continued long after the original act of provocation receded into the background. The propaganda that followed for the next few years was sometimes inaccurate, contradictory, and exaggerated; publicists painted in black and white, considering no middle ground, no extenuating circumstances, when judging men's motives or behavior. But there was also a maturing of the opposition's arguments. Propaganda changed from antitory to antiaristocracy, from attacks on legislation to attacks on legislators.

[37] John Sandford Dart to Ralph Izard, July 11, 1783, quoted in Rogers, *Evolution of a Federalist*, pp. 104–5.

[38] Ramsay to Benjamin Rush, July 11, 1783, quoted ibid., p. 105.

[39] Privy Council Journal, July 12, 1784, S.C. Dept. of Arch. and Hist., Columbia.

And, ultimately, within the propaganda contemporaries could find a political philosophy common in the eighteenth century but hitherto largely unspoken or unemphasized in South Carolina. The conflicts and rhetoric contributed to a further democratization of state government.

Almost always the biting, often sarcastic, diatribes were directed in general terms against the aristocracy and the legislature. One critic wrote about the "mal-administration of men in power or public trust"; another found "the *leading men*" intent on ruling "with a rod of iron."[40] When they focused their attention, newspaper correspondents lashed out at lawyers, since they were "more liable to corruption than other men." Lawyers enacted confusing legislation to increase their business and took money "to prevent" justice.[41]

Newspapers urged readers to be vigilant since slavery was "preceded by *sleep*." Benjamin Waller, who was involved in a volatile dispute with the Charleston city government, argued that vigilance might even require illegal actions. "A *subordination* to the laws," he wrote, "is always the cant word to enslave the people."[42]

To protect themselves against men who abused power and were "intoxicated" by it, voters were urged to take more care in choosing legislators. They were to examine candidates' beliefs and to withhold their votes from men who refused to abide by their constituents' directions. They were not to be awed by money and were to "shun all lawyers." Legislators, in turn, were reminded that they were dependent on and responsible to "the collective body of the people."[43]

The defenders of the government only partly joined the debate. They denounced "riot and faction" and "the snarls of invidious animals." They supported law and order and the

---

[40] *Gazette of the State of South Carolina*, Aug. 6, 1783, Aug. 19, 1784.

[41] *Charleston Evening Gazette*, Aug. 25, 1786; *Columbian Herald*, Nov. 26, 1784; *Gazette of the State of South Carolina*, Aug. 27, 1783.

[42] *Columbian Herald*, Nov. 26, 1784; *Gazette of the State of South Carolina*, June 13, 1785.

[43] *South Carolina Gazette & General Advertiser*, Sept. 16, 1784; *Charleston Evening Gazette*, Aug. 25, 1786; *Gazette of the State of South Carolina*, Aug. 27, 1783, Aug. 19, 1784.

city corporation's efforts to make the streets safe once more.[44] When Edward Rutledge attacked "the clamour of the worthless," he summed up what many advocates of law and order believed. The people, he said, have become "the dupes of a word. 'Liberty' is the motto; every attempt to restrain licentiousness or give efficacy to Government is charged audaciously on the real advocates for Freedom as an attack upon Liberty."[45] He was partly right.

Positions had become so polarized that government actions were denounced in terms that were out of proportion to the significance of particular policies. Thus, when William Thompson was jailed for issuing a challenge to John Rutledge, there was insufficient reason to argue that "the *grand hierarchy* of the State were not to be controlled, at least [not] by any of the *lower orders*."[46] Thompson had, after all, challenged a member of the House of Representatives to a duel while the house was in session. But men who thought like Edward Rutledge were too quick to denounce their opponents as advocates of anarchy and disturbers of society and ignored the justice of some complaints. There was reason to argue that the rulers were working for a government controlled by as few as possible. John Rutledge had vetoed the constitution of 1778 saying that the people did not want a government even "verging toward" democracy. Ralph Izard, a lowcountry leader who had expressed his dissatisfaction with backcountry representatives for their "opinion that a politician may be born such," opposed schemes to move the government inland because it "would strengthen the country interest in a proportion of four to one."[47] Nor would these men permit the country interest to be strengthened by sub-

[44] *South Carolina Gazette & General Advertiser*, Sept. 4 and 9, 1784.

[45] Rutledge to John Jay, Nov. 12, 1786, Johnston, ed., *Correspondence of Jay*, 3:217.

[46] *Gazette of the State of South Carolina*, Apr. 29, 1784.

[47] Izard to Thomas Jefferson, June 10, 1785, "Letters of Ralph Izard," *South Carolina Historical and Genealogical Magazine* 2 (1901): 197. Izard's remark about moving the government inland was made in the House of Representatives on Mar. 1, 1786, and printed in the *Charleston Evening Gazette*, Mar. 3, 1786.

stantially increased representation. Disregarding the constitution, the legislature did not reapportion representation in 1785 or in later years, although in 1789 it created two new backcountry counties. The inaction did not represent tyranny, but it did indicate an aversion to letting the people rule.

In 1784 the debate was sharply focused around a new issue in Charleston, when the opposition launched a newspaper war involving the supposedly oppressive treatment of Benjamin Waller. The defense of Waller involved protection of individual rights. The cry for liberty, although used to stimulate further opposition to existing authority, was not a demand for licentiousness. Waller had been imprisoned by the Charleston corporation for opening a "Chalking Office," considered a vendue, which was limited by law to Tuesdays and Thursdays. The corporation's prosecution of Waller intensified criticism of the powers granted the city government by the incorporation act of 1783 and a subsequent act of 1784. In 1783 the city corporation received not only ample legislative power but also the judicial authority exercised by justices of the peace. The 1784 act, which the wardens had requested, extended the city's judicial power to include jurisdiction over cases that did not exceed twenty pounds.[48]

Waller's remarks, offered in his own behalf, criticized the nature of the government. The act of incorporation "blended together" the powers of the legislative, judicial, and executive branches. The wardens enacted laws, appointed officials to enforce them, and tried the violators of those laws. "It is an alarming circumstance," Waller wrote, "when you consider that the *Prosecutor* sits judge." At his trial Waller found his "accusors, some of my enemies, set as jurymen and judges of a *Law enacted by themselves.*"[49]

Another feature of the city government considered unconstitutional and dangerous to freedom was the absence of jury trials. There was no jury when the wardens decided to jail Waller. His supporters cited the forty-first article of the state

[48] *Gazette of the State of South Carolina*, June 2 and 13, 1785; Thomas Cooper and David J. McCord, eds., *Statutes at Large of South Carolina*, 10 vols. (Columbia, S.C., 1836–41), 7:97–102.

[49] *Gazette of the State of South Carolina*, May 26, 1785.

constitution: "No freeman of this State [shall] be taken or imprisoned . . . but by the judgment of his peers or by the law of the land." "Judgment of his peers" meant trial by jury; "law of the land," they said, meant something equally specific. Despite the fact that the constitution, as "Old Homespun" pointed out, gave the legislature the power to decide the fate of any "great and atrocious villain [who] had by his property, connections or influence, acquired so much authority in a county or district, that he could not be proceeded against in the common manner," such power to proceed without a jury could not be delegated to a court of wardens.[50]

These criticisms produced some immediate effects. Both Benjamin Waller and Dr. John Budd, another opponent of the city government, were elected in early 1786 to represent Charleston in the legislature. Alexander Gillon was already a member. Adverse reaction to unsupervised spending forced the wardens to publish the city's receipts and expenditures in the fall of 1786.[51]

Gillon and other critics also had a long-range influence on the government. By stressing that men in government could become corrupt, they furthered the idea that officeholders needed to be freed from temptation. The legislature in 1787 prohibited officeholders from using their positions for profit, most sweepingly in an act to establish a civil list and to prohibit an elected state official with a salary above £150 from holding other paying offices under the state government or that of the United States.[52] That principle was even more widely applied in 1790. Specifying only a few exceptions, the state's new constitution excluded from the legislature people who filled offices "of profit or trust" under the state or national government.

Gillon, Budd, Waller, and their supporters became political forces, but they were never able to control the city or domi-

[50] Ibid., June 2, 1785.

[51] On the city council's budget, see ibid., Aug. 15, 1785; *Columbian Herald*, Sept. 7, 1786; House of Representatives, Feb. 9, 1787, in *Charleston Morning Post*, Feb. 15, 1787.

[52] Cooper and McCord, eds., *Statutes of South Carolina*, 5:21, 38–39, 49, and 60.

nate elections to the legislature. Their goals and arguments guaranteed them the opposition of the wealthy. Their rhetoric played down their own middle-class background and divided opposing forces into rich and poor, undoubtedly antagonizing those who expected to rise into the upper class and those who feared the lower orders more than they worried about aristocratic tendencies.

The Charleston opposition may also have failed to attract further support because, in their attacks on the aristocracy and government and in their defense of some freedoms and rights, they were too radical for some and not radical enough for others. When many people worried about riots and crime, John Budd and others stood forward in behalf of sailors, men who could do them little political good, protesting against the council's jailing sailors for being out after the evening gun.[53] But although they occasionally acted as spokesmen for the poor, they never suggested anything more than giving the lower orders a different set of rulers, more sympathetic perhaps, but rulers just the same. They never challenged the property qualification for city voting, payment of a tax of three-shillings sterling in the year preceding the election, or the requirement that no one could serve as warden unless he met the property qualification for representative, a requirement that excluded the lower class entirely from the legislature and city council.

While political life in Charleston was changing, the interior regions of the state, quiet for a few years after the war, were awakening politically. A few times in 1783 and 1784 the area exerted considerable influence. When the lowcountry eased the confiscation act in 1783, it passed another act, intended to satisfy the needs, emotional and economic, of backcountry settlers by confiscating the estates of former citizens who had "joined the enemies" of the state.[54] Perhaps more signifi-

---

[53] *South Carolina Gazette & General Advertiser*, Oct. 19, 1784; *Gazette of the State of South Carolina*, Aug. 15, 1785; House of Representatives, Feb. 9, 1787, in *Charleston Morning Post*, Feb. 12, 1787; *Columbian Herald*, July 26, 1787.

[54] Nadelhaft, "The 'Havoc of War,'" p. 113.

cantly, backcountry settlers secured alteration of the system of taxation. Before the war, they had been angered by the uniform property tax and had instead proposed a graduated tax placing heavier burdens on more valuable rice and indigo lands. The change came in 1784, when the usually quiet representatives from "the remoter and poorer" districts obstinately opposed an attempt to raise the land tax "equally over the entire state."[55] The act of 1784 placed a tax of 1 percent on the value of all land. In the Charleston area, land was valued from six pounds an acre down to five shillings an acre. Backcountry land was valued as low as one shilling an acre. The law also doubled the tax on slaves.

The effect of the change was soon apparent. In 1783 the planters of St. Paul's, a lowcountry parish, paid a tax of £163.7.5 on 70,018 acres of land. In 1787, the next year for which an itemized account exists, the planters paid taxes on 97,640 acres. At the old rate their land tax would have amounted to £227.16.4; instead it totaled £537.13.2. In 1788 the planters of Christ Church, also in the lowcountry, paid £402.19.8–1/2 on 68,549 acres; for the same land they would have paid only £159.18.9 in 1783. But while the land tax doubled for many in the lowcountry parishes, it decreased substantially for backcountry settlers on poorer lands. In 1788 settlers in Lexington County paid taxes on 165,148–1/2 acres. In 1783 they would have paid over £385; in 1788, however, the county tax amounted to only £189.16.2. The tax on 35,652 acres of land in a district between the Edisto and Savannah rivers amounted in 1787 to a little more than £22; it would have been over £83 in 1783.[56] The change could scarcely have been more drastic. The new law, in the words of one backcountry representative, levied "certainly the most equal [tax] that can be laid, because the rich must pay the chief of the same."[57]

Before 1785 the backcountry had seemed largely caught

---

[55] Schoepf, *Travels in the Confederation*, pp. 198–200.

[56] Tax returns, Records of the General Assembly.

[57] Gen. William Henderson to Capt. John Henderson, Mar. 10, 1784, Sumter Papers, Draper Manuscripts, State Historical Society of Wisconsin, Madison.

in the aftermath of the vicious civil war that had devastated the area. Many people there, as well as in Georgetown and Beaufort, were unable to rise above their immediate pressing circumstances to demand more from the legislature. The burning of houses, the plundering, the often wanton destruction of the war, "so reduced" people, wrote a backcountry legislator and tax collector, that they could not "procure even the necessarys of life."[58] Observers also pointed to problems caused by criminals who "peeled, pillaged, and plundered" the people. Judge Aedanus Burke was horrified to discover in December 1784 "how much the poor people . . . are worried & half ruined by . . . an outlying Banditti that constantly beset the roads, rob the inhabitants & plunder their dwellings."[59]

But as conditions improved, residents became more demanding. In 1785 the people around the Little River in Ninety-Six District demonstrated their new attitude when, in one petition, they suggested revising the constitution for the people's welfare; moving the government inland for the backcountry's convenience; reapportioning the legislature, since property was "larger represented than the free white inhabitants"; recording important votes in the legislature; establishing counties; reducing the fees and salaries of the officers on the civil list; and granting rewards for the heads of outlaws ravaging the frontier.[60] As settlers began to speak out, so also did their representatives. Perhaps the growing population gave the legislators confidence. Perhaps the widely reported activities of Charlestonians in opposition to their government inspired them, or perhaps a degree of economic recovery. Experience may have made them bold.

[58] Patrick Calhoun to the Commissioners of the Public Treasury, Jan. 31, 1784, Commissioners of the Treasury, 1778–91, Letters Received, S.C. Dept. of Arch. and Hist., Columbia.

[59] Rev. Archibald Simpson's Journal, quoted in George Howe, *History of the Presbyterian Church in South Carolina*, 2 vols. (Columbia, S.C., 1870, 1873), 1:466; Burke to Gov. Benjamin Guerard, Dec. 14, 1784, Penal System Papers, S.C. Dept. of Arch. and Hist., Columbia; Nadelhaft, "The 'Havoc of War,'" pp. 115–21.

[60] General Assembly, Petitions, 1785, No. 105, S.C. Dept. of Arch. and Hist., Columbia.

The earliest and probably the most important backcountry demand was to move the government out of Charleston. One such proposal was defeated in 1783, but the issue came up again in 1785 and 1786. Removal of the government was partly a matter of convenience for country members, many of whom lived more than 100 miles from Charleston. The trip was uncomfortable and the time away from home potentially ruinous to their economic affairs. Col. William Hill, who came down from an area bordering North Carolina, complained that gentlemen from inland regions could not afford to spend two or three months early every year in Charleston when they had to be home "to manage . . . rural concerns."[61]

Lowcountry senators and representatives could not deny the validity of Hill's position, but clearly it was power that was at stake. Ralph Izard focused attention on that when he opposed moving the government to the center of the state because it would increase the interior's power.[62] To an individual forced to decide whether to attend the legislature, the discomforts of a trip and sojourn at the capital might have been determining factors; to a section, the sum of all the decisions meant power or impotence. Charleston-area representatives could easily attend the legislature; their geographic advantage was enhanced when special sessions met. Non-Charleston legislators won a victory in 1786, when the legislature agreed to relocate near the center of the state as soon as residents bought enough lots to indicate that a settlement would be established.[63] But the capital was not established at "Columbia" until after the state adopted a new constitution in 1790.

Along with suggestions and demands to move the capital, to record votes in the legislature, and, as some Charlestonians were arguing, to elect only those who would bind themselves to follow instructions, came another attack on the lowcountry rulers: Backcountry settlers repeatedly petitioned for a convention of the people to write a new consti-

[61] Senate, Mar. 9, 1786, in *Charleston Morning Post and Daily Advertiser*, Mar. 11, 1786.

[62] House of Representatives, Mar. 1, 1786, ibid., Mar. 3, 1786.

[63] Senate, Mar. 6 and 9, 1786, ibid., Mar. 7 and 11, 1786.

tution. The pressure stemmed in part from the idea that the state had no fixed plan of government. The constitution of 1778, "being only an act of the legislature," was not "founded on proper authority." Furthermore, it was frequently "set aside" by the General Assembly and was "too subject to fluctuation."[64]

The first call for a state convention was rejected by the legislature in 1784. In 1785 backcountry forces were better prepared and organized; in separate petitions, settlers from the Spartan District, York County, the Little River region, and the areas between the Broad and Saluda rivers and the Broad and Catawba rivers joined in asking for a convention. The lower house responded favorably but the backcountry demands were defeated by the upper house, as they had been in 1784 and would be again in 1787.[65]

The votes on calling a convention were always sectional. Legislators in both houses knew that reapportionment, avoided in 1785 despite the constitution, would be a necessary consideration of any convention. Representation was not substantially altered before 1790, however, when the new state constitution was written. Charles Cotesworth Pinckney's attitude prevailed temporarily: A new plan would throw elections "into the hands of proprietors of barren acres, instead of persons possessed of real property."[66]

Outside the legislature and unmentioned by the newspapers, which were most accessible to Charlestonians, there may have been more radical demands. Judge Henry Pendleton, a representative of backcountry Saxe-Gotha, feared that the people might themselves call a convention, which would be attended by "consequent horrors" for "another revolution might be expected to follow." Another backcountry represen-

---

[64] *State Gazette of South Carolina*, Aug. 10 and 17, 1786; *Gazette of the State of South Carolina*, Jan. 24, 1785.

[65] House journal, Jan. 22 and Feb. 22, 1785, Records of the General Assembly; Senate journal, Sept. 29, 1785, Records of the General Assembly; Petition and Grievance of . . . Little River District, General Assembly, Petitions, 1785, No. 105; *Columbian Herald*, Mar. 28, 1785.

[66] House of Representatives, Feb. 3, 1786, in *Charleston Morning Post and Daily Advertiser*, Feb. 4, 1786.

tative was also apprehensive since "the general mass of the people were so much bent for a democratical government, that . . . a convention . . . would do more harm than good."[67] Possibly Pendleton and others who opposed or only reluctantly agreed to a constitutional convention were reacting to the harsh rhetoric in the Charleston newspapers in 1784 and 1785, perceiving radical proposals where none were made. Perhaps even more was implicit to them in backcountry calls for a new constitution. Backcountry representatives were asking for changes that would have altered the balance of power between east and west. New settlers might have pushed for more. Many had migrated from states with more democratic provisions for voting and officeholding, only to find themselves first without the right to vote for three years and then disenfranchised until the legislature saw fit to declare them full citizens of South Carolina. They might well have sought to abolish or lower the property qualifications for voting and officeholding, as well as the residency requirement for officeholding.

Although the backcountry did not force many changes in the 1780s, there were important developments. A new and revolutionary tax system put a greater burden on the lowcountry. Counties and county courts, demanded by westerners in the 1760s, were created in 1785. Equally important was the legislature's provision in 1786 for eventually moving the government inland. In general, the future looked good, politically, for the inland settlers.

Partly because of the attacks from Charleston dissidents and the demands of backcountry inhabitants, lowcountry political leaders began to think of strengthening the national government. In the writing and adoption of a new Federal Constitution, there was a strong element of reaction to the changes that had occurred and were continuing to occur in the state. At the Constitutional Convention the South Carolina delegates—all from the lowcountry—mirrored conservative pre-Revolutionary ideas. They were frightened by the

[67] House of Representatives, Feb. 3, 1786, ibid., Feb. 4, 1786; House of Representatives, Feb. 21, 1786, in *Charleston Evening Gazette*, Feb. 21, 1786.

anarchy, "or rather worse than anarchy," they found in South Carolina and other states. Charles Cotesworth Pinckney saw "a disregard for law" in every state. Charles Pinckney believed that "licentiousness" prevailed in Rhode Island.[68] Consequently, the state's delegates sought to decrease the role of the people in the proposed government. They unanimously denounced the popular election of senators and representatives because it was "impracticable" and because "the people were less fit Judges" than state legislatures.[69]

Antifederalists understood the completed Constitution. To them, the government to be established was not sufficiently responsive to the people nor did it adequately protect them from tyranny. Only one branch of the legislature was popularly elected, a provision that, as Rawlins Lowndes explained, Carolinians had done away with in their 1778 constitution. Another fault was the absence of a doctrine of rotation, an idea fundamental not only to the Articles of Confederation, but to many state constitutions, South Carolina's included. James Lincoln remarked that there was nothing to prevent a president from repeating his four-year term fourteen times. "You do not put the same check on him," Lincoln said, "that you put on your own state governor, a man born and bred among you, a man over whom you have a continual and watchful eye." The absence of rotation was more serious because the government was located far from Carolina. Liberty was entrusted to men "who live one thousand miles distant."[70]

Issues raised by the Constitution—the location of the capital, the rotation of officials, the election of senators—had divided Carolinians throughout the Revolutionary period. If Charles Pinckney favored, as citizens knew he did, a government with an absolute veto over all state legislation, and if he

---

[68] Charles Pinckney, "Observations on the Plan of Government Submitted to the Federal Convention in Philadelphia, on the 28th of May, 1787," printed in the *State Gazette of South Carolina* in October and November 1787, and reprinted in Max Farrand, ed., *The Records of the Federal Convention of 1787*, rev. ed., 4 vols. (New Haven, 1937), 3:115; Charles Cotesworth Pinckney, in Elliot, ed., *Debates*, 4:282.

[69] Farrand, ed., *Records*, 1: 50 and 137.

[70] Elliot, ed., *Debates*, 4: 288 and 314.

feared "pure democracy," Antifederalists could rightly conclude that he was interested not only in increasing the powers of the central government but also in depriving westerners of their newly won political power.[71] Their power decreased when state governments were weakened.

Regardless of the debate, ratification was effortless. The only potential allies for the backcountry spokesmen who led the attack were the Charlestonians who in the past had criticized the political ideas of the aristocracy. But the Charlestonians were willing to trade what must have been their constitutional objections to get a government with power to exclude competing British merchandise from American markets.

Ratification of the Constitution was not entirely a setback for those desiring to continue changing the state government. In fact, since the state government had to be altered to fit the requirements of the national government, ratification provided the irrefutable argument for calling a state constitutional convention. That convention met in 1790.

Because the legislature had finally agreed to move to Columbia in January 1790, despite the absence of adequate facilities, the constitutional convention met there. The new constitution introduced few changes, but these few, along with those in previous constitutions, gave South Carolina a government quite different from that existing before 1778. Even though William Loughton Smith, a Federalist member of Congress, thanked Edward Rutledge for inserting "such advantages for the Low Country" into a constitution that was "much better than the former one," the new plan was not an improvement over the government of 1778 for the old rulers.[72] If lowcountry leaders were satisfied, it was because they had not been forced to give up more. More than some contemporaries openly admitted and more than historians have subsequently realized, the constitution of 1790 was a major advance for the newer areas of the state.

[71] Pinckney, "Observations," Farrand, ed., *Records*, 3: 115.

[72] Quoted in Raymond Starr, "The Conservative Revolution: South Carolina Public Affairs, 1775–1790," Ph.D. diss., University of Texas, 1964, pp. 281–82.

Success for individuals or groups did not depend on the outcome of debates on such issues as rotation in office, pay for legislators, a veto power for the governor, property qualifications, or a provision for future amendments to the constitution. Lowcountry delegates, however, had their way only on the two last provisions. Rather, apportionment and the location of the government were the "advantages" people fought over.

It was probably obvious in 1789, when the legislature provided that each election area would send to the convention the same number of people as it sent to the legislature, that the bases of representation, wealth as well as numbers, would not be changed. Nonetheless, delegates for the backcountry, which in 1790 had over 110,000 whites compared to approximately 29,000 in the lowcountry, argued that representation be based on population. In its only real victory at Columbia, the lowcountry defeated that proposal. The constitution assigned the number of representatives and senators for each parish and county, making no provision for future changes. The lower house was reduced in size from 208 (as of 1789) to 124, the upper increased from 31 to 37.

With change in size came reapportionment. In 1778 the backcountry had elected almost 38 percent of the senators and representatives; in 1790 it elected 46 percent of the senators and over 43 percent of the representatives. The hitherto dominant Charleston District's share of senators dropped from 45 percent to 35 percent, and of representatives from 48 percent to under 39 percent.[73] The backcountry emerged from the convention of 1790 as the most powerful section in both branches of the legislature.

The reapportionment took on greater meaning and importance when combined with a related change. Western petitioners had requested removal of the capital from Charleston

[73] Historians have not generally noticed the reapportionment. See, for example, Fletcher M. Green, *Constitutional Development in the South Atlantic States, 1776–1860: A Study in the Evolution of Democracy* (Chapel Hill, 1930), p. 121; William A. Schaper, "Sectionalism and Representation in South Carolina," *Annual Report of the American Historical Association for the Year 1900*, 2 vols. (Washington, D.C., 1901), 1:380; John Harold Wolfe, *Jeffersonian Democracy in South Carolina* (Chapel Hill, 1940), p. 47.

as a matter of convenience. But the issue also involved power, so the fight over the location of the government was the longest and harshest of the convention. "All was violence and confusion," the *City Gazette* reported.[74]

Attendance at the convention reminded people of the issue's importance. Because of "ill health," "unexpected circumstances," private affairs "deranged" by past public service, or "business," conditions that had often affected backcountry legislators, at least nineteen lowcountry delegates informed the governor they would not go to Columbia, although many had had no prior difficulty serving in Charleston.[75] Elections were held to fill the vacancies, but the resignations highlighted both what was at stake and a lowcountry problem at the convention. The lowcountry lost the first vote on moving inland by one vote, 105 to 104. Eighty-six of the 87 backcountry delegates voted in favor of moving, while 103 of the 122 lowcountry delegates opposed the motion. The outcome, however, was determined as much by those absent as by those present. Twenty-two absentees were from the lowcountry and only eight from the interior.[76] Had the convention met in Charleston, the backcountry would have lost. Lowcountry spokesmen recognized the cause of their defeat. Christopher Gadsden was one who blamed the setback on "the impatience and Desertion of our lower members." He emphasized the point by adding, not very optimistically, that the remaining members "will endeavor to do the best" they can.[77]

The effects of the new constitution on legislative matters were apparent throughout the 1790s. There was startling evidence of the change in 1793 and 1794 when the legislature revised the state militia law to follow some general fed-

[74] Quoted in Starr, "The Conservative Revolution," p. 277.

[75] Governor: Correspondence Received, 1789, Letters of Acceptance and Declinature of Those Elected Delegates to the 1790 Constitutional Convention, S.C. Dept. of Arch. and Hist., Columbia.

[76] Schaper, "Sectionalism and Representation," p. 377.

[77] Gadsden to Thomas Morris, May 30, 1790, Richard Walsh, ed., *The Writings of Christopher Gadsden, 1746–1805* (Columbia, S.C., 1966), pp. 251–52.

eral guidelines. In the end, one could almost confuse South Carolina with Massachusetts. As passed, the law empowered the militia men to elect all officers under the rank of brigadier general. Polls would be open from 9 to 5 following at least a fifteen-day notice. Furthermore, the law established a scheme of scaled fines for nonattendance at musters. For absence from a regimental muster, a lieutenant colonel was to be fined a sum not to exceed £10 plus an amount not more than 5 percent of his last general tax. A noncommissioned officer or a private was to be fined not more than 14s. plus no more than 5 percent of his last general tax.[78]

The new provisions reflected the more democratic ideas of the backcountry and the Charleston opposition. When the vote on fines was taken in December 1793, the backcountry, with 72 percent of its representatives voting, supported the scaling 27 to 12. Charleston and the surrounding parishes, with only 52 percent of their representatives voting, cast 8 votes for the proposal and 17 against. Parishes in Georgetown and Beaufort, with 55 percent of their members participating, evenly divided 12 votes. The decision in May 1794 to elect officers was even more sectional. The 80 percent of the backcountry representatives voting favored the change 35 to 8. The Charleston area representatives, 58 percent voting, cast 27 of 28 votes against the change, while Georgetown and Beaufort districts, with 82 percent of their representatives voting, supported the change by a 10 to 8 vote.[79]

The votes on the militia bill reflected the decline of the old aristocracy's power. This decline had begun in the 1760s when England presented issues that simply could not be avoided. The danger had been recognized from the beginning. John Laurens, who returned home to fight, eventually to die, for America, expressed the dilemma of the ruling group as clearly as anyone. "Our country," he wrote in 1775,

[78] Richard H. Kohn, *Eagle and Sword: The Federalists and the Creation of the Military Establishment in America, 1783–1802* (New York, 1975), pp. 128–38; *Acts and Resolutions of the General Assembly of the State of South-Carolina Passed in April, 1794* (Charleston, 1794), pp. 1–7.

[79] While I have combined the votes of the distant lowcountry parishes, on both these militia votes Georgetown supported the backcountry and Beaufort the Charleston area.

was "a scene of the utmost confusion . . . every man thinking himself equal to a share in Government." Laurens "lament[ed]" the need to give to the people a greater political voice, but, he continued, "we must bear with these evils in order to avoid greater."[80]

In the 1780s, the "evils" Laurens had anticipated were apparent to everyone. The Charleston opposition constantly evaluated the operation of the legislature and city council; it criticized, protested, and participated. Backcountry residents pestered, voted, and saw their area gradually become the most powerful section of the state. Together, Charlestonians and settlers of the interior struck at the power of the colony's prewar ruling group.

These political newcomers worked to democratize state government. The changes incorporated in the constitutions testify to their success: a two-house legislature representative of all areas, a weakened executive, an inland capital, rotation in office, officeholders denied opportunities to exploit the people. Their political revolution was neither violent nor abrupt. But the effects were nonetheless dramatic.

[80] Laurens to Francis Kinloch, Mar. 10, 1775, *Charleston Yearbook*, p. 347.

RICHARD ALAN RYERSON

Republican Theory and Partisan Reality in Revolutionary Pennsylvania

Toward a New View of the Constitutionalist Party

NEARLY EVERY STUDENT of the American Revolution knows
that the Pennsylvania Constitution of 1776 was a dismal failure. It is the clear consensus of Pennsylvania historians that
immediately following Independence, politically naive zealots framed their organic law around the absurd concepts of

This essay is exploratory; its argument is a synthesis of my research on the
origins and growth of the Revolutionary movement in Pennsylvania and
my understanding, constructed from the work of several scholars, of the
behavior of the Constitutionalists in the years between Independence and
the Federal Constitution. In the course of revising this essay I have had
the benefit of excellent criticism from a number of colleagues and friends.
I would like particularly to acknowledge my debt to Robert J. Brugger,
Jack P. Greene, James A. Henretta, Ronald Hoffman, and Steven Ross-
wurm; approaching my argument from a broad spectrum of historical
perspectives, each has helped me avoid errors of fact or judgment. In addition, I would like to thank nearly a score of colleagues who criticized this
paper's earlier drafts at several scholarly meetings in 1979: Boston University's Colloquium on Early American History, the United States Capitol
Historical Society conference on the states during the Revolution, the
Charles Warren Center seminar at Harvard University, and the Philadelphia Center for Early American Studies seminar at the University of Pennsylvania.

95

unicameralism and legislative supremacy, and fourteen years of all-too-predictable horrors followed: A tyrannical assembly bullying a feeble plural executive and a dependent judiciary, the persecution of religious minorities, economic chaos, and class warfare. While several scholars of the Revolutionary movement throughout the thirteen states have expressed a qualified admiration for the democratic daring of Pennsylvania's revolutionaries, they, too, have ultimately concluded that the young commonwealth's adventure in radical democracy is an unhappy story that serves primarily to mark the outer limits of the Revolution.[1]

As their story is a sad one, so Pennsylvania's Constitutionalists appear a sad lot, though for reasons that differ from one interpreter to another. John Paul Selsam emphasized their lack of political experience and their devotion to anachronistic political institutions and visionary governmental structures. Robert Brunhouse saw them in class terms, with economically aspiring Constitutionalists arrayed against already wealthy Republicans. David Hawke boldly combined these approaches to argue that the Constitutionalists were an assortment of misfits and losers who sought through revolution to reshape a world they could not master. Breaking sharply with this economic determinism, Owen Stephen Ireland discovered in the Constitutionalists an ethnoreligious alliance directed against ethnic and religious antagonists. Most recently, Douglas Arnold has declared that the proud, elitist Republicans, Pennsylvania's proto-Federalists, espoused the pluralistic ideology of the future, while their Constitutionalist opponents were little more than backward-

---

[1] The citations for negative views of Pennsylvania's constitutional revolution appear in note 2. Important studies at the national level that discuss Pennsylvania's Revolution include Elisha P. Douglass, *Rebels and Democrats: The Struggle for Equal Political Rights and Majority Rule during the American Revolution* (Chapel Hill, 1955); J. R. Pole, *Political Representation in England and the Origins of the American Republic* (New York, 1966); Gordon S. Wood, *The Creation of the American Republic, 1776–1787* (Chapel Hill, 1969); Jackson Turner Main, *The Sovereign States, 1775–1783* (New York, 1973) and idem, *Political Parties before the Constitution* (Chapel Hill, 1973). Of the national-level studies, the most sensitive to the thought and attitudes of the defenders of Pennsylvania's radical new constitution is Wood's *Creation*.

looking bigots, zealots without important programs or noble goals.[2]

This almost universal condemnation is not without cause. Some Constitutionalists were religious zealots who took pleasure in persecuting their religious opponents; several felt class hatred keenly; and many were ignorant, narrow minded, and hopelessly idealistic. Yet by describing them in these terms, historians have merely declared their lack of interest in understanding them; nor are they now in a good position to do so, for three reasons. First, most students of Revolutionary Pennsylvania have shown a strong bias for the Constitutionalists' opponents. Second, the quality of their published scholarship is depressingly low; the two finest studies of the years after Independence in Pennsylvania, Ireland's analysis of the ratification of the Federal Constitution and Arnold's reading of the ideology of Pennsylvania's Re-

---

[2] J. Paul Selsam, *The Pennsylvania Constitution of 1776: A Study in Revolutionary Democracy* (Philadelphia, 1936), esp. chs. 4–5; Robert L. Brunhouse, *The Counter-Revolution in Pennsylvania, 1776–1790* (Harrisburg, 1942), esp. chs. 1–3; David Hawke, *In the Midst of a Revolution* (Philadelphia, 1961), esp. ch. 4; Owen Stephen Ireland, "The Ratification of the Federal Constitution in Pennsylvania," Ph.D. diss., University of Pittsburgh, 1966, pp. 7–8, 26, 30–44, 66–67, 71–74, 85–88, 116–17, and 212–19; and Douglas McNeil Arnold, "Political Ideology and the Internal Revolution in Pennsylvania, 1776–1790," Ph.D. diss., Princeton University, 1976, esp. chs. 3, 4, and 8, section 4.

Throughout this essay I will refer to the pro- and anti-Constitutionalist forces in Pennsylvania as the Constitutionalist and Republican parties, although these terms were not formally used until March 1779, when the leaders of the two parties formed the Constitutional and Republican societies. The Constitutionalists and Republicans were not modern parties, but they far more closely resembled the Democratic-Republican and the Federalist parties of the 1790s than they did the political factions of colonial America. Similarly, I will refer to Pennsylvania's Assembly (or Quaker) party of 1725–76 because that political force was unusually partylike for a colonial faction. For an effective brief discussion of Pennsylvania's Revolutionary parties, see Arnold, "Political Ideology," pp. 59–60. In the following argument, the term *constitution* will mean the Pennsylvania Constitution of 1776, while the national Constitution of 1787 will be labeled the *Federal Constitution*. In addition, I shall refer to the Commonwealth of Pennsylvania, as a government and as a political community, as "the commonwealth" or as "the state."

publican party, are unpublished doctoral theses. Finally, and perhaps most important, James Madison's Federal Constitution, regarded almost universally by historians as the quintessential expression of the political wisdom of the American people, has made America's most un-Madisonian constitution look too ridiculous for respectful scholarly study and has cast its authors in the roles of fuzzy-headed philosophers and unlettered country boobs, which Pennsylvania historians have assured us they richly deserve.[3]

The costs of this viewpoint are high; no one really knows who Pennsylvania's Constitutionalists were or what was wrong with their constitution. To understand these men and their Revolution, one must first answer several sets of questions. First, which Pennsylvanians became Constitutionalists, and why? Second, what were the origins of the attitudes and ideas that united and defined the Constitutionalists? Third, how well did the Constitution of 1776 work for Revolutionary-era Pennsylvanians, and how did it fail to meet their highest aspirations? Fourth, what forces shaped the positions Constitutionalists took on the controversial issues of this period? Fifth, what factors determined their many successes, and their ultimate failure, over fourteen years of struggle with their opponents? Finally, what did the Constitutionalists achieve? This essay will offer some tentative answers to each of these questions in the hope that they may stimulate a more penetrating inquiry into Pennsylvania's Revolution.

To the question, Who were the Pennsylvania Constitutionalists?, historians have given a confusion of answers. Selsam saw them as unlettered political neophytes; Brunhouse stressed their modest fortunes and rural, backcountry resi-

---

[3] The negative view of the Constitutionalists is clearest in Selsam, *Pennsylvania Constitution*, ch. 4, and in Hawke, *Midst of a Revolution*, chs. 4 and 9–10. In referring to "James Madison's Federal Constitution," I mean not only the document itself, but also Madison's defense of it in *The Federalist*. I count myself among those historians who regard Madison's Federal Constitution as "the quintessential expression of the political wisdom of the American people," but such admiration ought not to blind any historian to the importance and the merits of other organic laws that many Revolutionary-era Americans regarded, if only for a time, to be the distillation of their political wisdom.

dences; and Ireland has demonstrated that they were predominantly German Reformed or Scotch-Irish Presbyterian communicants, while their opponents came from virtually every other ethnic-religious combination. The respective adherents of these arguments perceive one another's hypotheses to be contradictory; this perception stems in part from their lack of attention to pre-Revolutionary Pennsylvania.[4]

Nearly all Constitutionalists shared one provincial experience: They were outsiders. These men, their fathers, and the communities in which they had grown to maturity had been firmly excluded from political power. Beginning in the 1760s, several spokesmen for these outsider communities attempted to enter the province's political elite, but they failed.[5] The Revolutionary movement finally opened the doors to full political participation for these groups, but not as quickly or as widely as they wished. The men who framed and defended the Constitution of 1776 were upstarts who lacked the traditional economic and social qualifications for political leadership that were honored even in Revolutionary Pennsylvania. Every early Constitutionalist leader from Philadelphia was a political unknown before April 1775. Few had served on the new radical committees of their city; almost none had held prominent positions on those committees or had ever served in city or provincial government. Their opponents, however, included nearly every local assemblyman, most officers of the Revolutionary committees, and many officers of the new militia battalions. Whatever po-

---

[4] Selsam and Brunhouse espouse the economic determinism of the Progressive school. Unlike many Progressive historians, however, both are clearly hostile to the upwardly mobile classes on the political left. Ireland, in contrast, follows the more recent ethnoreligious or ethnocultural interpretation of politics. These two perspectives may be incompatible for many times and places in American history, but in Revolutionary Pennsylvania they are highly complementary, as this essay will argue.

[5] See especially Dietmar Rothermund, *The Layman's Progress: Religious and Political Experience in Colonial Pennsylvania, 1740–1770* (Philadelphia, 1961); William Hanna, *Benjamin Franklin and Pennsylvania Politics* (Stanford, 1964); and James H. Hutson, *Pennsylvania Politics, 1746–1770: The Movement for Royal Government and Its Consequences* (Princeton, 1972), introduction and chs. 3–4.

sitions Philadelphia's Constitutionalists acquired in the Revolutionary movement came after Lexington and Concord, and often after the publication of Thomas Paine's *Common Sense*. The political experience of rural Constitutionalists was also recent; no pre-1776 assemblyman from the west was a Constitutionalist, but several western legislators were Republicans. The Constitutionalist party was born in the call to arms and the drive for Independence.[6]

Economically, too, the Constitutionalists had long been outsiders. In the fall of 1776 the Republicans claimed that nearly every man of property and understanding opposed the new frame of government. On the matter of property, the Constitutionalists did not refute them, but charged that their opponents were a "gentry," "aristocrats" who would not submit to the rule of the "leather aprons," the working men of Philadelphia.[7] While the economic differences between Constitutionalists and Republicans probably decreased slightly over the next decade, they remained substantial. Roland Baumann found the average assessed wealth of Republican

[6] See Richard Alan Ryerson, *The Revolution Is Now Begun: The Radical Committees of Philadelphia, 1765–1776* (Philadelphia, 1978), esp. chs. 4 and 6–9. The Constitutionalists' very recent political prominence is evident from a comparison of two lists of party leaders active between 1778 and 1787, constructed by Roland M. Baumann in "The Democratic-Republicans of Philadelphia: The Origins, 1776–1797," Ph.D. diss., Pennsylvania State University, 1970, pp. 592–97, with the lists of assemblymen and committeemen active between 1765 and 1776, in Ryerson, *Revolution*, appendixes B, D, E, G, I, J, and M. Of Baumann's thirty-six Constitutionalists, only ten had served on any Revolutionary committees, and only three sat on the relatively elitist committees formed before the First Continental Congress. Of twenty-seven Republicans, however, sixteen had served as committeemen or assemblymen, and only five had begun their service after the Congress. On the political affiliations of rural and western assemblymen, compare Baumann, "The Democratic Republicans," pp. 592–97, with *Votes and Proceedings of the House of Representatives of the Province of Pennsylvania*, Pennsylvania Archives, 8th ser., vol. 8 (Harrisburg, 1935), pp. 7024, 7148, and 7301–2 (assembly rosters of 1773, 1774, and 1775).

[7] On the Republican charges see Mathias Slough to Jasper Yeates, Mar. 28, 1777, quoted in Douglass, *Rebels and Democrats*, p. 277n, other quotations and references in the same note, and the citations in Arnold, "Political Ideology," p. 67n, covering 1776–79. For the Constitutionalist replies, see ibid., covering 1776–77.

leaders to be 164 percent greater than the average wealth of Constitutionalist spokesmen, and Ireland's study of ratification revealed equally significant differences between the electorates of the two parties. This distinction was starkly evident as late as 1787, as nearly every major study since Beard's *Economic Interpretation of the Constitution* has richly confirmed.[8]

Finally, the Constitutionalists were predominantly of German Reformed or Scotch-Irish Presbyterian background throughout the decade following Independence. Significantly, these were the most important ethnoreligious groups in Pennsylvania that had wanted political power and been denied it.[9]

This initial character of the Constitutionalist party changed little during the Revolutionary War, but the party was strengthened in 1777 and 1778 when three leaders from the Revolutionary elite joined its ranks. In 1777 Thomas Mc-

[8] The percentage figure compares the twenty-seven Republican leaders (average assessed wealth, £5,224) with the thirty-four Constitutionalists (average wealth, £1,978) in Baumann, "The Democratic-Republicans," pp. 592–97. On the economic and social differences between Federalists (Republicans) and Antifederalists (Constitutionalists) in 1787, see Charles A. Beard, *An Economic Interpretation of the Constitution of the United States* (New York, 1913), pp. 273–81; Jackson Turner Main, *The Antifederalists: Critics of the Constitution, 1781–1788* (Chapel Hill, 1961), pp. 187–93 and 289; Main, *Political Parties*, pp. 174–211, esp. p. 209; and Arnold, "Political Ideology," pp. 61–62. The only major quantitative dissent from this characterization of the two parties is Forrest McDonald, *We the People: The Economic Origins of the Constitution* (Chicago, 1958), pp. 163–82. Except on the narrow question of security holding, however, McDonald's analysis of the economic status of Pennsylvania's political leaders cannot withstand a rigorous quantitative critique. See Jackson Turner Main, "Charles A. Beard and the Constitution: A Critical Analysis of Forrest McDonald's *We the People*," *William and Mary Quarterly*, 3d ser. 17 (1960): 86–110, for a discussion of some of the problems with McDonald's methodology.

[9] Ireland, "Ratification," pp. 22, 30–44, 71–74, 85–88, and 214–19; Selsam, *Pennsylvania Constitution*, chs. 4–5; Brunhouse, *Counter-Revolution*, chs. 1–3. Pennsylvania's Lutherans had also attempted to participate in politics, but they were generally distrustful of German Reformed and Presbyterian Calvinist zeal during the Revolution, and after 1780 most of them, under the leadership of Frederick Augustus Muhlenburg, joined the Republicans (see Ireland, "Ratification," pp. 119–32). Other major white ethnoreligious groups in Pennsylvania were already insiders by 1775 or, like the German pietists, not interested in political power.

Kean was appointed chief justice of the state's Supreme Court, and John Bayard, chosen Speaker of the assembly in 1776, became an ardent Constitutionalist. In December 1778 Joseph Reed was elected president of the Supreme Executive Council, thereby becoming Pennsylvania's quasi governor. All three had opposed the constitution in 1776, but became loyal supporters of that document when they saw the new government urgently needed able, experienced, and widely respected leaders if the Revolution were to succeed.[10]

Beginning in 1784, however, the Constitutionalists began to take on the rural, localist, Antifederalist role for which they are best known. In that year the party leadership passed from well-educated Philadelphia Presbyterians of some social standing to obscure, western, immigrant and second-generation Scotch-Irish legislators. In 1785 Philadelphia's artisans began deserting the Constitutionalists for the more commercially oriented Republicans. By 1787 only a small Presbyterian speculator group defended the Constitution of 1776 in the city; most Philadelphians were now looking toward a quite different kind of national constitution. This last phase in the life of Pennsylvania's Constitutionalist party is the best known and understood. The present analysis will concentrate upon the Constitutionalists of the late 1770s, whose thought and behavior have been largely ignored.[11]

[10]See Brunhouse. *Counter-Revolution*, pp. 19 and 35 (McKean), 19, 20, 46, and 47 (Bayard), and 35 and 56 (Reed); John M. Coleman, *Thomas McKean, Forgotten Leader of the Revolution* (Rockaway, N.J., 1975), pp. 203–4, 205–6, and 210–12; Gail Stuart Rowe, *Thomas McKean: The Shaping of an American Republicanism* (Boulder, Col., 1978); and John F. Roche, *Joseph Reed, a Moderate in the American Revolution* (New York, 1957), pp. 115–22 and 143–50. McKean, and probably Reed as well, never overcame their reservations about the Constitution of 1776; in the late 1780s McKean worked openly for the adoption of the Federal Constitution and for a new, more conservative constitution for Pennsylvania. Both men, however, particularly Reed, became identified as Constitutionalists during the war years. For the inevitable Republician view that such men were merely self-serving opportunists, see Alexander Graydon, *Memoirs of His Own Time* (Philadelphia, 1846), p. 332, quoted in Douglass, *Rebels and Democrats*, p. 282.

[11]On the changing composition of the Constitutionalists, see Brunhouse, *Counter-Revolution*, chs. 6–7; Charles S. Olton, *Artisans for Indepen-*

At each stage in the development of their party, most Constitutionalists remained outsiders, too poor, too recently im-
migrated, and too Calvinist to join Pennsylvania's wealthy
Quaker-Anglican establishment. They remained something
else, too: zealous adherents of a radically democratic form
of republican government. These were not merely long-
excluded men; they were men with a particular view of the
good society and of the proper government for that society.
They began to acquire their outlook even before they sought
admission to Pennsylvania's political establishment, and the
province's history in the twenty years before Independence
strongly reinforced their early convictions.

Revolutionary Pennsylvania presents a striking paradox.
Its highly pluralistic, heavily immigrant population produced a prosperous economy and a lively but poorly inte-
grated society whose ethnoreligious communities should
logically have favored a republic constructed along conservative lines, replete with checks and balances designed to insure the political cooperation needed for social cohesion. Yet
in 1776 Pennsylvania's Constitutionalists chose to see their
pluralistic society as homogeneous; they believed that its diverse members would, in the purifying atmosphere of a virtuous Revolution, adopt the good of the whole society as
their overriding interest. Twenty years ago, historians widely
assumed that their naive faith arose out of political ignorance
and inexperience, but the recent work of several scholars
suggests a different cause. Pennsylvania's Constitutionalists
were misled about the character of their society both by the
culture in which they lived and the establishment that they
replaced.

The roots of the Constitutionalists' error ran deep into the
predominantly Quaker political culture of provincial Pennsylvania. Because the province was quietly pluralistic and enjoyed a unicameral legislature elected by a broad franchise,
historians have traditionally assumed that Pennsylvania was
as "democratic" as any colony in British North America. This

---

dence: *Philadelphia Mechanics and the American Revolution* (Syracuse, 1975),
chs. 8–9; Main, *Political Parties*, ch. 7; and Arnold, "Political Ideology," pp.
213–14, 216, 218, 220, 226, and 232.

view now appears untenable. From the time of its founding until the Revolution, Pennsylvania was dominated by men who had one overriding goal: the preservation of a civil society in which their sect, the Society of Friends, could live securely without compromising its religious convictions. Once Quakers became a minority in Pennsylvania early in the eighteenth century, the interest of one part of society became the object of the whole polity.

At the same time, Quaker control masked signs that Pennsylvania was not a peaceable kingdom. Following an initial period of class-based discord among themselves, Friends closed ranks and ran the assembly almost as a Quaker meeting. In the two decades preceding the Revolution, as Quaker domination of the legislature declined from absolute to merely impressive, conscientious Friends had to rely upon Anglican allies to carry out worldly measures that they would not perform. Even this loss of power, however, was more apparent than real. The assembly continued to work harmoniously and passed through the Seven Years' War without major damage to its Quaker-Anglican establishment. An observer visiting the house in 1774 described its members sitting "with their hats on, [in] great coarse cloth coats, leather breeches and woolen stockings in the month of July; there was not a speech made the whole time." It was a portrait that would have done justice to their fathers—or to their grandfathers.[12]

As their proportion of the population fell, however, the Quakers and their political allies became increasingly fearful of German and Scotch-Irish immigration and political activity, and their leaders set to work industriously to suppress

[12]Gary B. Nash, *Quakers and Politics: Pennsylvania, 1681–1726* (Princeton, 1968); Alan Tully, *William Penn's Legacy: Politics and Social Structure in Provincial Pennsylvania, 1726–1755* (Baltimore, 1977); Hanna, *Franklin and Politics*; Hutson, *Pennsylvania Politics*; Charles P. Keith, *The Provincial Councillors of Pennsylvania, 1733–1776* (Philadelphia, 1883), p. 228 (quotation). My own unpublished work on the Pennsylvania assembly shows that following their precipitous decline in power in 1755–56, Quakers made a strong comeback in overall membership and in legislative committee activity in the early 1760s and were dominant in the house from 1766 to 1773.

any bid for power by these new Pennsylvanians.[13] The Quakers also developed a more demanding peace testimony. Abandoning their traditional acquiescence in defensive warfare, they claimed an exemption from all burdens of war, including the payment of additional taxes or the handling of paper currency issued by governments engaged in conflict. In the Revolution they would publicly declare the superiority of their pacific principles to the demands of any larger society, or of any state.[14]

While Pennsylvania's Scotch-Irish Presbyterians and Reformed Germans gradually lost all respect for their legislative rulers in the 1760s and 1770s, they may unconsciously have learned an important lesson from them. The Quaker-Anglican establishment taught by example that it was legitimate to direct government toward an objective held by a minority of the whole society as long as that cause was morally superior, no matter how vigorously other minorities, or even a majority, opposed that objective. Pennsylvania's outsiders could certainly have drawn this lesson from Benjamin Franklin's arrogant attempt to have the province made a royal colony in 1764. Moreover, it was relatively easy for a dominant minority to maintain its control through a careful construction of electoral districts, as the Quaker establishment

[13] Benjamin Franklin, "Observations concerning the Increase of Mankind," in Leonard W. Labaree et al., eds., *The Papers of Benjamin Franklin*, 21 vols. to date (New Haven, 1956–), 4:234; Franklin to James Parker, Mar. 20, 1751, and to Peter Collinson, May 9, 1753, ibid., pp. 120–21 and 483–85; Samuel Wharton to William Franklin, Sept. 29, 1765, Franklin Papers, American Philosophical Society, cited in Hutson, *Pennsylvania Politics*, pp. 171 and 173; Abel James to Thomas Wharton, Sr., Oct. 16, 1773, Thomas Wharton, Sr., Collection, Historical Society of Pennsylvania, Philadelphia.

[14] See Hermann Wellenreuther, "The Political Dilemma of the Quakers in Pennsylvania, 1681–1748," *Pennsylvania Magazine of History and Biography* 94 (1970): 135–72; Wellenreuther, *Glaube und Politick in Pennsylvania 1681–1776: Die Wandlungen der Obrigkeitsdoktrin und des* Peace Testimony *der Quaker* (Cologne, 1972); *The Testimony of the . . . Quakers . . . at Philadelphia* (Philadelphia, 1775); *Ancient Testimony . . . Addressed to the People in General* (Philadelphia, 1776); and *A Testimony . . . from our Yearly-Meeting . . .* (Philadelphia, 1777).

had demonstrated.[15] The view that society had one morally superior interest group, when extended across several decades, could lead to the belief that the good society had but one proper interest. Great Britain had long operated upon this conviction. Many political theorists taught, and most members of Parliament believed, that the nation's true interest lay in preserving the vigor and prosperity of its landed elite.[16]

When the Americans began their Revolution, therefore, it was not surprising that the political outsiders among them quickly gravitated toward an ideology that would support their vision of a single-interest society. Avoiding philosophers of political pluralism and balance, these Revolutionaries drew upon a radical tradition that ran back to James Harrington and beyond and taught that the healthiest polity rested upon a virtuous, largely undifferentiated agrarian gentry and yeomanry.[17] This country myth was powerful;

[15] See Hutson, *Pennsylvania Politics*, chs. 3–4, on Franklin's royalization campaign; and Tully, *William Penn's Legacy*, p. 49, and Charles H. Lincoln, *The Revolutionary Movement in Pennsylvania, 1760–1776* (Philadelphia, 1901), p. 47, on the Quaker assembly's allotment of representation. By awarding each county an equal delegation in the assembly between 1776 and 1779, the Constitutionalists initiated their government with a similar, but geographically reversed, malapportionment.

In respect to the "lessons" suggested in this paragraph, it is instructive to compare the political experience of Pennsylvanians with that of colonists in Virginia and in New England, who had been learning throughout the eighteenth century that society was naturally composed of competing interests, each of which possessed a certain legitimacy and had therefore to be accommodated by the political process. Although Massachusetts Yankees could no more articulate this concept without anxiety than Pennsylvania's Quakers (see Michael Zuckerman, *Peaceable Kingdoms: New England Towns in the Eighteenth Century* [New York, 1970]), their legislature was in practice more committed to political pluralism—and to a more even distribution of assembly seats.

[16] See Pole, *Political Representation*, pp. 444–52; Lewis Namier, *The Structure of Politics at the Accession of George III* (London, 1929); Namier, *England in the Age of the American Revolution* (London, 1930); and such political classics as James Harrington's *Oceana*.

[17] On the complex history of this tradition, see Caroline Robbins, *The Eighteenth-Century Commonwealthman: Studies in the Transmission, Development, and Circumstance of English Liberal Thought from the Restoration of*

Samuel Adams early came under its influence, and Thomas Jefferson never freed himself from its spell. In 1776 Pennsylvania's Constitutionalists, relatively unfamiliar with a balanced constitution in their own province but filled with a sense of revolutionary virtue that would unite all citizens and overcome all differences between them, stepped forward to take their place as founders and defenders of their country.

Pennsylvania's Constitutionalists were not simply idealists, however; as frustrated outsiders many were angry idealists, and as the Revolutionary movement advanced they became angrier. The trouble began during the Seven Years' War when the Quaker-Anglican establishment failed, in the eyes of Pennsylvania's frontier settlers, to defend the province against Indian raids. The crisis deepened with Pontiac's Rebellion, exploding in the brutal massacre of Lancaster's praying Indians by the Scotch-Irish Paxton Boys, who then marched on Quaker Philadelphia, where they were only narrowly talked out of more violence by Benjamin Franklin. The next decade saw politically aspiring Presbyterians, artisans, and other Pennsylvanians of short pedigree and modest estate rudely rebuffed as the Assembly party of Franklin and Joseph Galloway attempted to "royalize" the province, accommodated themselves to the Stamp Act, and largely ignored the Townshend duties. In 1770 the Quaker mercantile elite broke Philadelphia's nonimportation boycott, thereby alienating the artisan class. In 1774 Galloway's assembly, in choosing delegates to the First Continental Congress, quietly ignored both the nominations and the advice of the widely popular committees of correspondence that had formed to oppose the Coercive Acts.[18]

Until the opening of the Congress, Pennsylvania's estab-

Charles II until the War with the Thirteen Colonies (Cambridge, Mass., 1959); Bernard Bailyn, *The Ideological Origins of the American Revolution* (Cambridge, Mass., 1967), esp. chs. 2–3 and 5; Wood, *Creation*, chs. 1–2, and pp. 226–37; J. G. A. Pocock, *The Ancient Constitution and the Feudal Law* (Cambridge, 1957) and idem, *The Machiavellian Moment: Florentine Political Thought and the Atlantic Republican Tradition* (Princeton, 1975).

[18] Brooke Hindle, "The March of the Paxton Boys," *William and Mary Quarterly*, 3d ser. 3 (1946): 461–86; Hutson, *Pennsylvania Politics*, chs. 3–4; Arthur M. Schlesinger, *The Colonial Merchants and the American Revolution*,

lishment checked every attempt of westerners, Germans, Presbyterians, and city artisans to play an active role in the province's political life. For a brief moment in 1774 and 1775 the success of the socially inclusive Revolutionary movement in taking over the assembly promised the more open polity appropriate to Pennsylvania's pluralistic society. But this last hope vanished when John Dickinson decided to lead the movement's moderate wing to oppose a complete break with England. When the assembly refused to allow Independence or to pass a strong militia law and the proprietary elite joined Dickinson and the more worldly Quaker assemblymen in an attempt to arrest the Revolution, Pennsylvania's outsiders rebelled.[19]

In four months, these outsiders brought Pennsylvania behind Independence, destroyed the old assembly, and wrote a radical new constitution. In the resolves that they passed in convention to implement this constitution, they made it clear that in their view Quakers and other pacifists, neutrals, and all members of the old elite who did not support Independence were no better than tories.[20] Not one of these groups formed a legitimate interest in society; each represented something else, something sinister in Pennsylvania life that must be controlled and, if necessary, suppressed or even excised.

In brief compass, this was the origin of Pennsylvania's Constitutionalists.

The central political and ideological achievement of Pennsylvania's Constitutionalists was the Constitution of 1776. One cannot assess their political behavior or their political contribution without first understanding their frame of government and determining the causes of its difficulties.

The constitution was framed by ninety-six delegates who

_1763–1776_ (New York, 1918), pp. 217–20 and 229–33; Olton, _Artisans for Independence_, chs. 4–5; Ryerson, _Revolution_, pp. 30–33 and 60–62.

[19] Ryerson, _Revolution_, chs. 5–9.

[20] Selsam, _Pennsylvania Constitution_, p. 221; Arnold, "Political Ideology," p. 56.

met in Philadelphia from July 15 to September 28. All persons qualified to vote for assemblymen and all militiamen who paid taxes could vote for the eight-man county delegations that composed the convention, a plan that overrepresented the thinly settled frontier counties much as the Quaker establishment had overrepresented the Delaware River counties in the old assembly. The constitution was largely the work of political novices like James Cannon and David Rittenhouse, perhaps with some assistance from the political veteran and nondelegate George Bryan. It was vigorously opposed in convention by George Clymer and George Ross, two leaders of the Revolutionary establishment, but it was finally approved by over three-quarters of the members.[21]

The constitution provided for a unicameral legislature of seventy-two members elected annually, and no legislator was allowed to serve more than four in seven years. Each county would have six representatives until the first septennial redistribution of seats, based upon a census of the taxable population, could be completed; this redistribution occurred in 1779. All bills except those dealing with "emergencies" had to be approved and printed for public consideration, and then reapproved by the next session of the assembly before becoming law. The executive was vested in a Supreme Executive Council of twelve members, one from each county, and each councilor was elected for a three-year nonrenewable term, with the terms staggered so that four seats fell vacant each October. Its president, chosen annually from its membership by the council and the assembly jointly, had little formal power beyond that of being presiding officer, although he was commander of the state's militia. Justices of the Supreme Court were appointed by the council to seven-year renewable terms. Local justices of the peace, who also served for seven years, were nominated by the voters; the council then selected one of the two most popular nominees in each district, usually the electoral winner. Any judge could be re-

---

[21] Selsam, *Pennsylvania Constitution*, pp. 138, 140–41, 147–55, 159–65, 185–87, and 201; Hawke, *Midst of a Revolution*, p. 186.

moved by the assembly for misbehavior in office. All adult white males who paid taxes or lived with a parent who paid taxes and who had resided in Pennsylvania for one year could vote; there were no specific qualifications for office. To insure the proper constitutional behavior of public officials and of the several branches of government and to provide for any necessary alterations in the constitution, each county would elect two men every seven years to form a Council of Censors. This body would report on the performance of the magistrates and recommend changes in laws and procedures, and it could, by a two-thirds majority, recommend the calling of a new constitutional convention. Every officeholder was required to take an oath of loyalty to independent Pennsylvania and to its new constitution; in a resolve separate from the document, the convention devised a similar oath for the voters.[22]

This constitution was attacked on a variety of grounds by several of Pennsylvania's most prominent Revolutionary leaders immediately upon its promulgation in September 1776. John Dickinson, Thomas McKean, Robert Morris, Benjamin Rush, and James Wilson objected to its lack of a governor, to its dependent judiciary, or to its Council of Censors, as well as to its oaths, which appeared to require the acceptance of the document without any real possibility of alteration. The one defect stressed by every critic over the next decade, however, was the new government's lack of an upper legislative chamber.[23]

Until recently no scholar had probed beneath the surface of this critique to discover why unicameralism frightened Pennsylvania's Republicans so deeply or why the Constitutionalists clung so tenaciously to their single chamber. The argument centered on the need for constitutional checks and balances, of course, but the Constitution of 1776 was not without checks upon the arbitrary exercise of power in the form of frequent elections and the rotation of offices. The

[22]Selsam, *Pennsylvania Constitution*, ch. 5.

[23]Ibid., pp. 212–25; Brunhouse, *Counter-Revolution*, pp. 18–21; Arnold, "Political Ideology," pp. 69–75 and 80–86.

Republicans, however, differed fundamentally from the Constitutionalists over what constituted an effective "check." The most penetrating discussion of their dialogue appears in Douglas Arnold's analysis of Republican ideology.[24] Republican spokesmen believed that the only reliable check upon man's innate desire for unchecked power lay in well-defined, carefully counterbalanced governmental institutions staffed by experienced public officials. Wary Constitutionalists, however, equated the Republicans' experienced officials with established elites who would bridge any chasm created by a separation of powers to form one upper-class magistracy that would ignore the interests and frustrate the will of the people. This was their reading of the alliance between Pennsylvania's two long-hostile elite factions, the executive-centered Proprietary group and the assembly's Quaker party, which attempted to check the Revolution in May 1776.[25]

In the decade following Independence, this constitutional argument manifested three prominent features. First, its consistently class-conscious rhetoric suggests that partisan divisions in Pennsylvania were always at least partly class-based. Equally significant is the repeated expression of ideological convictions about the proper form of sound government that go beyond the struggle between upper-class republicanism and middle-class democracy. What most commands one's attention to the controversy, however, is its ideological consistency over time. The strategies of each party

---

[24] See Arnold, "Political Ideology," ch. 3. It is worth noting that unicameralism was not new in Pennsylvania and was neither attacked nor defended in respect to its age. While the Constitutionalists defended unicameralism on ideological grounds, one must remember that Pennsylvania's legislature had been unicameral since 1701. Had the provincial legislature been bicameral, the Constitutionalists would probably have written a radically democratic constitution based on a bicameral legislature. Nor was the Republican critique of the constitution based on any illusions that a unicameral legislature could not work or that it could not be directed toward politically and socially conservative ends. The provincial Quaker assembly had proved beyond question that a one-house legislature could achieve conservative objectives.

[25] Ryerson, *Revolution*, pp. 171–73, 198–99, and 209.

changed with circumstances; the commitment of each to its favored checks and balances never varied.[26]

It was this enduring struggle which finally killed the Constitution of 1776 and which has caused historians to see it as unworkable. Yet only by asking the question, Was the Constitution of 1776 workable?—a question that does not appear to have been asked before—can one discover why this frame of government ultimately failed to command allegiance.

For a government operating under an "unworkable" constitution, Pennsylvania compiled a curious record. The commonwealth contributed heavily to the war effort for several years at a time when Congress made especially onerous demands upon it for men, material, and money. Its leader for three critical war years, the president of the Supreme Executive Council and ardent Constitutionalist Joseph Reed, effectively exercised the political and military powers of a governor despite his weak constitutional position. It had one energetic, well-qualified chief justice for nearly its entire existence under the constitution. And from a shaky beginning, it developed enough financial strength by 1785 to begin capturing that part of the national debt owed to its citizens. This last achievement caused dismay in Congress and disgust among Pennsylvania's nationalist Republicans, but it hardly indicates a weak or incompetent government. At the same time the state settled magnanimously with the Penns for their vast landholdings and presided over a generally booming, if often troubled, economy. The only time when Pennsylvania's radical new government did not work effectively was in 1776–77, when its Republican opponents tried every measure short of violence to sabotage it just as General Howe was invading New York, New Jersey, and finally Pennsylvania itself.[27]

Yet this thoroughly workable government probably had more enemies by the late 1780s than at any other time in its troubled course. Neither its survival nor its triumphs made it

[26] Arnold, "Political Ideology," esp. pp. 67, 72–73, 80–98, 111, and 153–73.

[27] Ireland, "Ratification," pp. 141–50 and 175–80; Brunhouse, *Counter-Revolution*, pp. 79–80; Selsam, *Pennsylvania Constitution*, pp. 223–54.

more loved, and the eventual repeal of its most obnoxious laws, the loyalty oaths, only gave more of its foes the vote.[28] More serious was the injudicious behavior of Pennsylvania's public officials. Not only were many magistrates petty and vindictive toward their partisan opponents, but several openly violated provisions of the constitution itself. Constitutionalists as well as Republicans remained in office when the rotation clauses required their departure, exercised powers that their branch of government did not possess, and repeatedly ignored the people, whose advice they were obligated to consult before enacting laws. Although the Republicans criticized Pennsylvania's unchecked assembly, weak executive, and dependent judiciary, they often abused the power of the legislative majorities that they enjoyed in the 1780s, pitted themselves as legislators against the Supreme Executive Council, and delighted in holding back or reducing the salaries of Constitutionalist judges.[29]

Too few Pennsylvanians of any political persuasion respected the Constitution of 1776 enough to save it. By combining an appreciation of the origins of Pennsylvania's Constitutionalists with Arnold's insightful analysis of the ideological wars fought over their constitution, one may discover deeper causes for the failure of Pennsylvanians to accord the document this respect than either its critics or its historians have afforded us.

In framing Pennsylvania's new government, the Constitu-

---

[28] The best study of the test oath legislation, and of its impact upon the voting strength of the two parties in Pennsylvania, is Ireland, "Ratification," pp. 74–82, 88–91, 153–56, 173–75, 190–93, and 198–203.

[29] James M. Aldrich, "The Revolutionary Legislature in Pennsylvania: A Roll Call Analysis," Ph.D. diss., University of Maine, 1969, pp. 18–19 and 179–83; Ireland, "Ratification," pp. 162–66; Arnold, "Political Ideology," pp. 153–73; *Journal of the Council of Censors* . . . (Philadelphia, 1783–[84]); James Madison, *Federalist Nos. 48* and *50*, in Edward Mead Earle, ed., *The Federalist* (New York, 1937). One should in fairness, however, point out that not all unconstitutional behavior in Pennsylvania was petty or partisan in origin. Wartime conditions created several real emergencies during which the assembly both passed bills into law in a single session without popular consideration (which the constitution permitted in an emergency), and gave the Supreme Executive Council broad quasi-legislative powers for limited periods of time.

tionalists drew upon their experience as angry, frustrated outsiders, excluded from power by an oligarchy which taught by example that the interest of the morally superior part of society could legitimately become the interest of the state. Reading in the radical whig tradition and more immediately in Thomas Paine's *Common Sense*, they encountered both the country myth of the single-interest society and the precept that the highest form of human endeavor is the defense of one's country against its enemies, both external and internal. There was but one theme in the life of that most celebrated of classical patriots: Cato the Younger dedicated himself totally to a heroic struggle against corruption and tyranny in the Roman republic. Cato appeared to eighteenth-century Americans as a wholly public man, unconcerned with the economic and domestic cares of ordinary mortals; and his patriotism was pure, unsullied by the slightest interest in personal power.[30]

Pennsylvania's Constitutionalists may not have attained the patriotic perfection of a Cato, but they tried. As the most idealistic of constitutional revolutionaries, they appear to have based their actions on three central assumptions about their countrymen. First, they believed either that all Pennsylvanians shared a common set of interests or, alternatively, that any differences in their interests were too insignificant to cause discord among virtuous men. Second, they presumed that Revolutionary Pennsylvanians would behave as citizens first and as farmers, artisans, or merchants, as young men or old, as Anglicans, Lutherans, or Presbyterians, second. All would act as vigilant watchdogs over the performance of their government, which consequently would have no need for institutional checks upon its actions. Finally, they

[30] Samuel Adams and Philadelphia's own Charles Thomson studied to become such men, with considerable success. On the origins and development of "country" ideology in the eighteenth-century British Empire, see Pocock, *Machiavellian Moment* and *Ancient Constitution*, and Robbins, *Commonwealthman*. On the image of Cato in eighteenth-century Britain and America, see Robbins, *Commonwealthman*, pp. 115–25 and 392–93; Bailyn, *Ideological Origins*, ch. 2, esp. pp. 43–44; and H. Trevor Colbourn, *The Lamp of Experience: Whig History and the Intellectual Origins of the American Revolution* (Chapel Hill, 1965), pp. 24 and 153.

were convinced that all who dissented from these assumptions, especially those who refused to defend their country and its new government against all its foes, were self-interested, corrupted men, morally unfit to be citizens.

Their steady adherence to these beliefs doomed sincere Constitutionalists to over a decade of self-righteous frustration. Their province had never been a single-interest society; in its first forty years it did not even enjoy a superficial harmony among its highly competitive inhabitants. The succeeding forty years of political apathy under the Quaker oligarchy, however, papered over the competitive aspirations of the province's increasingly pluralistic population. The decade before the Revolution saw real conflict, but this was cast in such morally black and white terms that political pluralism could develop no legitimacy.[31] During the Revolution the Constitutionalist vision of an undifferentiated citizenry was assaulted by the behavior of Pennsylvanians of every political persuasion. On the "right" were tories, neutrals, pacifists, and a large number of ardent patriots who vehemently opposed the Constitution of 1776. Within the Constitutionalist party, stalwart friends of the new government included Germans who saw it as pro-German, Scotch-Irish who saw it as pro-Scotch-Irish, and many others who only wanted to seize new political opportunities, or to get back at old enemies.[32]

This behavior invalidated both the Constitutionalists' first and second assumptions; not only were Pennsylvania's patriots displaying radically different interests, but many were placing their individual concerns above their civic obliga-

[31] Nash, *Quakers and Politics*; Tully, *William Penn's Legacy*; Richard Bauman, *For the Reputation of Truth: Politics, Religion, and Conflict among the Pennsylvania Quakers, 1750–1800* (Baltimore, 1971), chs. 1–8; Hutson, *Pennsylvania Politics*, chs. 3–4; Ryerson, *Revolution*, chs. 1–2.

[32] See Ryerson, *Revolution*, chs. 5–7 and 9, on conflict among the Revolutionaries before Independence. Selsam, *Pennsylvania Constitution*, ch. 6, Brunhouse, *Counter-Revolution*, pp. 18–38, and Arnold, "Political Ideology," chs. 2–3, discuss patriot opposition to the constitution. I am here interpreting Ireland's ethnoreligious argument in "Ratification," chs. 1–3 and 5, as evidence that Pennsylvania's religious groups saw the constitution in group-interest terms. For several examples of individual self-interest, see Brunhouse, *Counter-Revolution*, chs. 2–3.

tions. The twentieth-century American can calmly regard the issues that divided Revolutionary Pennsylvanians—which men would hold office; who would get what public favors; who would control taxation, currency, and trade; and what place the several ethnic and religious communities would secure in the economic and political life of their country—as the normal stuff of politics to which different citizens will naturally react according to their understanding of their individual interests. For Pennsylvania's Constitutionalists, however, each of these matters became a moral, patriotic question. They could not calmly discuss their differences like good republicans; they had to become zealous defenders of their country against all its enemies, wherever they saw them.[33]

This reaction, combined with their belief that all who did not think as they did were unfit for citizenship, brought on a tragically misguided policy. Every polity places limits upon permissible behavior, beyond which no citizen may go without penalty, but the Constitutionalists set their limits narrowly and even vindictively, and kept them intact long after the Revolutionary War had ended. Their test oaths disenfranchised not only tories but neutrals, pacifists, and even dedicated republicans who could not tolerate the imposition of the oaths. All were stripped of basic legal rights and consigned to second-class citizenship.[34] For over a decade the radicals fought to preserve their distinction between "citizenns" and "others" and to insure that only citizens partook of the full blessings of civil society and of their Revolution. This policy had as corrosive an effect upon Pennsylvania's civic happiness as any measure taken in the decade following Independence.

[33] It is perhaps this twentieth-century acceptance of conflict that has made it hard for Selsam, Brunhouse, and Hawke to understand their eighteenth-century subjects, men who had no tradition of competitive pluralistic politics behind them. James Madison also expressed a modern understanding of political pluralism in *Federalist No. 10*, but he and other pluralist thinkers were aware that their understanding of the problem was quite novel.

[34] On the provisions of the test oaths, see Arnold, "Political Ideology," pp. 105–8; and Ireland, "Ratification," pp. 74–77.

The Constitution of 1776 failed first because it neither grew organically out of nor fit comfortably upon the society it was designed to preserve and advance. This fundamental deformity led to obvious problems: unrealistic expectations of harmony and constitutional restraint among citizens and between the branches of government, emotionally charged battles over the proper function of normally beneficent institutions like the College of Philadelphia, and punitive loyalty oaths that stimulated the rampant growth of ethnic and religious antagonisms. Such intensely partisan behavior suggests that Pennsylvania's constitution never afforded its citizens the emotional security and sense of identity that Revolutionary Americans urgently needed and were increasingly coming to expect from their organic law. This constitutional shortcoming lies at the heart of the Constitutionalists' political failure.[35]

The foregoing analysis has suggested a new way of looking at the historical origins of the Constitutionalists and has hypothesized several assumptions upon which they based their constitution and their whole political behavior. Yet this characterization only brings these ardent patriots up to their first crisis when, in the fall of 1776, their opponents initiated a sustained attack upon their new frame of government. To understand the Constitutionalists' behavior during the war years and to appreciate what that behavior reveals about their fundamental motives, one must turn to the party's birth in the Revolutionary movement's later, more radical phase, from the spring of 1775 to Independence.

This brief period opened with preparations for war, the first armed conflict with Britain, and the first fears that all tories were potential traitors. A sudden polarization of Pennsylvanians followed, with most Quakers and older, wealthier Anglicans behaving conservatively, and most Presbyterians, younger Anglicans, Germans, and men of modest fortune behaving radically, culminating in a direct confrontation be-

[35] On the emotional need for constitutional security, see Wood, *Creation*, ch. 10, section 5, "Political Pathology."

tween individuals, social groups, and political institutions over both the war effort and Independence.[36] This polarization led directly to the Constitutionalist-Republican division of Pennsylvania, and the attitudes of the two parties toward the crucial issues of the next decade took definite shape in these months of intense, class-based ideological conflict. Owen Stephen Ireland has shown that virtually all Constitutionalist legislators demanded the harsh treatment of tories, neutrals, and pacifists, blamed inflation on monopolizers, were wary of commercial banks, and supported the reform of what they saw as the toryish, aristocratic College of Philadelphia. Republicans advocated leniency for neutrals and pacifists, and later for tories; blamed inflation on the uncontrolled emission of paper currency; favored commercial banks; and defended the College's charter. Constitutionalists were nearly all Antifederalists, and Republicans, Federalists, in 1787.[37]

In the positions they took and in the rhetoric they used to defend them, the Constitutionalists revealed their deep faith in certain perceptions of society. They held, first, that the most valuable members of society were those who would sacrifice their self-interest for the good of the whole; second, that the wealthier members of society, especially those with inherited wealth and social position, were seldom among its self-sacrificing citizens; third, that elites were invariably opposed to social, economic, and political equality of opportunity (and for the Constitutionalists, equality of opportunity was democracy); and fourth, that those who rejected equality of opportunity and self-sacrifice for the common good were easily recognizable by their social status and would be a threat to the preservation of the state whenever it came under attack by a foreign power.[38]

Two events convinced the Constitutionalists of the right-

[36] Ryerson, *Revolution*, chs. 6–9.

[37] Ireland, "Ratification," pp. 8, 86–91, 106–15, 119–40, 160–62, 164, 174–75, 183–85, 193–94, and 205; Main, *Political Parties*, ch. 7.

[38] For the expression of these sentiments, beginning in 1770 but only becoming numerous in late 1775 and in 1776, see Ryerson, *Revolution*, pp.

ness of these beliefs. The first was the confrontation between upper- and middle-class leaders over the issue of resisting Great Britain, which found its most dramatic expression in the sudden alliance of worldly Quaker spokesmen with the Proprietary and older Anglican elites against the campaign by Presbyterians, Germans, younger Anglicans, and rene- gade Quakers for Independence in the spring of 1776. The second event was Gen. William Howe's invasion of New York and New Jersey in 1776 and Pennsylvania in 1777, climaxing in his nine-month occupation of Philadelphia, where many local residents extended him a warm welcome.[39]

Howe's invasion had a powerful impact upon a broad spec- trum of Pennsylvania leaders. On the "left," three men who had been critical of the new constitution, John Bayard, Thomas McKean, and Joseph Reed, joined the Constitution- alists to save the war effort and preserve America's indepen- dence. All three were Presbyterian. On the "right," about twenty men were exiled to Virginia or to central New Jersey in 1777 as untrustworthy citizens, and in 1778 John Roberts and Abraham Carlisle were hanged for treason by the Com- monwealth of Pennsylvania. Most of the exiles and both exe- cuted men were Quakers. The two men chiefly responsible for sending Roberts and Carlisle to the gallows, prosecutor Joseph Reed and George Bryan, president of the Supreme Executive Council, were Presbyterians. When Pennsylvania's Revolution reached its fullest polarization, the poles were its Presbyterians and its Quakers.[40]

One could well connect the hanging of Roberts and Car-

32–33, 139, 145–47, 171, 174, 209–10, and 215–16; and Arnold, "Politi- cal Ideology," pp. 67, 87, and 158.

[39] Ryerson, *Revolution*, chs. 6–9, esp. 8 and 9; Brunhouse, *Counter-Revo- lution*, pp. 22–24; Roche, *Joseph Reed*, chs. 6–8, and pp. 144–47; Henry J. Young, "Treason and Its Punishment in Revolutionary Pennsylvania," *Pennsylvania Magazine of History and Biography* 90 (1966): 287–313.

[40] Brunhouse, *Counter-Revolution*, pp. 41–44; Young, "Treason"; Cole- man, *Thomas McKean*, pp. 214–16 and 229–31; Roche, *Joseph Reed*, pp. 144–47; Charles Page Smith, *James Wilson, Founding Father, 1742–1798* (Chapel Hill, 1956), pp. 117–23.

lisle with the march of the Paxton Boys fourteen years earlier, thereby relating the established Quakers' long exclusion
of immigrant Presbyterians from public councils to several
years of Presbyterian revenge; but in the context of the
Revolution, Presbyterian versus Quaker may have yet another meaning. The Revolution quickly acquired a unique
character for Pennsylvania's Presbyterians, and elicited an in-
tensity and a unanimity of commitment that was probably
not equaled by any other religious group south of New England. One could seek the roots of their behavior in the historic Scotch-Irish hatred of the English, but a recent study of
Presbyterian higher education in eighteenth-century America
by Howard Miller perceptively affords us a deeper explanation. Pennsylvania's Presbyterians, perhaps responding to
millenarian impulses that had lain dormant for over a generation since the end of the Great Awakening, believed that
the Revolution would, under divine Providence, create a new
feeling of American community. This great political struggle
would forge new social bonds of unprecedented strength;
and it would raise Americans, individually and collectively,
above the moral mud in which God had left man since the
Fall.[41]

Only citizens, however, only the faithful, could experience
this transformation. Many Pennsylvanians, sadly, chose to
spurn this heaven-sent opportunity to improve their country
and themselves. Following Independence, most of these dissenters were quiet. One large, visible community was not. In
their public "testimonies," Pennsylvania's Quakers attacked
the Revolution again and again, not only on the ground that
the accompanying war effort infringed upon their conscientious objection to violence but fundamentally because the

[41] See Howard Miller, *The Revolutionary College: American Presbyterian
Higher Education, 1707–1837* (New York, 1976), chs. 1, 3 and 5–6, and
Miller, "The Grammar of Liberty: American Presbyterians and the First
American Constitutions," *Journal of Presbyterian History* 54 (1976): 142–64.
The only Pennsylvania Presbyterians of any prominence who did not sup-
port Independence were the Allens, a long-established proprietary family.
The only prominent Presbyterian patriots who were not Constitutionalists
were James Wilson, who married an Anglican, and Benjamin Rush. Per-
haps significantly, neither man was of Scotch-Irish descent.

Revolution itself was an illegal insurrection in the sight of God.[42]

Nothing could have been better calculated to enrage the Presbyterian soul. The very act which this zealous Christian soldier saw as a sacred transformation of a corrupted world was being branded a sinful rebellion against divinely ordained authority. He could understand, although hardly forgive, the cowardly, self-interested behavior of royal and proprietary officials, Anglican clerics, and older, wealthier Anglican communicants who opposed the Revolution as an economically unwise, socially upsetting, and politically unjustified rebellion against their king. Pennsylvania's Quakers were saying something more disturbing; they made it clear that they were "others," that the transcendent vision of an American Jerusalem had no meaning for them.[43] In the 1770s it appeared that they would never value this new American citizenship, no matter how "successful" the Revolution might become, or feel any allegiance to the new nation that was being born.

The Presbyterian response was predictably bitter. When Pennsylvania's Constitutionalists hanged Roberts and Carlisle, they were acting out the role of angry, frustrated outsiders who had finally gotten through the doorway. They were acting out another role, too. These men were fearful patriots, defending a precious vision of a transforming society. This society, they were appalled to discover, was under assault by many Pennsylvanians at the very moment that the British enemy was at the gates. In a reaction that would inform their behavior for years to come, these apprehensive, deeply offended patriots lashed out at every refractory elitist and every humble neighbor who spurned Revolutionary citizenship, at Republicans, monopolists, neutrals, pacifists, and tories, and, finally and most tragically, at Quakers.

By 1778 the Pennsylvania Constitutionalist was part aspiring

---

[42] See *Testimony Addressed to the People, Testimony from our Yearly-Meeting*, and *From our General Spring Meeting . . . 1778* (Philadelphia, 1778).

[43] The language of the Quaker testimonies of 1776–78 forcefully conveys this sense of "otherness."

patriot, filled with the most exalted ambitions for the moral
future of his new country, and part fearful patriot, charged
with anxieties and hatreds that had taken root in his particular ethnic and religious background and had grown to maturity in the nourishing presence of greedy monopolists,
wealthy tories, outspoken pacifists, and British troops. An
appreciation of this heritage affords an explanation both for
the surprising durability of the new constitution and for its
eventual collapse; the Constitutionalist response to repeated
Republican attempts to revise the document richly illustrates
the role of this legacy.

The Constitution of 1776 survived four efforts to replace
it with a more conservative frame of government before it
succumbed to massive disapproval in 1789–90. The first two
attempts at revision were abortive. In the fall of 1776 outraged Republicans persuaded several newly elected members
of the Supreme Executive Council to resign so that no executive department could form and the new government would
be prevented from acting. At the same time these constitutional conservatives planned to have the new legislators take
the most unconstitutional step of amending the document
themselves. They failed to win control of this first assembly,
however, and the council, its vacated seats filled at by-elections, began functioning in the spring of 1777. The Republicans then changed their strategy. Tacitly admitting the
unconstitutionality of any alterations that the assembly might
make in the constitution, they persuaded the legislature to
schedule elections for a new constitutional convention. General Howe terminated this second attempt by invading the
state.[44]

Once the British army had left Pennsylvania, however, the
Republicans devised an attractive and persuasive plan to revise the constitution; attractive because of its essential fairness to both parties and persuasive because the price to the
Constitutionalists for rejecting it would be the loss of Republican votes needed to elect a Constitutionalist candidate for
president of the council. The Republicans proposed a two-

[44]Selsam, *Pennsylvania Constitution*, pp. 223–53; Brunhouse, *Counter-
Revolution*, pp. 18–38; Arnold, "Political Ideology," pp. 69–77.

part election; every voter would cast one ballot indicating whether to hold a new constitutional convention, and a second ballot listing the candidates he wished to have represent him in that convention. Each county would elect six delegates, thereby continuing the current malapportionment that favored the Constitutionalists. In November 1778 the Constitutionalist-dominated assembly approved this plan, setting the election for the following April; in December the Constitutionalist Joseph Reed was unanimously elected president of the council. In February 1779, however, after receiving the petitions of thousands of citizens that no changes be made in the constitution, the legislators canceled the April election, thereby ending the Republicans' third attempt at constitutional revision.[45]

The Constitutionalists never explained why, at a time when Pennsylvania sorely needed a rest from its partisan wars, they first accepted and then suddenly rejected the Republicans' conciliatory proposal, ultimately preferring partisan petitions to an open election as a referendum on their constitution. Coming immediately after Joseph Reed's crucial election, this decision has led historians to conclude that the Constitutionalists were hypocritical democrats who really feared the will of the majority.[46] Everything we know about these men, however, suggests that when all of their partisan guile is stripped away, they remain Pennsylvania's fearful patriots. The objects of their fear—monopolists and other men of wealth and power, Quakers, neutrals, open and secret collaborators with General Howe—had not departed, and some appeared to be getting richer in the inflationary crisis that was already beginning to bring suffering to so many humble patriots.[47] Constitutionalist legislators may have feared these

---

[45] Brunhouse, *Counter-Revolution*, pp. 53–60; Smith, *James Wilson*, pp. 123–24 and 129–30; Roche, *Joseph Reed*, pp. 148–50 and 163–65; Arnold, "Political Ideology," pp. 77–80.

[46] See especially Brunhouse, *Counter-Revolution*, pp. 58–60; Smith, *James Wilson*, p. 129; and even Roche, *Joseph Reed*, p. 164.

[47] On the inflation crisis of 1778–79, see Brunhouse, *Counter-Revolution*, pp. 68–76; Roche, *Joseph Reed*, pp. 157–60; Arnold, "Political Ideology," pp. 124–33; and John K. Alexander, "The Fort Wilson Incident of 1779:

enemies enough to reject any Republican plan to alter the constitution, no matter how fair that plan may have been. Moreover, the Constitutionalists could justly regard themselves as Pennsylvania's only reliable patriots. They alone had been willing to hold state office in the Revolution's darkest hours, when General Howe marched into their state just as their Republican opponents were making every effort to hobble the new commonwealth.[48] If they did not continue to govern Pennsylvania in the midst of a war for their nation's political survival, who would preserve the state? February 1779 was not the Constitutionalists' finest hour, but it was an hour that we can understand.

In 1779 the Republicans abandoned their attempt to reform the constitution through legislative initiative, took their partisan defeats stoically, and planned for the future. In that year they lost control of the College of Philadelphia to Presbyterian zealots, saw the assembly pass yet another offensive loyalty oath, and, after being branded the monopolistic malefactors of the current inflationary crisis, suffered a major defeat at the polls.[49] In the 1780s they fared better, winning elections regularly in the populous southeastern counties, and building a clear majority in the now popularly apportioned assembly and a narrow one on the Council of Censors by the fall of 1783. The meeting of this septennial body promised the Republicans the best chance they ever expected to have to amend the constitution. The Constitutionalists, however, secured enough seats on the council to block any plan to revise their frame of government, and in 1784 they refused once again to summon a constitutional convention.[50]

A Case Study of the Revolutionary Crowd," *William and Mary Quarterly*, 3d ser. 31 (1974): 589–612, esp. 593–600.

[48] For the campaign to frustrate the new government, see Brunhouse, *Counter-Revolution*, pp. 27–52; and for one angry Constitutionalist patriot's feelings in the summer of 1778, see Roche, *Joseph Reed*, pp. 144–47.

[49] Brunhouse, *Counter-Revolution*, pp. 76–82; Ireland, "Ratification," pp. 106–17, 119–33, and 277 (table 19).

[50] Brunhouse, *Counter-Revolution*, pp. 156–63; Ireland, "Ratification," pp. 162–65; Arnold, "Political Ideology," pp. 152–73.

It is richly ironic that the Republicans discovered that their only defense against Constitutionalist zeal lay in controlling the unicameral legislature that they so despised. In the 1780s they commanded either a majority or a rough equality in the assembly in every year but one. The Constitutionalists, however, were well entrenched on the Supreme Executive Council which, unlike the assembly, would never be reapportioned to reflect county population size. They were even more impressively fortified on the similarly constructed Council of Censors, where any majority under two-thirds could do nothing but talk. This curious incongruity between political ideology and constitutional structure allowed the "popular" party to secure themselves within the "elitist" branches of government whenever the "elitist" party won control of the legislature. It also insured that the Constitutionalists could block any revision of their frame of government as long as they controlled at least five of the state's thirteen electoral districts. They did somewhat better than this in the 1783 election, and by-elections to fill vacancies on the Council of Censors gave them a majority in 1784. Thus when they refused to summon a constitutional convention, they were fully within their constitutional rights. The interesting question, however, is why they refused this widely popular demand.[51]

Objective circumstances could well have prompted the Constitutionalists to consider revising their frame of government in 1783. That year Republicans achieved their first absolute majority in the assembly and an initial majority on the Council of Censors; this followed the 1782 election of John Dickinson, an early critic of the constitution, as president of the Supreme Executive Council. Such events left little doubt that most Pennsylvania voters wanted constitutional change. The Revolutionary War was now over, and so was the objective need to be on guard against tories and tory sympathizers.[52]

---

[51] On the ironic alignment of parties and institutions, see Arnold, "Political Ideology," pp. 162–64; on the shifting partisan balance on the Council of Censors, see pp. 153–54 and 158–60.

[52] Ireland, "Ratification," pp. 151–52 and 277; Arnold, "Political Ideology," pp. 153–54; Brunhouse, *Counter-Revolution*, p. 123.

The Constitutionalists, however, did not see matters this way. In 1784 they blocked the repeal of the state's harsh test oath by preventing a legislative quorum; as late as 1786 their leaders were openly hostile to all who had taken a tory, neutral, or pacifist stand during the war. They feared the mercantile elite in Philadelphia as deeply as ever, and they clearly understood Robert Morris's financial schemes and proposals as strategies to create a powerful national government. Strongly opposed both to Morris's means and to his ends, they used the one assembly majority they enjoyed in this decade (1784–85) to repeal the local charter granted to his Bank of North America. For Pennsylvania's Constitutionalists, neither the war nor the Revolution was over by 1784. Quite apart from their natural desire to hold on to public offices, they retained a compelling emotional need to defend their constitution and to see its enemies as America's enemies.[53]

The Constitutionalists' intransigence consigned the Council of Censors to ten months of frustration. Unable to summon a constitutional convention, the Republican majority in the opening sessions (November 1783 to February 1784) could only issue a report condemning the frequent violations of constitutional limitations by the assembly, the Supreme Executive Council, and individual magistrates over the previous seven years. The Constitutionalist minority then issued a dissenting report that cited still other abuses but denied that any or all of them justified amending the constitution. A popular resurgence of Constitutionalist strength in the spring and a change in party balance in the Censors' concluding sessions (June to September 1784) produced two more clashing reports. The council's published proceedings had little effect on Pennsylvania politics, but they did make three things clear: Violations of the constitution had been numerous, by both the legislative and executive branches and by many individual officeholders; both Republicans and Constitutionalists were responsible; and Pennsylvanians could not rely on the Censors to summon a constitutional conven-

[53] Ireland, "Ratification," pp. 153–56, 173–75, and 190–93, on the test oaths, and 181–88 and 193–94, on the bank.

tion until the Constitutionalist party became much weaker in the commonwealth. Thus ended one of the more curious experiments in American constitutional history. Pennsylvania's Council of Censors, created to keep a new government healthy, could effectively demonstrate that its young patient was ill, but it was powerless to prescribe a cure. In a final indignity, the patient protested his health: The assembly roundly attacked the Censors' criticisms of its behavior as partisan and erroneous.[54]

Four Republican efforts to secure the revision of the constitution, extending over eight frustrating years, had failed, and in 1784 the Constitutionalists again took firm control of the assembly. Short of an unconstitutional coup, the Republicans could only wait for some erosion of their opponents' popular support. Yet this last desperate hope was soon answered. A sharp and permanent decline in Constitutionalist strength among the electorate and in every branch of government began in 1785 and eventually forced the calling of a constitutional convention in 1789.

Two factors explain why the Constitution of 1776 survived as long as it did. First, despite widespread disapproval of the document in many quarters, it enjoyed the steady and zealous support of a large part of the population. In 1779 over eighteen thousand Pennsylvanians petitioned the assembly to cancel the convention called to amend the constitution. The Constitutionalists won five of the ten assembly elections held between 1776 and 1785 outright, split another evenly, and came close to an equality in three more; only in 1783 did they constitute less than 40 percent of the house. After 1786, however, the party never won as much as 40 percent of the assembly seats, and committed Constitutionalists became fewer both on the Supreme Executive Council and in the

---

[54] Arnold, "Political Ideology," pp. 154–58 and 160–62; also see pp. 150 and 151. Long after I had written this paragraph I discovered, in an essay that I had often read over before, that James Madison had already drawn the image that I present in the last two sentences. In *Federalist No. 50* he writes: "This censorial body, therefore, proves at the same time, by its researches, the existence of the disease, and by its example, the inefficacy of the remedy" (Earle, ed., *The Federalist*, p. 334).

judiciary.[55] After the Constitutionalists' failure to prevent the ratification of the Federal Constitution, they were in a hopeless position to defend their frame of government.

The second critical factor in the constitution's survival was the tenacity of its defenders. The determination to defend their frame of government that they had shown in 1776 and 1777, in 1779, and in 1784 remained firm until the end. They could not stop the Federal Constitution, but they tried, filling the newspapers with Antifederalist essays, abruptly withdrawing from the assembly in September 1787 in an abortive attempt to prevent a quorum in favor of calling a ratifying convention, and vigorously debating every point in that convention. In that body, their well-disciplined forces lost not a single man, but they were steadily outvoted two-to-one, a margin that probably accurately reflects the Federalist-Antifederalist division in Pennsylvania. The Constitutionalists continued to oppose the Federal Constitution in the press even after their state convention had ratified it, and in September 1788 they held their own convention in Harrisburg to discuss amendments that they believed essential in the national document. By 1789, when they were probably even weaker, their leaders struggled in vain to prevent the assembly from summoning a state constitutional convention. In that convention moderate Constitutionalists worked effectively with moderate Republicans to produce a frame of government that retained the democratic electoral features of its predecessor. Constitutionalist ideologues, however, continued their opposition to all constitutional alterations, even when losing by margins of ten-to-one.[56]

No one development terminated Pennsylvania's Constitution of 1776, but two immediate factors were crucial. First, the principle of using internal checks and balances, rather than relying on vigilant citizens, as the primary guarantor for the energetic yet safe operation of any constitutional govern-

[55] See Ireland, "Ratification," p. 277 (table 19). By 1787 Chief Justice Thomas McKean had become an open supporter of the Federal Constitution and by 1789 he was openly committed to revise Pennsylvania's constitution.

[56] Arnold, "Political Ideology," chs. 7–8.

ment received strong support from the ratification of the Federal Constitution. Under the Articles of Confederation the national government resembled Pennsylvania's own. After 1787, however, both the Articles and all unchecked and unbalanced constitutions appeared contemptibly weak and misshapen.

The second factor in the demise of Pennsylvania's constitution lay closer to home. Between 1786 and 1789, the assembly dismantled the Constitutionalists' punitive test oaths step by step, thereby bringing thousands of new anti-Constitutionalist voters to the polls to end the Constitutionalists' career as a popular party.[57] There is, moreover, a symbolic significance in the repeal of the test oaths that has not been appreciated. The party that wrote and defended the Constitution of 1776 based its behavior on the concept that Pennsylvania must have a government of, by, and for its "citizens"— men whose first interest was the happiness and prosperity of the whole society and whose dedication to that society was proved by their patriotic behavior and their willingness to subscribe to loyalty oaths. Many Constitutionalists intended this division between "citizens" and "others" to be permanent. The rejection of this principle in the late 1780s did more than increase the constitution's opponents; it attacked an important part of the Constitutionalist's reason for existence. When Pennsylvanians repudiated the Constitutionalists' exclusive brand of militant patriotism, they said, in effect, that the Revolution was over.

Pennsylvania's Revolutionary constitution survived for over a decade because, despite its flaws, it enjoyed strong popular support until the mid-1780s, when Philadelphia's artisans and many other Pennsylvanians deserted it for a strong national government just as many of its longtime opponents were rejoining the electorate. It survived, too, because despite frequent Republican charges that it created a government that was unduly subject to pressures by the people, it was carefully designed to withstand anything short of a nearly unanimous demand that it be changed. It expired only when Pennsylvanians approached that level of una-

[57] Ireland, "Ratification," pp. 198–203.

nimity; even then it was not terminated by the explicitly constitutional means of a convention called by the Council of
Censors but by a constitutionally dubious agent, a convention
called by the assembly.[58] Its poor image in historical scholarship notwithstanding, the constitution was indubitably popular until the mid-1780s and was at the same time surprisingly
resistant to popular attack.

This brief examination of Pennsylvania's Constitutionalists
has reached the point where a general assessment of their
central achievement, the Constitution of 1776, and of the political behavior which that constitution informed should be
possible.

At a fundamental level the new constitution was a failure.
It never achieved the nearly universal acceptance that any
constitution must have to become a firm basis for popular
government. But it did not fail because it was unworkable,
because it created a powerless executive, because it was too
easily subject to popular pressures, or even because it created
a unicameral legislature. Each of these allegations is either
untrue or without explanatory power. It failed because its
proper operation depended on two factors: a society with
either one or a few very similar interests and a body of citizens who would place their civic obligations ahead of the normal mix of individual and group ambitions, selfishness, and
pride that make up the human condition. The Constitutionalists never denied that mankind possessed these faults, but
they believed that the Revolution would transform Americans into something better, a belief that they shared with
many of their contemporaries throughout the new nation.[59]

The constitution began to fail at the point when thousands
of Pennsylvanians sensed that its underlying assumptions
were false. Pennsylvania had never been a single-interest society, and neither the Revolution nor the new constitution
could make it one. More critical, however, was the insecurity
that arose from the sudden realization that the one poten-

[58] Arnold, "Political Ideology," pp. 91–98, esp. p. 94.

[59] On the widespread belief that the Revolution would transform
America into a kind of "Christian Sparta," see Wood, *Creation*, pp. 114–24.

tially effective check upon the new government was the vigilance of its citizenry. In the fall of 1776 most powerful and wealthy Pennsylvanians understood that the only thing standing between them and their economic and social inferiors' envious desire for their property and status was their inferiors' "virtue." Terrified, they attacked the constitution hastily and irresponsibly, and they failed miserably.

Over the next decade, however, their insecurity spread down the social ladder as ordinary citizens began to experience the inconvenience and confusion of living under a constitution that generated no deep respect in any quarter. As they observed their commonwealth, many Pennsylvanians also felt deeper emotions—anxiety and shame. The Pennsylvania constitution did not perform that first function of effective organic law: It did not express the political wisdom of its people. For Americans in the 1780s, such feelings were particularly disturbing. Their new nation lacked symbols that effectively embodied its pride and its aspirations. They were too close to their victory over Great Britain to see this triumph as heroic myth, for they could vividly remember their often confused, tight-fisted, and sometimes cowardly patriotism. Their flag was but a piece of cloth; their army just soldiers; their heroes still real men. Even George was not yet the Washington he would become. The one potentially pure and aspiring creation within every American's reach was a state constitution that expressed who he was, how he behaved, and what he thought he might become.[60] For too many Pennsylvanians the Constitution of 1776 failed this test. They saw it, instead, as a visionary document that made false assumptions about Pennsylvania society and impossible demands upon its magistrates and its citizens.

To appreciate the role that their disappointment in their constitution played in their political behavior, one need only to compare the experience of Pennsylvanians in the 1780s with that of all Americans a decade later. Despite several important parallels in their public concerns and in their partisan activity, the constitutional conditions of the two polities were radically different. Eight years after the creation of the

[60] See Wood, *Creation*, pp. 413–15, 423–25, 428–29, and 431.

Constitution of 1776, Pennsylvanians were divided into two largely class-, religion-, and region-based parties that battled over paper money, banks, tories, and the nature of citizenship. One of those parties took the name of their constitution; the other party hated the Constitutionalists—and despised the constitution behind them. Eight years after the creation of the Federal Constitution, Americans were also divided into two largely class-, religion-, and region-based political parties that battled over paper money, banks, taxes, Anglophiles and Francophiles, and the nature of citizenship. One of those parties took a name that was inseparably associated with the national Constitution, the other party hated the Federalists—but revered the Federal Constitution that they claimed the Federalists were distorting and violating. However the Federal Constitution had been created, it quickly became America's Constitution, and was universally felt to express the political genius of the American people.[61] However the Pennsylvania constitution had been created, most Pennsylvanians eventually decided that it did not express their genius and that it was not truly their constitution.

What, then, did Pennsylvania's Constitutionalists achieve? And on what basis can the present discussion claim to present a more favorable view of the Constitutionalists than previous historical scholarship?

The Constitutionalists' accomplishments have perhaps been neglected because they are so casually accepted in twentieth-century America. They were controversial in 1776. The Constitutionalists introduced the taxpayer franchise, something that closely approached white manhood suffrage, into the American political tradition. They introduced the regular reapportionment of legislative seats solely upon the basis of the taxable population. They dispensed with all special qualifications for office. In short, they created the first large, radically democratic republic in the modern world. Moreover, they incorporated each of these innovations into

[61] On the rapid and total acceptance of the Federal Constitution by the Antifederalists, and later by the Republican-Democrats, see Lance Banning, "Republican Ideology and the Triumph of the Constitution, 1789 to 1793," *William and Mary Quarterly*, 3d ser. 31 (1974): 167–88.

the more balanced, conservative Pennsylvania Constitution of 1790.[62] In its Revolutionary-era context, Pennsylvania's democracy made the commonwealth's neighboring sovereign states, from Massachusetts to South Carolina, look either gentrified or positively aristocratic. Pennsylvania was America's cutting edge of democracy, advancing that political condition to a Jacksonian level fifty years before Jackson.[63]

Yet the strongest political and social forces in America were running against the Constitutionalists' basic social objectives in the 1780s. This makes it fitting for historians to see the Constitution of 1776 as a failure. It does not justify their lack of interest in sensitively understanding its defenders. Angry, frustrated outsiders rushing through the doorways to the power and status they so desperately craved, idealistic patriots who sacrificed gladly for a bright new vision of their nation, fearful patriots who saw enemies, real as well as imagined, all around them—such men are seldom a revolution's winners, either in their own day or in the historian's narrative. They are, however, among a revolution's most characteristic and creative actors. Pennsylvania's Constitutionalists contributed early and heavily to the equality-of-opportunity democracy that Americans like to think they have created. Their mistake was to presume, in James Madison's familiar words, "that by reducing mankind to a perfect equality in their political rights, they would, at the same time, be perfectly equalized and assimilated in their possessions, their opinions, and their passions."[64]

[62] Arnold, "Political Ideology," pp. 299–317.

[63] I am not referring to any particular interpretation of Jacksonian democracy here but simply to the fact that between 1828 and 1840 virtually all adult white males could vote and large numbers did so.

[64] *Federalist No. 10*, in Earle, ed., *The Federalist*, pp. 58–59.

EDWARD C. PAPENFUSE

The Legislative Response to a Costly War

Fiscal Policy and

Factional Politics in Maryland

1777–1789

THE COST OF Independence to state governments and the people they served was high. Funding the Revolution forced the states to accept a multitude of new or expanded responsibilities. The ensuing controversy over what services government ought to provide and how those services ought to be paid for placed great strain on what hitherto had been an affordable parochial experiment in representative government. Before 1776 provincial government cost little and was left largely to a small, relatively affluent elite to manage and to quarrel about in leisurely fashion. To understand what state government became during and after the American Revolution, we must look closely at the economic consequences of war as they interacted with the existing factious climate of state politics.

The single most important economic problem that the new state legislatures had to grapple with from their inception to the assumption of the debt by the new federal government in 1790 was devising means by which the staggering cost of the Revolutionary War could be paid. Between 1776 and 1783, Maryland incurred a war-debt principal of £1,647,750, an annual average of £329,550, that, if not paid, caused an additional yearly drain of about £20,000 in interest.[1] In 1783

[1] Edward C. Papenfuse, *In Pursuit of Profit: The Annapolis Merchants in the Era of the American Revolution, 1763–1805* (Baltimore, 1975), pp. 80–81, n. 8.

the white population of the state was 179,177, making the annual per capita rate of indebtedness between 1779 and 1783 £2, including interest. The average per capita wealth among whites in Maryland in 1783 was £68.14.0. Assuming that, at best, average per capita income was 6 percent of per capita wealth, the average annual cost of the war effort to each white Maryland resident between 1779 and 1783 was almost 50 percent of gross per capita income. Not until very recently in Maryland history would the debt burden on taxpayers again be so great. In 1977 the average per capita income of Maryland residents was $7,572 while the gross per capita public debt of the United States was $3,233 or 42.7 percent of per capita income.[2]

In *Prospects on the Rubicon* (1787) Thomas Paine reflected on the decade or so that had passed since the publication of *Common Sense*. "War," he wrote, "involves in its progress such a train of unforseen and unsupported circumstances that no human wisdom can calculate. It has but one thing certain, and that is to increase the Taxes." In the twelve years from 1777 until 1789, the outlook for Maryland taxpayers was indeed potentially bleak. Not only did the government have to come to grips with a totally unfamiliar debt burden of disquieting proportions but after 1781, when it reluctantly created the mechanism for collecting and enforcing taxes, it was tempted to postpone amortizing war-related debts and to enlarge the uses to which the money raised would be put. As long as the economy remained relatively healthy (as it did until November 1785), the legislature seemed more than willing to appropriate monies for civil salaries, county courthouses, and public improvements, while increasingly supporting measures to defer payment of any but locally held war debts. In November 1786, near the end of the yearlong controversy over the merits of printing vast quantities of paper money backed by nothing more than the good faith of

[2]Based upon an analysis of the 1782 and 1783 tax lists. See "Summary Accounts of the Valuation of the Assessments in the Several Counties Returned by the Commissioners of the Tax, 1782, [and] 1783," Scharf Collection, Maryland State Papers, series Z, box 95, folder 56, Maryland Hall of Records, Annapolis. *The World Almanac and Book of Facts, 1979* (New York, 1979), pp. 97 and 108.

the state, a letter signed "Poverty" appeared in the *Maryland Gazette* (Baltimore). It pleaded with the legislature to attend to the needs of the poor and charged that hitherto the assembly's principal concern had been to "found the college, to improve the public buildings at Annapolis, and the navigation of the potomack." Tax revenue in hand or anticipated formed a powerful inducement to politicians to discover ways in which it might be spent rather than to pay the public debt and reduce the tax burden.[3]

Charles Carroll of Carrollton, Maryland's arch-conservative in more than fiscal matters, as early as 1777 predicted difficulties arising from a rapidly mounting war debt but saw no other recourse than high taxes. In a series of letters written between 1777 and 1779 to William Carmichael, a protégé in the congressional foreign service, Carroll took an increasingly pessimistic view of the effect of stringent tax collection. He calculated that property taxes would bring about £120,000 annually into the treasury but warned that under British rule taxation was "very moderate." He suggested that people would make unfavorable comparisons. "The bulk of mankind only judge by their feelings and cannot see into the remote consequences" of low taxes. They were sure to resist paying "what they can even bear."[4] Until 1781 the legislature

[3] Statements concerning the nature of legislation passed during the years 1780–89 are based upon an issue analysis of legislative activity, made under the terms of grants from the National Endowment for the Humanities, and a correlation of lower house proceedings with the session laws, the original recorded versions of which are in the Maryland Hall of Records, Annapolis. *The Maryland Gazette or The Baltimore Advertiser*, Nov. 14, 1786.

[4] William Carmichael Papers, Maryland Historical Society, Baltimore. See also Memorial of Alphonsa F. A. Blake, Record Group 233, National Archives. While correct about the discontent high taxes would cause, Carroll typically misread the consequences. He felt strict collection of high taxes would lead to mass migration from the older settled areas to "new confederacies" in the West that would be reluctant to ally with the seaboard states. The ultimate disposition and settlement policy for the lands west of what Carroll called "the appalachian hills," a policy in large measure shaped by the Maryland delegation in Congress, did not fulfill his gloomy prediction that the new western states would "pay . . . little or none of our taxes." In fact the adoption of the Constitution led to a quite equi-

of Maryland demonstrated a great reluctance to fund the war effort and avoided collecting all but token taxes. Consequently inflation became more severe than it has ever been since in the United States, although not as bad as in Germany in 1923. In August 1780 a bed with clean sheets and breakfast in Annapolis at the regulated rate cost forty-seven times what it would once inflation was controlled. By the early months of 1781 the exchange rate in Annapolis reached a peak of 135 Continental dollars for one dollar specie. Creditors like John Galloway, who was attempting to collect the debts owed a deceased relative, simply refused to accept payment in Continental dollars.[5]

Congress appointed a superintendent of finance in the spring of 1781 with broad powers to bring fiscal stability to the national war effort. The Maryland legislature followed suit in January 1782 by appointing an intendant of the revenue after passing in 1781 a tory property confiscation law that provided some capital for funding the debt beyond the anticipated collection of taxes. Both measures served to bring inflation within acceptable bounds. Confiscation, however, did not promise to raise more than a third of the principal of the war debt, and money from the sale of confiscated property could only be collected over a considerable length of time. Few purchasers had the means to pay cash and most could only post interest-bearing bonds. Taxes had to provide the difference. Even Charles Carroll underestimated the revenue that could be generated by property taxes. In 1782 the estimate of gross tax receipts was £264,348, or £1.11.0 for every white person in Maryland, about 50 percent of per capita income. If collected, property taxes could just barely pay the accumulating war debt; as time would prove, however, the revenue collected was not exclusively earmarked for paying for the war. Tax revenue proved too great a tempta-

---

table distribution of the tax burden caused by the war, but in 1779, on the eve of a greatly accelerated war effort in Maryland, neither Carroll nor anyone else could have predicted precisely what the consequences of an expensive war would be.

[5] Annapolis Records, 5:190 and 9:13, Md. Hall of Rec., Annapolis; Papenfuse, *In Pursuit of Profit*, pp. 103–4; "Summary Accounts."

tion, and Maryland's new intendant of the revenue found himself embroiled in controversy almost from his first day in office.[6]

On January 20, as the session of the assembly that established the office of intendant ended, State Senator James McHenry wrote George Washington that the "only novelty which [the assembly] has given birth to, is a man called Intendant, whom we have vested with great powers & who is to destroy that disorder in our affairs, which has arisen chiefly from a bad money & a want of money. You, who know the confusion which reigns very generally throughout the States, will suppose that Daniel of St. Thomas Jenifer, the Maryland Intendant, must have a very embarrassing time & that he shall be uncommonly fortunate, should his administration be successful."[7]

The legislature instructed the intendant to oversee the collection of taxes, the sale of specifics (wheat, pork, and tobacco) accepted in payment of taxes, and the collection of all debts to the state, including those arising from the sale of confiscated property. It also expected him to oversee the payment of the state's creditors. Inevitably, Daniel of St. Thomas Jenifer, who held office until 1788, first as intendant responsible to the legislature and then as agent for the governor and council, found himself frequently at odds with the governor, the governor's council, dissident elements in the legislature, and taxpayers in general, who either blamed him for their plight or asked him for relief. In September 1782 a prominent Anne Arundel County tobacco planter, Samuel Chew, with whom Jenifer had long been acquainted, went so far as to ask for a loan with which to pay his taxes. "How Times are alter'd since we used to meet often at our City. But so it is. Things are turn'd upside down & when they will come Right again God knows. If theire be not Some altera-

[6] E. James Ferguson, *The Power of the Purse: A History of American Public Finance, 1776–1790* (Chapel Hill, 1961), p. 118; November session, 1781, ch. 27, passed January 22, 1782, Recorded Laws of Maryland, Md. Hall of Rec., Annapolis.

[7] Bernard C. Steiner, *The Life and Correspondence of James McHenry* (Cleveland, 1907), pp. 41–42.

tion in affairs soone I do not know what will be ye Consequence. These heavy taxes we shall never be able to comply with unless ye Country produce will fetch a better price."[8] If it was difficult for Chew to pay taxes in 1782 because of the low price of tobacco, it must have been impossible by November of 1785. Tobacco prices fell by a third and remained there for some time after a sustained period at an exceptionally high 40 shillings per hundredweight. In November 1785 Maryland settled into a temporary yet severe recession, accentuated by Jenifer's policy of retiring the debt with as much dispatch as he could command.[9]

Shortly after his appointment as intendant in 1782, Jenifer received a congratulatory letter from his counterpart at the national level, Robert Morris. Morris cautioned that Maryland's method for supporting the war effort was a "bad one" since it allowed people to pay taxes in kind (specifics) instead of money. Morris pointed out that the articles submitted for taxes were never of the highest quality and the public costs of marketing them soon consumed most, if not all, of their worth to the state. "It is a vain thing," he wrote, "to suppose that wars can be carried on, by quibbles and Puns and yet

---

[8]Samuel Chew to Daniel of St. Thomas Jenifer, Sept. 5, 1782, Scharf Collection.

[9]The causes of the recession of 1785–86 are well known and were not surprising even to knowledgeable contemporary observers. In April 1784 John Ridout of Annapolis wrote to his patron, former Governor Sharpe, that he would "easily conceive how much distress't the people are in general & how unable to pay the heavy taxes imposed on them in consequence of the late unhappy ruinous War. Money was never more scarce, much having been exported last year by the foreign adventurers who poured in Quantities of goods from Europe on the Cessation of Hostilities & got for them most of the specie that was then in circulation" (John Ridout to Horatio Sharpe, Apr. 17, 1784, Ridout Papers, Md. Hall of Rec., Annapolis). The full impact of the high taxes and acute shortage of coin was not generally felt, however, until coupled with the sharp reduction in the market price of tobacco that occurred in November 1785. "Maryland tobacco at Baltimore through 1785 would average for good quality 24/- sterling per nite hundr. –for common or inferior 21/-. . . . In Nov. price suddenly reduced at least ⅓ and remains [early 1786] at that reduced price" (Chalmers Papers, Maryland, 1:16 and 17, New York Public Library).

laying taxes payable in specific articles is little better, for with great Sound they put little or nothing into the Treasury."[10] Jenifer learned this lession only too well, for he was soon criticized roundly for the low return on the sale of specifics. He came under most fire, however, for placing the demands of Congress before those of local creditors of the state and, more importantly, ahead of salary payments to civil officers. Within months of his appointment he was engaged in a bitter, vituperative debate with Gov. Thomas Sim Lee and the council, a debate that momentarily raised to a philosophical plane the only two discernible elements of political principle consistently in evidence in the factious squabbles among legislative interests of the 1780s: Should national needs take precedence over local spending priorities? To what extent should local, state, and national government be permanently expanded? Slightly modified, Carl Becker's well-known paradigm for the origins of the Revolution in New York applies to Maryland politics in the late 1770s and the 1780s. From 1777 to 1789 two questions of roughly equal prominence affected the course of political events in Maryland. The first was whether essentially parochial and provincial interests should prevail over what could be termed the national interest. The second was by whom, for whom, and at what expense state government should be conducted. The first was the question of home rule. The second was the question of what factions and fiscal policies should rule at home.[11]

[10]Morris continued, "Experience will however evidence before long to every understanding, the folly of levying specific Supplies, for it will be found that those states which tax in *money only* will grow rich whilst the others continue poor. You must provide the ways and means of turning your Specific Articles into money. Congress have required money, and I will strictly adhere to their requisition through out the States" (Robert Morris to Daniel of St. Thomas Jenifer, Mar. 12, 1782, Adjutant General's Papers, Md. Hall of Rec., Annapolis).

[11]Maryland State Papers. Jenifer's conflict with the executive on the matter of spending priorities continued through William Paca's terms as governor. It was only under Gen. William Smallwood that Jenifer could feel comfortable in the executive branch. Smallwood understood well the need to support the war debt and had defended army spending priorities in 1782 and 1783 against a governor and council that had other concerns (Edward C. Papenfuse and Gregory A. Stiverson, "General Smallwood's

From 1782 until 1785 the legislature left the management of the state's finances largely to Jenifer. At almost every session it expanded Jenifer's powers and it annually reappointed him. Morris's advice was taken and at Jenifer's insistence a law was passed requiring specie in payment for taxes. When money became scarcer and taxpayers more dissatisfied, however, the prevailing view in the assembly of Jenifer's duties shifted. Laws passed in the assembly of 1784 assigned equal status to local obligations—including expanding the civil list—and taxes owed Congress.[12]

Yet the assembly of 1784 felt no impending economic crisis and concerned itself with only minor adjustments to the tax *rate*, raising money through excise duties. In fact it increased public expenditures by establishing institutions of higher learning with specific taxes dedicated to that end. Throughout the 1784 assembly there was a prevailing consensus, perhaps more aptly seen as the calm before the storm, which was reflected in large voting blocks rarely found in the fifteen sessions between 1780 and 1789. The subsequent assembly of 1785 was radically different. Not only were there more roll-call votes indicating considerable dissension in a long, tumultuous session, but the specter of inadequately funded paper money returned as the assembly struggled to find a way to meet the increasing clamor for tax and debtor relief. Instead of the narrow majorities Jenifer's efforts to pay the national debt had hitherto received, only five members could be found who were willing to vote "yes" on three roll calls that successively called for compliance with the requisitions of Congress, increasing the appropriations to pay Congress, and imposing a tax for the payment of debts to Congress.

Recruits: The Peacetime Career of the Revolutionary War Private," *William and Mary Quarterly*, 3d ser. 30 [1973]:117–32; Carl Lotus Becker, *The History of Political Parties in the Province of New York, 1760–1776* [Madison, 1909], p. 22).

[12] Jenifer accepted the shift in priorities even if, in all probability, he did not agree. In a broadside dated September 1784 he wrote, "Having to the best of my judgment performed . . . my duty, I shall be perfectly satisfied with any system which the legislature, upon mature consideration of the circumstances of the state, may think just and wise" (Wheeler Pamphlets, No. 317, Md. Hist. Soc., Baltimore).

Finally the 1785 assembly voted to abandon the task of supervising the payment of the state's debts and the collection of tax revenue, although it did recommend that Jenifer be appointed to perform those tasks within the executive branch. A deepening recession made Jenifer's office politically awkward. As long as some effort of the kind could be continued without the assembly having to shoulder all the blame for the economic consequences, a slim majority felt his work should continue under the governor and council.[13]

Jenifer's primary concern, apparent from his correspondence and accounting records, was the retirement of the national debt, with other demands on the public treasury considered secondary.[14] He accepted the transfer of power from assembly to executive as the only viable means of continuing the work he had begun as intendant. When he agreed to become the agent of the governor and council in April 1786, Gabriel Duvall, a member of the council, resigned in protest on the grounds the agent's powers were too broad and were unconstitutional.[15] Even without Duvall, Jenifer continued to have problems with the council and in January 1787 barely survived a highly critical resolution that read in part: "Whereas it appears that from the low condi-

[13] The assessment of political behavior throughout this essay is based upon the biographical files of the Maryland Hall of Records Legislative History Project and my hand analysis of matrices showing legislator agreement in each of the sessions of the Maryland House of Delegates between 1776 and 1779. The matrices were created under the direction of David Wise for the Legislative History Project with funds granted by the National Endowment for the Humanities. The tables documenting the pattern of factionalism between 1776 and 1788 are on file at the Maryland Hall of Records, Annapolis. In looking at alignments on roll-call votes, I concentrated on the distribution of agreement and degree of success on all roll-call votes.

[14] Records and Papers of the Intendant, Md. Hall of Rec., Annapolis. Also see Edward C. Papenfuse, Gregory A. Stiverson, and Mary D. Donaldson, *The Era of the American Revolution, 1775–1789, an Inventory of Maryland State Papers*, vol. 1 (Annapolis, 1977), for an index to loose papers relating to Jenifer.

[15] Aubrey C. Land, ed., *Journal and Correspondence of the State Council of Maryland: Journal of the State Council, 1784–1789*, Archives of Maryland, vol. 71 (Baltimore, 1970), p. 96.

tion of the State in point of credit and finances he has been able but in a small degree to carry the purposes of his appointment into effect, and as it appears by his letter of this day in answer to the enquiry of the Board that he believes the two principal objects of this appointment are not further attainable," therefore, Jenifer's salary should cease and "the Board will hereafter make him reasonable compensation for any services contrary to present expectation he may be able to perform."[16] The motion failed, but in some respects Jenifer agreed with his opposition in the legislature and on the council. It was difficult to pursue anything like a sound fiscal policy that included payment of the national debt within a local context where priorities were constantly shifting and local needs were forever being brought to the fore. When Jenifer at last gave up the onerous responsibilities of his office in November 1788, it was after he had transferred his energies to the support of a Federal Constitution, a new national government that at least in theory could accomplish what he had been unable to attain within a local framework: satisfactory resolution of the fiscal consequences of a war that his personal preference had been to avoid.[17] In 1773, as the proprietor's primary fiscal agent, Jenifer's income had been, at minimum, £833 a year. In 1786 his yearly salary with commission probably was no more than £600.[18] His motive in pursuing a postwar career as Maryland's minister of finance had not been one of personal financial gain, although there were always sufficient detractors to argue that it was. In truth, Jenifer spent the hot summer of 1787 in Philadelphia as a Maryland representative to the Constitutional Convention, advocating the balancing of local revenue-raising authority with a national government having fiscal power sufficient to fund the national debt. It was no wonder that

---

[16] Ibid., p. 183.

[17] Nov. 7, 1778, Maryland State Papers.

[18] The figure for 1773 is taken from Donnell MacClure Owings, *His Lordship's Patronage* (Baltimore, 1953), p. 79, converted to currency. That for 1786 comes from Land, ed., *Journal and Correspondence of the Council*, p. 183, with the commission figured on the basis of the probable rate of sale of the remaining confiscated property.

exasperation with the vagaries of local politics as they im-
pinged upon the execution of his duties led Jenifer into the
camp of those who called for a stronger, more viable, national government powerful enough to transcend local interests.[19]

If throughout the late 1770s and 1780s Daniel of St. Thomas
Jenifer represents the vanguard of nationalist sentiment in
Maryland concerned with pursuing and *paying for* the national debt, Capt. Charles Ridgely stands at the other extreme in the House of Delegates as a champion of parochial
and provincial interests in favor of ignoring the war debt and
constricting the fiscal policies of state government altogether.
In the assembly the prevailing point of view vacillated between the two extremes depending upon temporary alliances
among many different factions, alliances often forged by faction leaders like Samuel Chase, Thomas Johnson, and William Paca, who by themselves could transcend a provincial
outlook but could rarely convince a majority of their peers in
the legislature to follow their lead. The well-known contro-
versies over the issues of debtor relief and the emission of
paper money which dominated the first session of the 1786–
87 legislature exemplify this. Shortly after the assembly convened in November 1786, Uriah Forrest, a prominent merchant and delegate from St. Mary's County, described the
controversy's impact on the business of the lower house:
"T[homas] J[ohnson] appears to me to be almost as much
afraid of S[amuel] C[hase] and W[illiam] P[aca] as they really
are of him. I am fixed to do my duty not only faithfully but
attentively, yet I will steer so clear of party as rather to [be]
out with all than in with any. There will be no paper nor no
installments. Chase is for the one. T[homas] J[ohnson] in-
clines for the other. I am yet to be convinced of either."[20]

---

[19] Jenifer died in Annapolis in 1790 at the age of sixty-seven. His obitu-
ary was flowery, but short (*Maryland Gazette*, Nov. 18, 1790). Today no one
even knows where he is buried.

[20] Edward C. Papenfuse, "An Undelivered Defense of a Winning Cause:
Charles Carroll of Carrollton's 'Remarks on the Proposed Federal Constitution,'" *Maryland Historical Magazine* 71 (1976): 220–51.

Factions of from five to fourteen men who consistently agreed with one another over 70 percent of the time were the rule in the Maryland lower house from 1777 until at least 1788. Only in rare sessions did anything like "parties" with working majorities make an appearance. Between 1781 and 1788, for example, in only three out of fifteen sessions did any one faction predominate, but even these majorities were an illusion of "party" that primarily arose from a momentary consensus on critical economic issues. The moments of cohesion do, however, bring into bold relief intransigents like Ridgely, who, while able to establish their county's claim to state revenues, on balance stubbornly held to a minority opinion that taxes should be lower, government less powerful, churches unsupported by the public purse, and government-funded higher education avoided.[21]

To observe political alliances among legislators, it is necessary to encompass the whole of political behavior (at least as reflected in recorded votes) rather than to select issues that bring a ready-made bias to any analysis. Between 1780 and 1789 there were 425 men who participated in 1,183 recorded votes in the House of Delegates. The pattern of agreement and degree of success of delegates on those roll calls, adjusted by the attendance of each legislator, is one of small alliances. Except for temporary surges of majority consensus in three out of fifteen sessions between 1781 and 1789, fragmentation prevailed, and the degree of success of each faction, or "interest," depended upon temporary alliances on a kaleidoscopic array of local, state, and national issues.[22] From one session to the next the immediate concerns could range from reestablishing formally and financially the ties between church and state to the building of a market house in Baltimore City with what amounted to taxes paid by county landholders. The importance of issues could shift dramatically too, as was the case with paper money. What was vital one session could become inconsequential the

[21] For a distinctly different view of Maryland politics, see Norman K. Risjord, *Chesapeake Politics, 1781–1800* (New York, 1978).

[22] Summary tables and documentation of factional alliances in the Maryland legislature between 1776 and 1788 at the Maryland Hall of Records.

next. Majorities normally arose out of a coalition of interests agreeing for the moment on the matter at hand. The net effect of those majorities as reflected in the laws passed was often begrudging support in principle for Jenifer's efforts to meet national fiscal needs offset by a steady growth in the powers and financial obligations of state and local government. In the 1780s, with a momentary pause of critical self-evaluation in 1785 and in the first session of 1786–87, the Maryland General Assembly became increasingly irresponsible on fiscal matters. Instead of paying the war debt, it expanded the use of the public purse to include higher education, a greatly accelerated public-building program, and a larger, better-paid civil service. The taxpaying public had never seen anything like it before and would find it difficult to reverse the trend.[23]

The inability of the legislature to respond constructively to both the public outcry over taxes and the need for a sound fiscal policy is illustrated by a proposal set forth by the lower house in the spring of 1787. In a classic abdication of responsibility, the delegates announced a complicated scheme for issuing paper money. When the Senate refused to adopt the plan, the lower house, in an unprecedented move, appealed to their constituents in seven and a half pages of small print. The address began: "We, your immediate representatives in the General Assembly, think ourselves responsible to you for our conduct, and that on all subjects that materially concern your welfare or happiness, you are to be consulted, and your opinions, freely and fairly delivered, ought to govern our deliberations."

The Senate, it went on, feared that the broadside, distributed in an edition of 1,800 copies, 100 to each county, was likely "to weaken the powers of government and to disseminate divisions and discord among the citizens of this state, at a crisis, when the energy of the one, and the union of the other, are more than ever necessary. Appeals to the people upon a diversity of opinion arising between the two branches of the legislature upon any public measure are unprecedented." The Senate need not have worried. If the broadside

23 Ibid.

was read with any comprehension, the only lesson voters would have learned was that their representatives had over-committed the public treasury and now could not find the means to meet their obligations. After listing without evaluation the components of what seemed to be an insuperable public and private debt, the broadside concluded that

> the result of our opinions on this inquiry was, that you could not discharge your private and your public engagements; and that you must neglect your private obligations, or your public duty. For if you paid your debts, you would thereby be unable to discharge your taxes; and if you paid your taxes, you must thereby be rendered unable to discharge your debts. Your honour, welfare, and safety, required that every exertion should be made to support the union. We thought it imprudent and useless to lay on you further taxes, unless some expedient could be devised to assist you in the payment of them, also in the discharge of your private debts.

The solution to the lower house was paper money, funded by a complicated formula requiring nine years of careful monitoring and creditor indulgence to achieve payment of the existing debt. It ignored the fact that for almost four years, when the economy was reasonably healthy, the legislature had given too low a priority to paying off the national debt and had concentrated upon spending tax revenues in other ways. For example, it did not mention that the cost of state government between 1776 and 1779 was only £11,000 specie a year while the "annual expences of our own government" in 1786 were £16,000 specie, an increase of 45 percent.[24]

The inability of the legislature to deal effectively with economic issues or to limit new public expenditures was to be expected. Strong leadership and coherent fiscal programs, focused nationally or statewide, could only emerge with a strong, highly disciplined, majority party organization. The rule in the Maryland legislature was shifting coalitions of

[24] *Votes and Proceedings of the House of Delegates . . . November Session 1786* (Annapolis, 1787), pp. 85–92.

small groups of men whose spokesmen were numerous and often at odds. Indeed there were discernible regional patterns to alliances among factions, as Norman Risjord's recent work on Chesapeake politics points out.[25] Over the twelve sessions of the legislature between 1780 and 1789 in which Samuel Chase served, for example, almost 60 percent of his voting allies in the legislature were drawn from seven out of a total of eighteen counties and Annapolis: Worcester, Calvert, Somerset, Dorchester, St. Mary's, Prince George's, and Queen Anne's. Charles Ridgely served nine sessions in the same period as a delegate from Baltimore County. His band of regular associates was geographically more concentrated and smaller than Chase's. An estimated eight dependables voted with Ridgely over 70 percent of the time, while Chase could count on an average of thirteen. Ridgely drew his support primarily from his own, Harford, Washington, and Montgomery counties, but he was not without allies even in Worcester County, a Chase stronghold. Rarely could either muster a working majority, for most assemblies between twenty and twenty-eight votes.[26]

What must be taken into consideration in explaining regional patterns, however, is why delegates allied with a Chase or a Ridgely. Indeed Chase had more than a local following, perhaps created by his oratorical and leadership powers, but family ties to the Eastern Shore where his support was greatest (Worcester, Somerset, and Dorchester counties) must not be ignored either. Ridgely was far from charismatic and perhaps is more representative of the norm among faction leaders than Chase. He could neither speak nor write exceptionally well.[27] His political success lay in the strength of his local political organization, an organization which probably was duplicated in many areas other than those from which his vot-

[25] *Chesapeake Politics.*

[26] Based on an analysis of Chase's and Ridgely's voting behavior and roll-call allies in all assemblies to which they were elected.

[27] Chase's speaking talents are well known. See Samuel Chase biographical files, Md. Hall of Rec., Annapolis. For evidence of Ridgely's poor spelling, hot temper, and inability to express himself well among his peers, see Ridgely Papers, Md. Hist. Soc., Baltimore.

ing allies were drawn and which preceded any of the major economic issues he confronted in the 1780s.[28] This organization was in evidence as early as the constitutional convention of 1776, at a time when the future of the Revolution was in considerable doubt. During the convention Ridgely was an advocate of what he assumed would be a temporary government to oversee a war of limited duration and purpose. At its conclusion he evidently hoped politics would resume as usual, perhaps with decreased interference from proprietary and Crown interests.[29] Ridgely and probably the majority of politicians of his day saw events within the context of a highly personal and very limited perspective. When the call came in 1777 for him to be more active in the war effort, Ridgely reportedly voiced his disgust freely:

> Capt. Ridgely being asked by Mr. [William] Lux [a prominent Baltimore merchant] if he was not getting himself ready to March to assist General Washington and prevent the Enemy geting to Philadelphia, he replied he should go when the Congress went or at least the younger members, for that old Col. Harrison and such were enough to do the business of Congress and said he thought they ought to March with the rest, for that his Life was as dear to him as theirs to them—and that the Congress ought to have made peace last Summer with Lord Howe as the Kings Commissioner—that they had an opportunity to do it upon honorable terms when Lord Drummond proposed a plan; but that the men sent by Congress to Lord Howe were such as he knew would not Treat with him.[30]

When questioned by the assembly, Ridgely did not deny the charge. He apologized for not appearing to explain himself in person and offered the excuse of a bad case of poison oak contracted while working in the fields. Although the conver-

[28] Edward C. Papenfuse and Gregory A. Stiverson, *The Decisive Blow Is Struck* (Annapolis, 1977).

[29] Charles Ridgely biographical file, Md. Hall of Rec., Annapolis. There were two Charles Ridgelys who served in the General Assembly at the same time, Captain Charles and Charles of William known as "Blackhead" Charles.

[30] Revolutionary War Papers, Md. Hist. Soc., Baltimore.

sation with "Pretty Boy Billy" Lux did take place because "that flaming patriot would not receive Continental Dollars for the Ballance Due on Bond for Spannish Dollrs," Ridgely asserted that he said nothing disloyal: "As Common passing money was allways Rec'd by him before, his Refusing made me warm & gave the flesh [no] small advantage. . . . But thanks be to god I said nothing that I am ashamed of [and] . . . I trust in God he never will spar me to live to be a Enemy of my dear Country knowingly, nor to do one act that I am ashamed of."[31]

Apart from a large block of delegates with a low roll-call failure rate that controlled the writing of Maryland's first constitution, there were three small opposition factions in the convention of 1776: those like William Fitzhugh who wished to obstruct the war effort; like Rezin Hammond who sincerely wished to radicalize the political process by broadening the suffrage and lowering officeholding qualifications as much as possible; and like Charles Ridgely who wanted as little government as possible to conclude a war he fervently wished would be over quickly.[32] In stark contrast to the normal voting patterns of the 1780s, the pattern of voting at the constitutional convention of 1776 could easily obscure the importance of factions in the subsequent political arena of the 1780s. There was a broad consensus on issues and lopsided majorities on most roll-call votes during the convention. But rather than focus on the temporary illusion of party, we should look more closely at the political base of the Ridgely faction which, in contrast to the other two minority factions extant in 1776, persisted at least until Ridgely's death in 1790. In most respects the Ridgely faction was also philosophically consistent and this gave it more coherence than any other faction in the lower house. With Ridgely it is possible to predict with some certainty how he and his band, composed mostly of delegates from Anne Arundel, Baltimore, Montgomery, and Harford counties, would vote on a given matter.

Throughout Ridgely's career in the house he persistently

[31] Ridgely Papers.

[32] Papenfuse and Stiverson, *The Decisive Blow Is Struck.*

voted in the minority, for less government, reduced government spending (except in his own district and other pork barreling trade-offs), and for measures that would facilitate the payment of his own debts. To Ridgely, paper money was desirable as long as it could be easily acquired and was generally accepted at face value. Ridgely's local political machine was a marvel at bringing out the vote. It was said by his detractors that if he put up a stone it could win. He had "precinct," or neighborhood, captains who regularly shepherded his supporters to the polls, and he in turn gave particular attention to the needs of those "precincts" he won. Even traditional enemies like George Lux, son of the merchant with whom Ridgely quarreled in 1776, came with cap in hand. In December 1786 George Lux wrote that Mr. McMechen, a delegate from Baltimore Town, had informed him that Ridgely "had taken a warm & decided part in favor of our Precinct Petition, and that only one obstacle can prevent our being redressed." The obstacle was the rate at which land was currently being taxed, and the "Precinct Men" wanted Ridgely's support for a more favorable arrangement, if not in terms of the rate at least by facilitating the manner in which the rate could be appealed. Lux went on to provide a glimmer of the political machinations that went on at the local level, behavior that is not unfamiliar today.

> Blackhead Charles [Ridgely, another Baltimore County delegate] had made me uneasy by telling me he & you suspected me of twisting some of the Hooks Town People from you at the last elections [November 1786]—for this reason only, because I promised you at your own House, that I would not make interest against you, even if included in the Reisters Town Arrangement so that you, nor your Friends struck at me, and if not included, I should be neutral, which would be almost equivalent to making interest for you, as they were naturally prone (if not prevented) to vote for you, because they were of opinion, you had incurred [Thomas Cockey] Deye's [another Baltimore County delegate and Ridgely opponent] enmity [by] you & your Friends having supported Howard as a Senate Elector.[33]

George Lux's primary concern was to further his own po-

[33] George Lux to Charles Ridgely, Dec. 27, 1786, Ridgely Papers.

litical career. He was exasperated because Ridgely had won in precincts near Baltimore City even though Ridgely was not in complete sympathy with the local interests. Now elected, he was seeking to have those precincts transferred to Baltimore City for future elections. Lux was attempting to impress Ridgely with the lengths to which he *might* have gone to oppose Ridgely's election, and he did manage, with some exaggeration, to convey a rather timeless picture of a political manipulator at work playing off urban against rural interests.

> What would have ruined you among the [town] Precincts, had I reminded them of it, was that at that time an objection was made against me by one of your men because I lived near the *Town*, & would not be a suitable Member for *Farmers* thus declaring yourself decidedly against the [town] Precincts—I could easily prove both you & Hollidays having repeatedly declared, that the Good of the County required the annexation of the [Reisterstown] precincts [to Baltimore]. You may remember also that in your answer to Tom Cradocks charge against you for thinking all men of education should be excluded from public life, you explained it in such a manner as to offend the Precincts beyond conception by saying in your Hand Bill, that you thought none but FARMERS should be in [the] Assembly, and so they were only Farmers, you had not objections to their being Men of education—by this doctrine you showed yourself at that time an Enemy to the Precincts, for none of them are FARMERS and by your arguing in that manner you certainly could not consistently vote for Howard—he is no FARMER.[34]

The greatest test of Ridgely's political wisdom probably came in the assembly of 1785 when his particular view of how government ought to be run momentarily met with more support than it ever had before or ever would again in his lifetime. During the session his block of regular allies rose to an all-time attendance-adjusted high of over thirteen. Only in 1789, when uncertainty about the future course of national politics gained him some new support, did almost as many legislators agree with him.

[34] Ibid.

The assembly of 1785 was forced to confront the deepening recession with some measures of relief for taxpayers and debtors. Most of the session was taken up attempting to adjust the tax rate but not the tax base, while sentiment grew for legislation to aid debtors and to emit paper money despite the haunting memories of wartime inflation. For the first time Ridgely found himself often in agreement with Samuel Chase. Although they had previously been unsuccessful business partners, joining together in the purchase of confiscated property thought to be useful in the manufacture of iron, Ridgely and Chase were forever voting with opposing factions. Chase was an expansionist at the level of state government. He was in favor of increased government spending and an enlarged government role in other matters, including a state-supported church. Ridgely was not. Yet for a time in 1785 their divergent views evaporated and both men joined first an apparent majority within the assembly, and then, in 1788, a determined minority outside that body when the question of who should control the course of national affairs shifted beyond the assembly to ratification of the Federal Constitution.[35]

During the 1785 session Ridgely allowed himself to swap votes with Chase on Chase's promise that he would support the removal of the seat of government to Baltimore. This angered some of Ridgely's constituents, who charged him "with the unpardonable guilt (both as to this world and the next) of being a friend to Mr. S. Chase."[36] Ultimately he survived constituent outrage over such an unseemly alliance, but not before exhibiting a voting behavior distinctly contrary to his career norm. As might be expected, Ridgely voted during the 1785 session for an unfavorable report on the intendant's efforts to manage the state's finances, voted against a motion absolving the intendant, and against enlarging the powers of the governor to encompass the work of the intendant. Yet he voted to continue the office of intendant with Jenifer as the incumbent and to recommend that Jenifer

[35] For Chase's business dealings with Ridgely, see Ridgely Papers and Ridgely Family Papers, Md. Hist. Soc., Baltimore.

[36] Robert Gilchrist to Charles Ridgely, ca. Nov. 1786, Ridgely Papers.

be appointed agent by the governor and council.[37] It was a temporary phenomenon.

When the purchases of tobacco by Robert Morris for his monopoly with the French quietly infused coin and acceptable paper money, known as "Morris Notes," into a sluggish economy in the summer of 1786, political unrest subsided. The assembly of 1786–87 abandoned paper money and the number of Ridgely's voting regulars dropped sharply by the second session.[38] His alliance with Chase disintegrated. Between the assemblies of 1785 and 1786–87 Chase moved to Baltimore, where the twelve-month residence requirement barred him from immediate election as a delegate. Instead he successfully ran for election from Anne Arundel County, surviving an attempt to oust him for nonresidency. Inside the assembly he and Ridgely resumed their adversary roles, although they would again join in opposition to ratification of the Federal Constitution. What led Chase to oppose the Constitution is complex, but on balance he probably desired to amend it rather than defeat it altogether.[39] Ridgely's opposition to the Constitution was of a far different kind and is rooted in the nature of his political environment and a preference for limited government at all levels.

Ridgely represented a county with one of the lowest delegate turnover rates in the General Assembly; such areas of the state ultimately proved to be the Maryland strongholds of anti-Constitution (Antifederalist) sentiment. It is likely, however, that the voting behavior of delegates from localities that Norman Risjord has labeled "debtor" (in the assembly) and "Antifederal" (outside it) was not governed so much by the needs and desires of their constituents as by successful political machines of the Ridgely type. Ridgely mustered

---

[37] *Votes and Proceedings of the House of Delegates . . . November Session 1785* (Annapolis, [1786]).

[38] See Papenfuse, "An Undelivered Defense," pp. 224–25, for a discussion of the voting behavior of two large factions in the 1786–87 assembly, one led by Chase, the other by Thomas Johnson. Both Johnson and Chase lost support between the assemblies of 1785 and 1786–87 and neither could consistently command a majority in either.

[39] Ibid., pp. 225–26.

votes by any available means at election time. The "safeness" of his seat allowed him freedom to pursue a basically anti-government stance from as early as 1776. There were, of course, boundaries beyond which machine-backed politicians could not stray for long, such as those Ridgely encountered in the reaction to his alliance with Chase. But the principal determinant of consistent legislative behavior between 1776 and 1789 was the degree to which like-minded men could be reelected from the same district over and over. Possibly such machines were most successful only in those rural areas where neighborhoods remained largely stagnant economically, or at least much the same as they were in 1776. But to argue that one particular point of view about government consistently emerged from neighborhoods having similar socioeconomic profiles is to miss the point altogether.[40]

The pressure for debtor relief was almost universal by the 1785 General Assembly. It cannot be shown that the areas represented by Ridgely and other future Antifederalists were in greater need of relief than others. Ridgely's Antifederalism was logically consistent with the voting behavior of his minority faction in the General Assembly and was rooted in his highly personal view of government. Since at least 1776 his faction had been articulating, with varying degrees of success, a concern over an increasingly powerful state government levying high taxes to pay for more than purely local

[40] Jackson Turner Main, in *Political Parties before the Constitution* (Chapel Hill, 1973), pp. 212–43, looks at selected roll calls and a large but not complete sample of legislators for the period 1780–88. He concludes that various "interests" and loose "coalitions" of "like-minded individuals" were the norm between 1780–88 but sees polarization within the legislature into two somewhat nebulous but sizable blocks of "cosmopolitans" and "localists." While Main's chapter represents some of the best work published to date on the socioeconomic characteristics of legislators, it does not look at factional alignments over time among *all* legislators on *all* issues. I would argue that in addition to emphasizing selected issues and legislative behavior with respect to those issues, it is necessary to examine the careers of legislators and how they aligned with other legislators on all issues during their entire length of service. In the end, I suspect that instead of cosmopolitan versus localist, the major philosophical division or clustering with the assembly will prove to be between government expansionists and restrictionists, but unquestionably more work needs to be done before any conclusive answer is given.

needs. Other constituencies with socioeconomic profiles similar to Ridgely's county produced factions with views differing sharply from his. A good example are the five men who in 1785 stood alone in favor of assigning a high priority to the payment of the national debt even to the extent of raising taxes. All five—Brice T. Worthington and Nicholas Worthington from Anne Arundel County, Michael Taney from Calvert, John Bracco from Talbot, and John Stevenson from Baltimore County—served constituencies that are indistinguishable from those of Ridgely's allies.[41]

The rapid growth in the functions, personnel, and cost of government commencing with the Revolutionary War, at least in Maryland, must be viewed in the context of a predominant pattern of highly fragmented and personalized political behavior that left little room for coherent fiscal policies and strong legislative or executive leadership. That out of such a tumultous, pervasively factious political environment could arise a movement for strong national government with broad fiscal powers is a tribute to men like Daniel of St. Thomas Jenifer who had a larger vision of what could and ought to be, and to a general public apathetic at that moment about anything other than local matters. In April 1788 a national "interest" did indeed triumph in Maryland as the state overwhelmingly ratified the Constitution. Jenifer's fiscal policies had succeeded in spite of the legislature, and the economy was healthy enough to dampen any significant opposition. If the ratification movement were to be examined in detail, it might even be seen as the first victory of party in an organizational sense, a victory that would in turn lead to the development of major political parties as they are known today. But it cannot be interpreted as anything more than the fragile beginnings of party, born of frustration with factious local political behavior, the onerous fiscal burden of a costly war, and the inability of the legislature at the state level to offer any long-range solutions to complex economic issues involving other states and other nations.

[41] Based upon a comparison of wealth holding patterns as reflected in the 1783 tax lists, "Summary Accounts."

EDWARD COUNTRYMAN

Some Problems of
Power in New York
1777–1782

THE PROBLEM OF power, of men's ability to influence and control other men, is central to any study of politics, whether the politics be past or present. Who makes initiatives, who ratifies or rejects them, in and against whose interests they are made, are questions that both political historians and political scientists have long asked. Students of power within representative assemblies have developed a specialized set of tools for their task. Their interest has centered on measuring the particular influence exerted by palpably important members, such as Speakers and the members and especially chairmen of weighty committees. Their goals generally have been to find the social characteristics that separated such men from their lesser colleagues and to determine the ways in which front- and back-benchers have related to each other. Their working assumptions have been three: first, that differentiation into the powerful and the powerless is normal in any parliamentary body; second, that the distribution of internal offices and honors is the best measure of how such a body differentiates itself; and third, that the institution under study is fully legitimated, both in terms of outsiders ac-

I want to thank Jeanne Chase, Meg Beresford, and the members of the American history seminar at St. Catherine's College, Oxford, for comments on earlier drafts of this essay.

cepting the right of the men within to make authoritative decisions and in terms of insiders regarding differentiation among themselves as proper.[1]

The study of power is also central to the study of revolution, but in a very different way. The essence of a revolutionary political process is to smash existing power relationships. It does this by destroying offices, positions, and hierarchies and creating something else in place of them.[2] That such a process took place in Revolutionary America has become clear from the studies of the past decade. The angry crowds and the popular committees that destroyed the power of Britain and the colonial elite have been shown to be "revolutionary manifestations of the most fundamental sort." It has also been demonstrated that rather than disappearing after Independence, those crowds and committees coexisted uneasily for several years with the new state governments. At least part of the uncertainty of those first years of American republicanism stemmed from the tension between two tendencies that were fundamentally opposed. The dominant and ultimately triumphant one was toward constitutional sta-

[1] For a historian's discussion of the enormous social-science literature on power, see Allan G. Bogue, "Some Dimensions of Power in the Thirty-Seventh Senate," in William O. Aydelotte et al., eds., *The Dimensions of Quantitative Research in History* (London, 1972), pp. 285–318. The classic analysis by a political scientist is Nelson W. Polsby, "The Institutionalization of the U.S. House of Representatives," *American Political Science Review* 62 (1968): 144–68. For use of these concepts by historians see Jack P. Greene, "Foundations of Political Power in the Virginia House of Burgesses, 1720–1776," *William and Mary Quarterly*, 3d ser. 16 (1959): 485–506; Robert M. Zemsky, *Merchants, Farmers and River Gods: An Essay on Eighteenth-Century American Politics* (Boston, 1971); and L. Ray Gunn, "The New York State Legislature, 1777–1846: A Developmental Perspective" (Paper presented at the Twenty-first College Conference on New York History, Albany, 1977).

[2] See Samuel P. Huntington, *Political Order in Changing Societies* (New Haven, 1968); Peter Amann, "Revolution: A Redefinition," *Political Science Quarterly* 77 (1962): 36–53; Isaac Kramnick, "Reflections on Revolution: Definition and Explanation in Recent Scholarship," *History and Theory* 11 (1972): 26–63; and V. I. Lenin, *State and Revolution* (1917; reprint ed., Moscow, 1972).

bility. The other, weaker but still noteworthy, was toward some form of popular council democracy.[3]

In studying the state legislatures, the most important institutions of the new order that began to emerge after 1776, one is accordingly not justified in making the assumptions that are normal in legislative analysis. In particular, one cannot assume that they were fully legitimated, either vis-à-vis their constituents or within themselves. There is ample material on which to use the conventional tools, in the form of committee assignments and voting records. But in using it one must be open to the possibility that the legislatures were as much revolutionary bodies, the products of the tumultuous forces that surged around them, as they were parliamentary ones.

Analysis of the New York state legislature during its first years demonstrates that this was precisely the case. The legislature did its business while the state it was supposed to rule was in extreme disarray. The British had occupied the five southern counties. The Vermonters had seceded with two and a half more. Militant loyalists carried on armed resistance in the Hudson Valley and on the western frontier. For none of these people was republican New York in any sense legitimated. Among New Yorkers who accepted the Revolution the problem was scarcely less acute. At least until 1779 they were torn when seeking remedies for their problems between turning to their state government and taking direct action themselves.[4] This paper will show that such uncer-

[3] See the following: Dirk Hoerder, *Crowd Action in Revolutionary Massachusetts, 1765–1780* (New York, 1977); Ronald Hoffman, *A Spirit of Dissension: Economics, Politics, and the Revolution in Maryland* (Baltimore, 1973); Richard Alan Ryerson, *The Revolution Is Now Begun: The Radical Committees of Philadelphia, 1765–1776* (Philadelphia, 1978); Eric Foner, *Tom Paine and Revolutionary America* (New York, 1976); and Alfred F. Young, ed., *The American Revolution: Explorations in the History of American Radicalism* (DeKalb, Ill., 1976). The point about "revolutionary manifestations" was made by Ted Robert Gurr at a conference on the interdisciplinary study of the American Revolution, Harvard University, May 1975.

[4] See Edward Countryman, "Consolidating Power in Revolutionary America: The Case of New York, 1775–1783," *Journal of Interdisciplinary History* 6 (1976): 645–77.

tainty extended into the legislature. It will demonstrate that the legislators were profoundly suspicious of any concentration of power among themselves, that they took steps to prevent such concentration, and that the single figure most clearly identifiable by conventional standards as a "powerful" man was forced to use his talents and influence for causes just the opposite of those that he and the group he represented wanted to further. To demonstrate these things is to show that the early legislature was in fact as much a revolutionary as a parliamentary body and provides further evidence that far from being unique the shattering Revolution Americans went through had much in common with those of other peoples.

New York's republican constitution of 1777 provided for a bicameral legislature. There was to be a Senate of twenty-four men chosen in four great districts by freeholders worth £100 and an Assembly of seventy members chosen in county delegations of varying sizes by freeholders worth £20. Events modified these precepts even before the document went into effect. The secession of Vermont reduced the Assembly's working maximum to sixty-five. The British occupation of the southern counties led to the naming of their senators and assemblymen by an ordinance of the same Revolutionary convention that wrote the constitution. These "ordinance members" held their seats until the redcoats finally evacuated at the end of 1783.[5]

Within the legislature the signs of power that analysts usually seek out prove much less useful than one might expect. The Assembly named its own Speaker, as had its colonial predecessor, and at the start of each session it picked standing committees. Before Independence the speakership had been the prime indicator of the condition of provincial politics; when Philip Livingston was replaced in the chair by John Cruger after the election of 1769, the change symbolized the defeat of Livingston's party. But after Independence the

[5] The text of the constitution is conveniently available in William A. Polf, *1777: The Political Revolution and New York's First Constitution* (Albany, 1977), pp. 44–61.

speakership bore no such partisan weight. In the first two sessions, between late 1777 and early 1779, the post was held by Walter Livingston, a nephew of the earlier occupant. We know from William Smith's diary that the new Speaker was terrified by the Revolution and that he was loathe to accept even his nomination to the Assembly, let alone its leading position.[6] In the third, fourth, and fifth sessions, which covered the rest of the period of actual warfare, the Speaker was the undistinguished Evert Bancker, a New York City merchant and one of the "ordinance" members. Bancker was never opposed for the seat, and the journal of the Assembly indicates that he was a neutral presiding officer rather than a partisan leader. Alexander Hamilton significantly did not include Bancker in a list of powerful New Yorkers that he prepared for Robert Morris in 1782.[7]

The legislature's choice of these men is probably best read against the fact that New York's internal politics in these years were based on coalescence rather than on partisanship. The Revolutionary movement included many diverse groups, and these all had good reasons for conflicting with one another. The movement's leaders agreed, however, that the important immediate points were to win Independence and to keep the coalition together. Picking Livingston had the symbolic effect of honoring his family and the practical one of assuring nervous members of the landed elite of their place in republican political society. The election of Bancker took place as the Revolutionary coalition was beginning to fray. It had the effect of removing the speakership from the increasingly competitive political life of the unoccupied counties, made a gesture toward the idea of harmony between upstate and down, and told downstate citizens that despite the occupation their counties were still part of New York. But the

[6] Patricia U. Bonomi, *A Factious People: Politics and Society in Colonial New York* (New York, 1971), pp. 257–58; William H. W. Sabine, ed., *Historical Memoirs from 16 March 1763 to 25 July 1778 of William Smith*, Apr. 8, June 14 and 27, 1777, 2 vols. in 1 (1956 and 1958; reprint ed., New York, 1969), 2:107–8, 160–61, and 167.

[7] Alexander Hamilton to Robert Morris, Aug. 13, 1782, Harold C. Syrett, ed., *The Papers of Alexander Hamilton*, 26 vols. to date (New York, 1961–), 3:132–43.

important point is that the choice of these two men as Speaker told nothing about who was on top in state politics. Not until the end of the Confederation period would the speakership again be a prize sought by contending sides.[8]

The standing committees are not much more help, though a cursory reading suggests that they might be. Thirty-two places on such committees were created in the first session and thirty in each of the others. Picking the men who would fill these seats was among the earliest actions of a newly elected session. The titles of the committees are as one would expect: ways and means, grievances, courts, privileges and elections. In addition to these there was always a committee to draft a reply to the governor's opening address and one to report on what laws were on the point of expiring and to recommend new laws "for the benefit of the State."[9] The naming of these committees presents the strongest evidence that the Assembly was differentiating itself in exactly the way that parliaments do. An analysis in terms of systemic political theory would treat the men who sat on them, especially their chairmen, as the Assembly's front-benchers. The object of such an analysis would be to identify the factors which made

[8] In the seventh and eighth sessions, immediately after the liberation of the southern district, the speakership was held by two obscure country members, John Hathorn of Orange County and David Gelston of Suffolk. But the elevation to the chair of the prominent Federalist Richard Varick in the tenth and eleventh sessions (1787 and 1788) probably betokened a partisan triumph for his group.

[9] For the picking of the standing committees see *The Votes and Proceedings of the Assembly of the State of New-York . . . Begun . . . on . . . the Tenth Day of September, 1777*, Sept. 17, 1777 (Kingston [and Poughkeepsie], N.Y., 1777[–78]), *The Votes and Proceedings of the Assembly of the State of New-York . . . Begun . . . on . . . the First Day of October, 1778*, Oct. 13, 1778 (Poughkeepsie, N.Y., 1779), *The Votes and Proceedings of the Assembly of the State of New-York . . . Begun . . . on . . . the Ninth Day of August, 1779*, Aug. 24, 1779 (Fishkill [and Loudon], N.Y., 1779[–80]), *The Votes and Proceedings of the Assembly of the State of New-York . . . Begun . . . on . . . September 7th, 1780*, Sept. 7, 1780 (Albany, 1859), and *Votes and Proceedings of the Assembly . . . October 24th[–November 23d,] 1781*, Oct. 24, 1781 ([Poughkeepsie, N.Y., 1781?]), William Sumner Jenkins, ed., microfilm *Records of the States of the United States of America* (Washington, D.C., 1949).

them a group and which separated them from their lesser colleagues.

But to analyze them in that way would be a mistake, for the Assembly went to some lengths to keep those committeemen from becoming an internal elite. In the first place, the members of the standing committees formed a heavy majority rather than a small minority of the assemblymen actually in attendance at the start of a session. Secondly, the Assembly never formally designated a member as a committee chairman. Presumably the first-named man on each list held the chairmanship, but he received no public honor or distinction for it. Thirdly, there was no tenure from session to session of either the putative chairmanships or of seats on particular committees. A man whose name came first on a committee in one session might be a member of another or of no standing committee at all in the next.

But most important, the Assembly gave its standing committees very little to do; it seldom referred problems to them. Instead it picked an ad hoc board and directed it to draft a bill or a proposal. The drafting committee's proposal would be debated by a committee of the whole house, and the deliberations of the committee of the whole would be considered by the house in normal floor session. The topics on which the Assembly charged such committees to draft bills ranged across the whole set of problems that faced the state. They included the confiscation of loyalist property, raising military supplies, defending the frontier, collecting overdue taxes, settling the public accounts, and stabilizing the state's paper currency. Though there were times when a major policy proposal did come from a standing committee, such occasions were rare.[10]

The Assembly's choice of this way to go about its business presents even more of a puzzle than does its devaluing of the speakership. Why the house should have bothered to name standing committees if it was going to give them nothing to

[10] This judgment is drawn from a careful reading of the Assembly and Senate journals for the first eleven sessions, 1777 to 1788 (Jenkins, ed., *Records of the States*).

do is not explainable by evidence from its records, from the writings of the men involved, or even from the larger context. Several things are clear, however. One is that the method was practicable, which it might not have been in a larger body. Though the Assembly was more than twice the size of its colonial predecessor it was dwarfed by the assemblies in other states, such as Massachusetts and Virginia, and was considerably smaller than the Revolutionary congresses that had preceded it in New York itself. With a working size not much larger than a major committee of the modern House of Representatives, it was small enough to do most of its business in committee of the whole.[11]

Furthermore, this was not simply a carry-over of colonial practice. The record of the opening days of the Assembly, when it was setting its precedents, shows that the house avoided adopting a rigid internal structure as a matter of choice. Doing business through ad hoc committees and committees of the whole rather than standing committees made it much easier for any assemblyman to participate actively in shaping policy. By avoiding a situation in which a few regularly and as a matter of right proposed and the rest consented, it obliterated any working distinction between front- and back-benchers.

The house's adoption of this and a number of other practices that had the same effect was a result of dispute rather than consensus. The members who supported them indicated by their votes that they wanted to guarantee working equality among themselves, for they were rejecting moves by a few of their number toward differentiating the house in the way that systemic theory would consider normal. The record of the Assembly's earliest weeks, in September and October 1777, is one of continual debate over how to name committeemen, delegates to Congress, and the four state

[11] The four Revolutionary congresses that met between 1775 and 1777 varied in size, but the largest of them, the third, had ninety-four members. On other state legislatures see Jackson Turner Main, "Government by the People: The American Revolution and the Democratization of the Legislatures," *William and Mary Quarterly*, 3d ser. 23 (1966): 391–407; on committees in the modern Congress see Richard F. Fenno, *The Power of the Purse: Appropriations Politics in Congress* (Boston, 1966).

senators whom the Assembly was required to select as a Council of Appointment. Almost as soon as the house convened, Assemblyman Egbert Benson of Dutchess County tried to preempt the questions both of how the councilors of appointment would be named and of who they would be by nominating four senators for service. The house postponed action on his proposal, and a few days later it decided that instead of voting on these four it would take four nominations from each of its members, in rota. Gouverneur Morris, of Westchester, tried again to seize the initiative by putting forward nominations out of turn, but the house rebuffed his intervention. It adopted the same method, each member nominating a candidate for every vacancy, for filling both the seats in Congress and the vacancies among the ordinance senators. In every case a formal division was required to resolve the issue.[12]

The evidence on the naming of committeemen is less explicit, but it suggests a division of opinion along the same lines. The journal never states whether committeemen were elected from the floor or picked by the Speaker, and the house voted down an early motion to postpone selecting committeemen until it had resolved the problem of how to choose them. But at the same time it decided not to act on a motion to name standing committees immediately. This was put by Gouverneur Morris, who on the same day made the second of the two attempts at preempting the naming of the Council of Appointment. One cannot avoid the conclusion that Morris and Benson had sought to seize the initiative and that their colleagues had refused to let them do it.[13] To the

[12] *Votes and Proceedings, 1777*, Sept. 11, 16, and 30, and Oct. 2, 1777.

[13] It seems significant that the drive against the positions taken by Benson and Morris was led by Abraham Brasher, a New York City silversmith and former Son of Liberty; by Robert Harpur, a Scottish immigrant who had taught mathematics at King's College; by Thomas Tredwell, a member from Suffolk; and by Henry Williams, a delegate from King's County. Bernard Mason has identified Brasher and Harpur as playing radical roles during the Independence crisis. See his *The Road to Independence: The Revolutionary Movement in New York, 1773–1777* (Lexington, 1966), p. 247n. It may also say something about Brasher that he sought to style the Assembly's response to the governor's first message as simply an "answer" rather

majority in the Assembly, active participation was more important than procedural efficiency. The contrast between such a mentality and that of the minority who followed the lead given by Benson and Morris suggests that within the legislature as much as outside it, a revolutionary thrust toward participatory democracy vied with a conservative one toward ordered regularity.

The same tension expressed itself in day-to-day practice throughout the Assembly's first five years. Some members did enjoy more esteem, have more say in the drafting of bills, and carry more weight in setting policy than others. They did not, however, operate from publicly recognized chairmanships or even from tenure within a stable committee system, and thus their marks of identity were far different from those that single out a John Robinson in the Virginia House of Burgesses, a William Pitt Fessenden in the Civil War Senate, or a Sam Rayburn, a Lyndon Johnson, and a Richard Russell in the twentieth century Congress. Such men can be found, but both the difficulty of finding them and the problems one sees them facing once they are identified illustrate this essay's contention that power in Revolutionary New York was a problem, not a certainty.

The way to locate these men is to scan the listings of all committees, standing and ad hoc alike, for names that recur frequently. One member who turned up with unusual frequency during the war years was Egbert Benson, who represented Dutchess County from 1777 to 1781. Benson was the only member of the house who sat on more than one standing committee in each of those four sessions.[14] In addition he was regularly named to temporary committees; during his last two sessions, especially, he was appointed to them at a rate highly disproportionate to that of all other

---

than the "respectful address" that it became (*Votes and Proceedings, 1777,* Sept. 12, 1777). William Smith judged Tredwell's politics by his reported refusal to sign the state constitution on the ground that it was not levelling enough (*Historical Memoirs,* Apr. 26, 1777, 2:121).

[14] For Benson's career see his entry in the *Dictionary of American Biography.*

assemblymen. In the first and second sessions he served on nine such committees, but in the third he sat on thirty-one and in the fourth, on forty-one. At busy times he worked at a rate that must have been staggering. To take two examples: On October 13 and 14, 1779, he was appointed to three separate committees and reported back to the house on behalf of two of them. One of his reports included the draft of a bill. On January 27 and 28, 1780, he was named to two committees, both of them of major policy importance. Over those two days he reported on behalf of one of those committees and also brought in a bill of his own. No other assemblyman approached such a pace, either during Benson's four sessions or in the years immediately following. If being named to committees was a measure of what the legislators thought of a colleague's abilities and of his own potential for influencing events, Benson was the single most powerful man in the early legislature.[15]

The names of some other members do appear in the journal with unusual frequency, though not as often as Benson. In the second session he was joined in service on more than one standing committee by Assemblymen Stephen Ward of Westchester, John Tayler of Albany, Ezra L'Hommedieu of Suffolk, and Robert Harpur of New York. In the third and fourth sessions the house gave multiple permanent assignments to L'Hommedieu and to Thomas Tredwell of Suffolk as well as to Benson. In the fifth session, the last of the war years, it gave two seats each to Tredwell, Charles DeWitt of Ulster, Jonathan G. Tompkins of Westchester, Thomas Storm of Dutchess, and Matthew Adgate of Albany. Permanent seats that meant nothing may not indicate much, but the careers of these men do bear the marks of unusual political success. They had been prominent members in the congresses during the Independence crisis. They went on from the Assembly to service in the state Senate, the Confederation Congress, and the federal House of Representatives. In 1785 Alexander Hamilton spoke of one of them, Adgate, as

[15]*Votes and Proceedings, 1779*, Oct. 13 and 14, 1779, and Jan. 27 and 28, 1780.

the hidden driving force behind postwar radicalism.[16] But Benson ran far ahead of all others in the frequency with which he was named to both major and minor committees. Despite their demonstrated reluctance to permit formal concentrations of power among themselves, his colleagues gave him a unique chance to influence their deliberations. The ways in which he used that opportunity demonstrate, however, that rather than being a free agent who could get the legislature to do his will he was often constrained into doing precisely the opposite of what he privately wanted.

Benson held a degree from King's College and had studied law in New York City under John Morin Scott. A "young man of the Revolution," he was only thirty-one in 1777 when he began his legislative career.[17] In some ways his public life seems a minor-key variant on that of John Adams. Both began as college-educated country lawyers. Both committed themselves early to the movement of resistance, though "early" meant different things in Boston and in Poughkeepsie. Both were active in changing the movement of resistance into one of revolution. At the same time both changed themselves from men of local prominence to men of much larger importance. Once Independence was a fact, both strove to quell domestic radicalism.

Benson's home county of Dutchess exemplified the internal tensions of Revolutionary New York. It was dominated by the estates of great landed gentlemen, but it also included the bustling town of Poughkeepsie and some stretches of freehold farms. Before Independence it had been split on class lines between landlords and tenants, with yeomen and townsmen uneasily in the middle. During the war it split on political lines into tory and patriot. The two splits were not parallel; instead, each side on the question of Independence was made up of a coalition of class fractions.[18] Benson, as a

[16] Alexander Hamilton to Robert Livingston, Jr., Apr. 25, 1785, Syrett, ed., *Papers of Hamilton*, 3:608–9.

[17] See Stanley Elkins and Eric McKitrick, "The Founding Fathers: Young Men of the Revolution," *Political Science Quarterly* 76 (1961): 181–216.

[18] See Staughton Lynd, "Who Should Rule at Home? Dutchess County, New York, in the American Revolution" and idem, "The Tenant Rising at

whig lawyer with connections to the landlords, played an active part in framing the Revolutionary coalition. He was in the fore during the creation of the Dutchess County Committee of Safety in late 1774 and early 1775 and he served several times as its chairman. In April 1775 the county elected him to the convention that began the task of revolutionizing politics on a provincewide level. At the end of 1777, when a British incursion up the Hudson Valley shattered the new state government, Benson joined an impromptu group of legislators that formed a convention and seized what little power could be found. The convention elected him to its Committee of Safety. After his four terms in the legislature he went on to the Confederation Congress and eventually to the House of Representatives and the federal bench.

Both his own letters and the comments of observers show that he was on the right wing of the Revolutionary coalition. William Smith noted in April 1778 that Benson was in alliance with John Jay; in Jay's own correspondence he, Benson, Robert R. Livingston, and such men as Gouverneur Morris and William Duer emerge as men in close cooperation throughout the late 1770s.[19] The collaboration of Duer, the aspiring merchant prince, Livingston and Morris, the scions of landed families, and Jay and Benson, the highly professional lawyers, symbolizes the union of merchant capital, landed interest, and conservative intellectuals that would be the basis of New York's Federalist movement a decade later.

These men delayed writing the state constitution in order to get a document that suited their taste,[20] and over the three years after it was promulgated they intervened again and again in the state's public life. When they did, it was on behalf of three main principles. The first was that the written constitution was to be established in practice as superior to the immediate will of either the people or the legislature. The

---

Livingston Manor, May 1777," in his *Class Conflict, Slavery, and the United States Constitution: Ten Essays* (Indianapolis, 1967), pp. 25–77.

[19]Smith, ed., *Historical Memoirs*, Apr. 10, 1778, 2:345. For the correspondence of the figures named see the letters in Richard B. Morris, ed., *John Jay: The Making of a Revolutionary, 1745–1780* (New York, 1975).

[20]Mason, *The Road to Independence*, ch. 7.

second was that the state's economic life must be organized as much as possible around a free private sector rather than around publicly regulated commerce. The third was that "radicalism" must be moderated in any way that this might be done. Jay and Livingston defended these principles from their positions as chief justice and chancellor. These gave them seats on the Council of Revision, which had a qualified veto on laws that the legislature passed. Benson worked with them from his seat in the Assembly.

But Benson was also attorney general of the state throughout the Confederation. He was known as an intimate advisor of Gov. George Clinton, a man almost the personification of Antifederalism in 1787 and 1788. Observers noted that Benson had a major part in shaping not only conservative laws but most legislation that the state passed while he was in the Assembly, including such radical measures as the confiscation of loyalist lands, taxation at double rates of what property remained to tories, taxing all property in a way that hit the rich harder than they had ever been hit before, and the imposition of precisely the corporatist economic controls that Benson and his associates loathed.[21] His involvement in such things stands in profound contradiction to the conservative stance he took on their constitutionality and to the opinions he expressed in his private correspondence.

So does the part he took in the famous suit that Elizabeth Rutgers brought against Joshua Waddington before the mayor's court of New York City in 1784. Mrs. Rutgers, a widow who had fled the city when the British occupied it in 1776, claimed damages against Waddington for the use he made of her brewery during the British occupation. She based her claim on the Trespass Law, a piece of punitive antitory legislation that the state enacted as part of its general policy of putting former loyalists, collaborators, and neutrals in an inferior position to patriots in the postwar order. The case marked a testing of the law's validity, and Benson, as the

[21] For comments on Benson's importance see William Kent, *Memoirs and Letters of James Kent, LL.D.* (Boston, 1898), p. 20, and Alfred F. Young's assessment in *The Democratic Republicans of New York: The Origins, 1763–1797* (Chapel Hill, 1967), pp. 14 and 16. For the radical laws and their context see Countryman, "Consolidating Power," pp. 667–69.

state's attorney general, argued on Mrs. Rutgers's behalf. Waddington's lawyer was Alexander Hamilton. Studies of the dispute usually focus on Hamilton's argument and on the decision that Mayor James Duane handed down, which together marked a major development in the Federalist assault on the idea of unlimited state sovereignty. Benson would be the active colleague of such men in 1787, as he had been in 1777, but he did a creditable job both for Mrs. Rutgers's claim against Waddington and for the state's insistence that as a sovereign political entity it might enact any law it wished.[22] The contradiction between his argument and his role in the passage of early radical legislation, on the one hand, and the social and political conservatism that formed the basis of his career points toward another dimension of the tangled power situation that he confronted as a legislator. It underscores the fact that this was a time when the normal rules of political behavior did not apply and when the normal assumptions of political study cannot be made.

Two keys are needed to resolve the contradiction. The first is that Benson was a professional who could do a good job on either side of most questions. His colleagues thought of him in those terms.[23] The second is that he, like Jay and Livingston and perhaps even more than them, fully understood the revolutionary nature of their time and what men of their social standing had to do if they wanted to survive. Looking about them in the late 1770s, they could see how tentative was the state government's hold on the active loyalty of even republican New Yorkers. They could see that despite the constitution, crowds and committees were still active, and that even in the free counties militant loyalism threatened what was left of the state's fabric. New York was not the only

[22] On the Rutgers case see Gordon S. Wood, *The Creation of the American Republic, 1776–1787* (Chapel Hill, 1969); and E. Wilder Spaulding, *New York in the Critical Period, 1783–1789* (1932; reprint ed., Port Washington, N.Y., 1963), pp. 128–29.

[23] In February 1784, just before Benson argued on behalf of Mrs. Rutgers, Hamilton invited him to join in the defense of "clients who are British Merchants" and who were "anxious" to have the attorney general's assistance (Hamilton to Benson, Feb. 18, 1784, Syrett, ed., *Papers of Hamilton*, 3:511).

state to face such problems, and it has been shown that similar men elsewhere, such as Samuel Chase and Charles Carroll of Carrollton in Maryland, recognized the "wisdom of sacrifice" in confronting them. Disdaining mere short-run interests, they led the way in passing radical domestic measures, knowing that only in that way could they conserve their ability to influence any measures at all. Benson and his colleagues, whom I have elsewhere called "constitutionalist patriots" to describe their situation in the late 1770s, found themselves in a similar predicament. Robert R. Livingston summed up their project when he spoke in 1777 of "swimming with a stream it is impossible to stem" and of yielding "to the Torrent" in order to "direct its course."[24] Their tactic worked. It gave them the constitution they wanted, put them in most of the high offices of state, and gave Benson his chance to become their foremost spokesman in the Assembly. It must not be thought that they formed a totally disciplined group or that they agreed on the best approach to all issues.[25] But they did share a point of view that gave them a coherent sense of what the Revolution ought to mean and of what they ought to do in it.

Benson's actions as a legislator took two main forms. In many instances he can only be understood as a man who was both a professional attorney, with skills for hire, and an intelligent conservative who knew that the most important thing to conserve was his own ability to influence events. But on a number of occasions he made interventions that reflected the orientation and the policy goals of his group. Their strategy, which governed his actions, was to give away as much as they had to when they had to, and to recoup whatever they could when they could.

[24] For the Marylanders see Hoffman, *A Spirit of Dissension*, ch. 9; for Benson's group as "constitutionalist Patriots" see Countryman, "Consolidating Power"; for the metaphor of the torrent see Robert R. Livingston to William Duer, June 12, 1777, Robert R. Livingston Papers, New-York Historical Society, New York City, quoted in Young, *The Democratic Republicans*, p. 15.

[25] See, for example, the material cited in notes 26 and 27.

They had to give away a great deal and often they regained little. We can see this by looking at the part Benson took in the confiscation and redistribution of the great tory estates. This was the central action in a general radicalization of New York's social policy that took place in the winter of 1779–80, but the bill that finally passed was not the first attempt at a seizure. That had been made half a year earlier, at the end of the previous session. Robert R. Livingston thought that "never was there a greater compound of folly, avarice and injustice" than that bill, and with Governor Clinton's support he and Jay were able to stop it in the Council of Revision. Though the house voted to override the veto, the Senate did not and the bill died.[26]

Here was a point where Benson and his colleagues diverged. Livingston blamed Benson's "compromising genius" for the first bill's passage in the Assembly and Benson was among the members who voted to override. But the difference did not turn on principle; rather it sprang from the two men's different readings of the state's political situation. Benson thought the bill "far from being unexceptionable" but realized that public pressure made it necessary. After it failed he told Jay he wished it had passed, for "the loss of it has occasioned some Clamor and Uneasiness." Even Livingston had seen that tide of discontent and predicted that Benson himself would lose his seat because of it. That Benson did not probably was due to his visible support of confiscation.[27]

Though Benson had not written the first confiscation bill, he was the author of the second one, which became law in October 1779. The bill that passed was not materially different from the one that failed. Though it directly attainted fewer people, it still contained most of the provisions the

[26] For the second session's attempt at confiscation see *Votes and Proceedings, 1778*, Nov. 2, 1778–Mar. 15, 1779, and *Votes and Proceedings of the Senate of the State of New-York ...* , Mar. 9–15, 1779 (Fishkill, N.Y., 1777[–79]), in Jenkins, ed., *Records of the States*; for Livingston's opinion see Livingston to John Jay, Apr. 21, 1779, Morris, ed., *John Jay*, pp. 583–84.

[27] Compare Livingston to Jay, Apr. 21, 1779, Morris, ed., *John Jay*, pp. 583–84, with Benson to Jay, June 23, 1779, pp. 604–6.

council had objected to in the first bill.[28] Yet it met neither the legislative opposition that had delayed the first bill's passage nor a veto from the council. One reason why no veto took place may have been the absence of Jay, who had resigned the chief justiceship and thus given up his seat on the council, but Livingston, who had written the first veto message, raised no objection. The conclusion must be that he, his colleagues, and the men in the Senate whose support had enabled them to stop the first bill had realized that passage of the second was an absolute necessity. In the chancellor's case one can watch the turnaround taking place. In early and mid-October 1779, Livingston was still casting futile, solitary votes on the council against other punitive antitory laws, but by the time the confiscation bill was considered he had given up. Benson's victory over him did not present a triumph for radicalism over conservatism. Rather it marked the chancellor's acceptance of a pragmatic wisdom that had come sooner to his friend.[29]

That Benson's attitude on confiscation was pragmatic rather than principled can be demonstrated from the larger context of his actions. When he could either postpone the confiscation process or weaken it, he did so. Even before the first bill was introduced, the house named him to a committee to deal with a massive petition that demanded seizure of the tory estates before that meeting of the legislature adjourned. Though Benson's name came last among the committeemen, he was the one who brought in their report. In it he maintained that the time remaining before adjournment would be too short for a bill to be drafted and passed. Time, indeed, was short, but the argument contrasts oddly with

[28] The text of the second session's bill does not survive, but compare the objections raised against it by the Council of Revision with the text of the third session's bill. The council's objections can be found in the "Minutes of the Council of Revision, Jan. 1778–March. 1783," Mar. 14, 1779, in Jenkins, ed., *Records of the States*. The text of the third session's law can be found in *Laws of the State of New York*, 3d sess., ch. 25 (Poughkeepsie, N.Y., 1782), pp. 85–91, in Jenkins, ed., *Records of the States*.

[29] For Livingston's changing position see the positions he took on three separate bills for punishing loyalists in the "Minutes of the Council of Revision," Oct. 3, 15, and 22, 1779.

Benson's riposte to an adjournment motion at the next session when he argued that the assemblymen should remain in session until their work was accomplished "in Pursuance of the Trust reposed in them by their constituents."[30]

The real sign of a radical friend of confiscation was his position on whether and how to sell the forfeited lands. As long as the property remained in the possession of the state, a chance remained to restore it eventually to its pre-Revolutionary owners. When the war was over the Assembly received many petitions from the law's victims for restitution of what was left of their estates.[31] Benson consistently acted to postpone sales and to make them more difficult. During the passage of the second bill he voted against allowing the commissioners of forfeitures to sell unimproved lands. Later in the session, after the bill had passed, he opposed the introduction of a bill for selling the forfeitures at all. Despite that opposition he was put on the drafting committee for a sales bill, but in debate in February 1780 he once again voted against sales, at least for unimproved lands. In the following month, when the Senate sent down a resolution in favor of postponing sales or, if possible, avoiding them altogether, Benson was one of the minority who wanted the Assembly to concur. A year later, in March 1781, he voted against a proposal to double the time allowed to purchasers of forfeited land for the payment of what they owed on it.[32]

Benson found himself torn the same way on the problem of managing the economy. His tenure in the legislature coincided with both long-term and short-term crises in American economic history. The long-range crisis, only now beginning to be appreciated, turned on the transition from a corporatist economy in which state intervention was re-

[30] *Votes and Proceedings, 1778*, Nov. 2, 1778, and *Votes and Proceedings, 1779*, Oct. 12, 1779.

[31] *Votes and Proceedings of the Assembly [October 4–November 29, 1784]*, Oct. 29, and Nov. 6, 8, and 15, 1784 ([New York, 1784]), in Jenkins, ed., *Records of the States*.

[32] *Votes and Proceedings, 1779*, Feb. 4 and Mar. 10, 1780, and *Journal of the Assembly of the State of New York, for the Year 1781*, Mar. 27, 1781 (Albany, 1820), in Jenkins, ed., *Records of the States*.

garded as normal, to one based on the operations of an un-restricted market. Corporatist economic practice included action to ensure a ready and cheap supply of such basic com-modities as bread and salt. Free market practice imposed no such duty. The shift that was underway was thus from a so-ciety in which the needs of the community were superior to the rights of private property to one in which the reverse was effectively true. The problems that this shift posed were ex-acerbated between 1776 and 1780 by a short-term crisis springing from the wild inflation that accompanied the col-lapse of the Continental dollar.[33]

Men like Benson, firmly committed to the coming rather than the waning order, were convinced that it was futile to fight either of these crises by traditional corporatist devices like embargoes on trade, wage and price regulation, or the revival of the Revolutionary committees. They had many reasons to oppose that committee revival when it came in 1779. Though they were republicans, none of them were democrats, and these committees were as close as New York ever got to direct democracy. Benson and his colleagues were dedicated to stability and to a restricted rule of law, and they associated the committees with unrest and with immediate power. The persistence of the committees after the constitu-tion was proclaimed and their revival in 1779 conflicted di-rectly with the state constitution, which described them as "temporary expedients" that produced "many and great in-conveniences." This made it possible for the constitutionalist patriots to take high ground and make no concessions in their battle against any recognition of the committees by the state laws. They might lose; in fact they usually did. But they would not agree to any compromise.[34]

It needs to be stressed, however, that political economy as

[33] On the long-term crisis see Foner, *Tom Paine and Revolutionary America*, ch. 5, and Howard B. Rock, "The Perils of Laissez-Faire: The Aftermath of the New York Bakers' Strike of 1801," *Labor History* 17 (1976): 372–87. On the short-term crisis see Richard B. Morris, *Government and Labor in Early America* (1946; reprint ed., 1965), ch. 2, and Thomas C. Cochran, *New York in the Confederation: An Economic Study* (Philadelphia, 1932).

[34] The quotations are from the preamble to the state constitution, in Polf, *1777*, p. 44. For the resistance of Benson's group to any legitimation

well as abstract constitutionality lay behind their hostility to the committees. During the crisis of 1779, particularly, the committees openly blended corporatist economics with revolutionary popular involvement. Several times during that year Benson juxtaposed a hostility to the committees based on constitutionality with one based explicitly on economics. He was sure that the revived committees threatened "the subversion of the constitution," and he was equally sure as the price control movement was getting underway in Albany that he wanted "the *limitation*" to be "*limited*" to that city. Over two consecutive days in March 1780 he voted against going into committee of the whole on "An Act to Prevent Monopoly and Extortion," whose very title placed it in the corporatist tradition, and tried to have the house establish "A Committee for Preserving the Constitution." This, he proposed, would have power to investigate any actions outside the legislature that might reflect on the constitution. Every member of the house knew that the foremost of such actions would be a committee revival.[35]

Not all matters of political economy involved the problem of committee power. When his belief in the need for the absolute supremacy of the constitution did not dictate a rigid stand, Benson's record again shows him acting according to the strategy of giving in to the other side—even leading it where he had to—and acting on his own ideas where he could. Early in the second session he was the author of a bill to post guards at the state borders in order to prevent the export of foodstuffs. Later he served on a committee to investigate violations of that embargo. In 1780 he drafted a law to reinstitute the price controls that he loathed. But here, as on the forfeitures question, the larger background of his actions forces a distinction between things he did because ex-

---

of the committees by the state laws and for their inability to win their point see Countryman, "Consolidating Power."

[35] John Lansing to Philip Schuyler, Aug. 4, 1779, Schuyler Papers, Manuscript Division, New York Public Library, the Astor, Lenox, and Tilden Foundations; Egbert Benson to John Jay, July 6, 1779, Henry P. Johnston, ed., *Correspondence and Public Papers of John Jay*, 4 vols. (New York, 1890–93), 1:213; *Votes and Proceedings, 1779*, Mar. 8–9, 1780.

pediency required them and things he did because they were in accord with his long-term goals. The prime alternative to price controls as a weapon against inflation was heavy taxation, and in every debate on a tax bill Benson took the fore in efforts to collect as much as possible and to impose the most demanding terms. His proposals for the sums to be collected were consistently the highest that any member put forward, often running to twice as much as other legislators wanted to raise. He worked against taxation on the radical principle of assessment by "circumstances and other abilities to pay taxes, collectively considered." He even opposed allowing a stay of taxes to hard-pressed people who were already creditors to the government as a result of loans or of impressment of their animals, wagons, and crops.[36] These were the actions of a man who was convinced that the real solution to the crisis of the dollar was to abandon corporatism and tax the economy dry, regardless of the social cost.

It can be seen that Benson governed his legislative actions by an overall strategy. His group included men at the highest levels of both the state and Continental governments; he himself moved to a seat in Congress at the end of his four sessions in the Assembly. These men had learned the importance and the techniques of staying in communication and coordinating things among themselves. When Benson made personal interventions in the legislature, he acted to realize their prime concerns. But his repeated demonstrations that he could vote for and even draft laws he personally disapproved of demonstrates the flexibility, the recognition of the need to "ride the torrent," that saved him and his kind from the rout their counterparts suffered in Pennsylvania in 1776 and from the rigidity of the comparable group in Massachusetts that in 1786 provoked Shays's Rebellion. Their guiding principle was that the stronger the state government and the central Congress, and the more secure the working supremacy of the state constitution, the more likely their social group would be to emerge from the Revolution with the

---

[36] *Votes and Proceedings, 1778*, Oct. 19, 1778, and Feb. 27, 1779, *Votes and Proceedings, 1779*, Jan. 27, 1780, *Votes and Proceedings, 1778*, Feb. 6, 1779, *Votes and Proceedings, 1779*, Feb. 9 and 16, 1780.

power and the policies that it would need to safeguard itself and to control future American development. Wise sacrifice, they realized, was a matter of frequent necessity, but when events made it possible they acted to secure the policies that they really wanted. We know that such things as delaying confiscation, avoiding other punitive tory laws, and taxing the state out of the inflation crisis were what they "really wanted" because they said so to one another, whatever their judgment as politicians forced them to do in the public arena.

Benson's power as the man whom the Assembly named most often to committees was thus far more dilute than a first glance at the journal would lead one to expect. The dilution bears out this paper's working assumption that for all its parliamentary trappings, the legislature in its first years is best understood as a revolutionary body. Analysis of its committees shows that the distribution of power within it was not a matter of a structure regulated by recognized norms. Rather it was a problem over whose resolution men of different viewpoints struggled.

The other conventional method of analyzing power within legislatures is through study of roll-call votes. Which members could regularly convince their fellows to vote with them? Which could not? Such analysis is usually a matter of inference from patterns whose existence the student demonstrates statistically, and a number of methods have been developed for doing it. Most of those methods were employed at one stage or another in the larger project for which this essay was a study,[37] and it would be out of place here to undertake a comprehensive report on their application or to

[37] For a detailed and critical discussion of such methods see Bogue, "Some Dimensions of Power in the Thirty-Seventh Senate." For use of such methods in my project on New York see Edward Francis Countryman, "Legislative Government in Revolutionary New York, 1777–1788," Ph.D. diss., Cornell University, 1971, idem, "The Shaping of Party System in Post-Independence New York" (Paper presented to Twenty-first College Conference on New York History), and idem, *A People in Revolution: The American Revolution and Political Society in New York, 1760–1790* (Baltimore, 1981), appendix 2.

indulge in an abstruse discussion of quantitative method. By using a very simple method, however, it can be shown that power relationships at the moment of decision were as fluid as they were in the naming and operation of committees.

The method used here consists of nothing more than computing the percentage of roll calls in each session on which each member voted and the percentage of those roll calls on which he voted with the majority. The working assumption is that the higher the percentage of a member's majority votes, the greater was his ability to influence controversial decisions. That assumption can be faulted, or at least qualified, but it provides a simple and readily intelligible measure of the assemblymen's positions relative to one another at the moment when they made their decisions. The rates of two sorts have been selected for careful study. One group includes the few whom systemic theory would single out as power wielders. These are the Speaker and, in the absence of recognized chairmanships, the men whom the Assembly named to more than one standing committee. It has been shown that these honors were empty in terms of giving their holders any clear institutionalized ability to influence the shaping of policy. It can also be shown that holding them in no way predicted that a man would often have a majority voting with him. The other group consists of the members who voted with the majority at high rates, whatever the issue. These have been defined as members who were present for at least 70 percent of all roll calls and who were on the winning side at least 70 percent of the times they voted.

A number of points emerge from these data. One is that none of the first four sessions was strictly polarized into a majority and a minority. Though the assemblymen who served during these sessions can be grouped into blocs whose members agreed virtually regardless of issue, it would not be impossible to take several members out of any bloc and put them into another. The roll calls on major issues might divide members into opposing groups, but there was no continuity from issue to issue. Of the assemblymen who voted on at least 70 percent of all divisions, only a minuscule number were not with the majority at least half the time. Counting everyone who took part in even a single roll call, there were only five men in the fourth session who voted on the winning side less than half the time. These statistics do not offer the comprehensible simplicity of numbers that show a clear partisan opposition. They are confusing because the voting alignments within the legislature were confused. Politics during the war years were founded on something other than straightforward, unchanging partisanship. That is in no way to argue an overall consensus interpretation; there were fierce disputes and some of them marked the first beginnings of a partisanship that would flourish in the 1780s and the 1790s. But in the short run all measures indicate a pattern of shifting coalitions rather than one of flat confrontation.[38]

The members who have been picked out, perhaps artificially, as front-benchers showed no sign of being able to influence their fellows. The Speaker voted only on tied divisions and in committee of the whole, and as a result neither of the wartime Speakers took part in anything like 70 percent of all roll calls. In the first session Walter Livingston was with the majority on only 35 percent of the votes in which he took part; only two members who voted did worse. In the second his rate of majority voting increased to 56 percent, which was barely more than average. Evert Bancker did better, voting with the majority on 67 percent of his roll calls in the third session, on 60 percent in the fourth, and on just over 70 percent in the fifth. That was the only wartime session when the Speaker voted with the majority at a rate that can be considered outstanding.

[38] The comments in this and the following paragraphs are based on the following techniques: cluster-bloc analysis for all Assembly and Senate sessions from 1777 to 1788; Guttman scale analysis by hand for the Assembly and Senate sessions from 1777 to 1783; Guttman scale analysis by computer for all Assembly sessions from 1777 to 1788, using a purpose-written program to compute Yule's Q between all pairs of roll calls and using the scaling program in the *Bio-Medical Data* package BMD 05S to build scales on the basis of the Q programs; and computation of the rate at which each member of each Assembly session from 1777 to 1788 voted with the majority on all roll calls and on roll calls in which he took part. A detailed statement of the problems involved in using these methods is included in my book *A People in Revolution*. I want to thank Keith Halstead and Rachel Countryman of the Warwick University computer unit for patient professional help with this analysis.

Roughly the same is true of the men who enjoyed multiple assignments to the standing committees. Ezra L'Hommedieu of Suffolk had the best record among them. His rate of majority voting in the second session was 75 percent, and in the fourth it was 77 percent. In both of those sessions his attendance record was extremely good. In the third session he took part in only 45 percent of all roll calls, but he was still with the majority 72 percent of the time that he voted.

Egbert Benson had the second-best record in the group. In the third session he voted with the majority on 71 percent of his roll calls, a rate second to that of only one other member in that session who voted more than 70 percent of the time. In the fourth he was on the winning side on almost 70 percent of his responses. But in the second session his rate of majority voting was less, standing at 67 percent, and in the first it was only 57 percent. In all four sessions, it might be noted, his attendance record was within a few percentage points of perfect. The rest of the putative front-benchers voted with the majority at far lower rates, as low as 20 percent in one case and falling below 50 percent in at least five. Despite the performance of L'Hommedieu and Benson, the receipt of multiple appointments to standing committees in no way indicated that an assemblyman would be able to carry his fellows with him on divisions.

The members who voted with the winning side at very high rates tended to be not front-benchers of any description but rather men of obscurity. The highest rate of all, 92 percent, was achieved in the second session by John Coe, who represented Orange County for two terms. The men who voted with the winning side at rates above 80 percent included such figures as Joseph Crane, Samuel Drake, and Joseph Benedict of Westchester, Roeluff Van Houten of Orange, William B. Whiting of Albany, Cornelius C. Schoonmaker and John Cantine of Ulster, George Henry Bell of Tryon, Samuel Dodge of Dutchess, and Burnet Miller of Suffolk. These were not men who went on to greater and higher things in politics. By and large they seem to have been reliable workhorses during the sessions for which their voting rates were high. They attended faithfully, and if the Assembly was forming a spectrum of opinion, they took positions toward the middle of it, where their chances of voting with the majority were greatest, rather than at either extreme, where the probability was less. That a measure which in a "normal" legislature might be expected to pick out the power-wielders instead picks out men like these is another indication that for these years the normal rules of parliamentary sociology do not apply.

There has never been any doubt that in military terms New York was an uncertain place during the Revolution, and it has been shown by recent studies that it was equally uncertain in terms of its political society.[39] What has been argued here is that uncertainty extended into the heart of the constitutional republican structure, the state legislature, and that this made the legislature something other than a stable, differentiated parliamentary body. The assemblymen recognized the need for some differentiation and specialization of function within their house, but they took elaborate care lest specialized positions become posts of public honor, or the permanent possession of one man, or even the source of more than a few aspects of public policy. They recognized that Egbert Benson, and perhaps Ezra L'Hommedieu and a few others, possessed talents and skills that most of them did not have, even on the level of being able to put a proposal into proper legislative form. They gave such men, especially Benson, much more to do than they expected of the average member. But frequently they called on him to use his skills on behalf of causes that he personally disliked. When he did intervene in support of an issue about which he felt strongly, whether it was constitutionality, confiscation, price control, or taxation, the probability was not high that he would be able to carry the house with him.

Without question Benson aspired to be leader of the house, but his aspiration sprang from something other than mere careerism. He, Jay, Livingston, and others of their persuasion recognized that they were living through a time that was fully revolutionary. Benson knew that even if he could gain the leadership of the Assembly, it would be worthless

[39] See the essays in Lynd, *Class Conflict*, and Countryman, "Consolidating Power."

without the assembly's having the people's consent to its rule. He knew that often the most he could hope for was to lead an assault on a position that he would have preferred to defend. Technically he was a "new man" of the Revolution, coming to state-level prominence with no background in provincewide affairs. But unlike most of the new men in the legislature, he had many reasons to be conservative. He brought to his Revolutionary experience the confidence that came from widespread contacts in the world of affairs and from a superior education. He also brought to it strong opinions about the direction in which the Revolution should go. The other new men whom he sought to lead had nothing like his sophistication, his education, or his conservatism, and they showed often enough that they recognized this. They had not yet come to the coherent perspective and the self-organization necessary to make a political party. They thought of themselves instead as members of a Revolutionary coalition that included and needed men like Benson. But they learned during those first republican years to suspect what Benson stood for and to use his talents to achieve their own ends. Further, they recognized that a coalition was not the same thing as a perfect, harmonious union, and that theirs contained the seeds of its own destruction. Loyalist militance, the British army, and Vermont secession had given New York's republicans many reasons for standing close together at the point of Independence, and men like Benson took advantage of that to guide the Revolution in the direction they wanted. They achieved exactly what they wanted with the state's constitution of 1777. What is more, they did so without meeting serious opposition. But the complications of political sociology within the legislature suggest that the conservatives' victory was neither permanent nor complete. Full partisanship that pitted republican New Yorkers against one another would not come until the next decade, but even in these earliest years its basis was being laid as the members of the Revolutionary coalition began discovering that with Independence achieved they now had different ideas about what was to be done.

EMORY G. EVANS

Executive Leadership in Virginia
1776–1781

Henry, Jefferson, and Nelson

THE EXECUTIVE BRANCHES of the new state governments during the American Revolution were weak; Virginia's was no exception. Virginia's constitution provided for a governor, elected annually by a joint vote of the legislature, who could not serve more than three terms successively. The governor was to be assisted by an eight-member Council of State, again elected by the legislature; two members were to be replaced by the legislature at the end of every three years. The governor and the council could exercise no significant authority except when they acted together. The executive branch was, in the words of the constitution, to "exercise the Executive powers of government according to the laws of this Commonwealth." In 1776 these powers were few. The governor, with the consent of the council, could grant reprieves and pardons; call out and direct the militia; fill militia officer vacancies and suspend those officers for misconduct or "inability"; appoint, when the legislature was not in session, ad interim administrative and judicial officials; and appoint justices of the peace, sheriffs, and coroners on the advice of the county courts. The governor could not prorogue, adjourn, or dissolve the legislature, but, with advice of council, he

Professor John Selby of the College of William and Mary shared with me his notes on governmental organization in Virginia during the Revolution.

could call them back into session early. The executive had no veto power.[1]

James Madison was to call Virginia's executive branch "the grave of all useful talents." But in 1776 there was little disagreement regarding the propriety of a weak executive. The prevailing view, which had emerged from the experience of colonial legislatures with royally appointed governors, was that the representatives of the people were the best judges and that a strong executive was not desirable. As one contemporary commented, the representatives in the assembly "are the People's men (& the People in general are right)." So Virginia's General Assembly was where the power rested, and in the assembly the House of Delegates, where all legislation was to originate, was the more powerful body. The Senate could only approve, reject, or, with the House of Delegates, amend legislation.[2]

In this context the executive branch of Virginia's government does not appear very important. But the form of government established in 1776, which was perfectly adequate for peacetime (it lasted half a century) left something to be desired for a period of war. Virtually everything depended on legislative action, and rapid response to crisis situations was difficult when the assembly was not sitting. Still, the executive did play an important, even crucial, role during the war, and it did so despite the problems associated with democratic government and its own limited powers.

Virginia had three governors in the period under consideration: Patrick Henry (1776–79), Thomas Jefferson (1779–81), and Thomas Nelson, Jr. (June–November 1781). They were among the one hundred wealthiest men in Virginia,[3]

[1] Robert A. Rutland, ed., *The Papers of George Mason, 1725–1792*, 3 vols. (Chapel Hill, 1970), 1:304–9.

[2] Irving Brant, *James Madison*, vol. 1, *James Madison: The Virginia Revolutionist* (Indianapolis, 1941), p. 316; Roger Atkinson to Samuel Pleasants, Nov. 20, 1776, Roger Atkinson Letterbook, 1766–77, University of Virginia Library, Charlottesville; Merrill D. Peterson, *Thomas Jefferson and the New Nation* (New York, 1970), p. 105; Edmund Randolph, *History of Virginia*, ed. Arthur H. Schaffer (Charlottesville, 1970), p. 255.

[3] Jackson Turner Main, "The One Hundred," *William and Mary Quarterly*, 3d ser. 11 (1954):354–84.

had long legislative experience, and were effective in their executive roles. Their effectiveness resulted from four factors. First, from time to time the legislature extended executive powers in response to obvious administrative needs and emergency situations. This extension of authority came largely in the area of military operations and supply but also included such things as the power to appoint state officials and maintain fair prices. Second, the executive had the central responsibility for keeping the government functioning, and this, as well as the fact that it had the best overall view of the state and the nation, could give it influence far beyond its delegated powers. Third, the three governors who served in this period were all seasoned politicians who dealt flexibly with a good deal more unrest, even insurrection, in Virginia than has previously been recognized. Virginia's stable political experience during the eighteenth century, which had seen the colony's government deal tolerantly with such problems as religious dissent, no doubt served these men well. The fact that their political astuteness allowed them to deal effectively with a highly unstable political situation needs to be emphasized. Finally, the governors saw the war in broad perspective. They understood that it would be fought both in the east and the west, that supplies and money would have to be obtained at home as well as abroad, and that a high degree of cooperation between the states was going to be necessary. Perhaps this understanding can be explained by the fact that the commander in chief was a Virginian and that all of the state's wartime governors had national experience. But whatever the case, they rarely suggested that congressional requests were not necessary, objected to sending Virginia's troops out of the state, or failed to try to cooperate with their sister states. Sometimes they objected to the way Congress was doing things, and frequently they were not able to deliver all that was desired, but they tried, and any assessment must conclude that they did a remarkable job.

Patrick Henry, who assumed office in July 1776, was Virginia's most popular public figure. A consummate politician, his political career had been built as a leader of the protest movement against British actions in the 1760s and 1770s. This role often obscures the fact that he was a political conservative and initially had not been in the forefront of the movement for a declaration of independence. His legislative career both before and after his terms as governor demonstrated that he more often opposed than initiated legislation. Yet he was excelled by no one as an orator and could sway his colleagues one way or the other when the vote on legislation came. It remained to be seen how effective he would be once he was removed from his natural habitat in the legislature.[4]

Henry had no administrative experience, and he was not known for his love of hard work. But during his three terms, except for one or two periods of sickness, he was regular in attendance, efficient, and seemingly hard working. When compared with his successors, he had both the easiest and the most difficult task. On his shoulders rested the awesome responsibility of being the first governor. But he was a popular choice, and with public enthusiasm high it was easier to mobilize support for the war effort than it would be for Jefferson and Nelson. Another advantage was that a Committee of Safety, similar to the Council of State, had been carrying on the affairs of government for nearly a year before Independence. Two of the members of that committee, John Page and Dudley Digges, were elected to the council. Henry had the benefit of their experience. Further, the legislature had been more powerful than the executive in Virginia for a number of years. The new House of Delegates was a mirror of the old House of Burgesses, and it was accustomed to a position of leadership. Initially at least this was also an advantage because the House of Delegates did not have to learn its role; it did what it had always done. Henry had argued in the debates over the constitution that "a governor would be a mere phantom" without a veto, but he lost this battle and seems to have accepted his reduced role.[5]

---

[4] See, for example, Robert Honyman, Diary and Journal, 1776–82, July 4, 1780, Library of Congress; Randolph, *History of Virginia*, pp. 178–81 and 278. The standard biographies of Patrick Henry are Robert D. Meade, *Patrick Henry*, 2 vols. (Philadelphia, 1957–69), and Richard R. Beeman, *Patrick Henry* (New York, 1974).

[5] David J. Mays, *Edmund Pendleton, 1721–1803: A Biography*, 2 vols. (Cambridge, Mass., 1952), 2:76; Randolph, *History of Virginia*, p. 256.

The constitutionally designated job of the executive branch was, in any case, to carry out the will of the legislature. The functions of the executive during the Revolution, which this paper will examine, were largely those associated with the overall direction of the military establishment and keeping both that establishment and the Continental one supplied with men, equipment, and provisions. Within this context Henry and his council of eight, who like him were men of wealth and experience, worked primarily with the various county lieutenants, who headed the county militia, to get troops into the field; with the state commissary of stores, who was charged with obtaining and disbursing supplies; and with a legislatively appointed board of naval commissioners, who were in charge of building all naval vessels and keeping them equipped and supplied.[6] And these significant functions were given added importance when very early in Henry's administration the legislature began to broaden executive authority.

The assembly, beginning in the fall of 1776 and in each subsequent session, granted power to the governor and council that the Committee of Safety had exercised earlier, "to direct such military movements as in their judgment shall be necessary for the safety and security of the commonwealth," including sending militia out of the state in the case of invasion. From time to time this general authority expanded for limited periods. For example, in December 1776, with the American army retreating toward Philadelphia, the governor and council were authorized to respond to requisitions from Congress for the purpose of "encountering or re-

[6] William Waller Hening, ed., *The Statutes at Large; Being a Collection of All the Laws of Virginia, from the First Session of the Legislature, in the Year 1619*, 13 vols. (Richmond etc., 1809–23), 9:50 and 149–51. William Aylett to George Mason, Sept. 29, 1775, Rutland, ed., *Papers of Mason*, 2:253; H. R. McIlwaine et al., eds., *Journals of the Council of the State of Virginia*, 4 vols. to date (Richmond, 1931–), 1:29; H. R. McIlwaine, ed., *Official Letters of the Governors of the State of Virginia*, 3 vols. (Richmond, 1926–29), 1:76n. During Henry's three terms sixteen men served as members of the council. Ten of those sixteen are listed in Main's "The One Hundred" and Jack P. Greene's, "Foundations of Political Power in the Virginia House of Burgesses, 1720–1776," *William and Mary Quarterly*, 3d ser. 16 (1959):485–506.

pelling the Enemie"; to send existing forces in the state to the aid of the Continental army or elsewhere; to raise additional troops for similar purposes; and to spend whatever money was necessary to pay and supply them. These emergency powers were to be in effect until ten days after the next assembly met.[7]

Similarly the power of the Committee of Safety to appoint commissaries or contractors to supply military needs was extended to the executive in the fall of 1776 and was continued in each subsequent session of the legislature. That same fall the executive was empowered to employ ships to export the state's produce and import necessary articles, not only for the army and navy but for the entire population.[8]

In 1778, when supplying the military became more difficult, the governor and council were allowed to place an embargo on the exportation of produce and to seize from any "forestaller, engrosser or monopoliser" all grain and flour necessary for the use of the army and navy provided that they paid prices deemed proper by "three reputable freeholders." These acts, too, were continued by later assemblies, and during Jefferson's administration the one allowing seizure of grain and flour was broadened to provide for the impressment of necessary produce from anyone.[9]

It is clear from the foregoing discussion that the legislature, while extending power to the executive, kept it on a very short rein. Virtually no additional power of any importance was granted for longer than the next meeting of the assembly. Henry and his council do not seem to have been concerned about the temporary nature of their increased au-

---

[7] Hening, ed., *Statutes*, 9:49–53, 178–79, 309, 429, 462, and 477–78, 10:106 and 141–42; McIlwaine, ed., *Official Letters*, 1:82–83; Rutland, ed., *Papers of Mason*, 1:325–27; Pendleton to Richard Henry Lee, Dec. 28, 1776, David J. Mays, ed., *The Letters and Papers of Edmund Pendleton, 1734–1803*, 2 vols. (Charlottesville, 1967), 1:204.

[8] Hening, ed., *Statutes*, 9:50 and 178; McIlwaine, ed., *Official Letters*, 1:59.

[9] Hening, ed., *Statutes*, 9:530–32 and 580–85, 10:105, 107, 140, 142, 233–37, 306, 344–45, and 376.

thority. They were sensitive to and respectful of the fact that the power rested in the legislature. They frequently referred to the assembly matters that they were not authorized, or were not certain that they were authorized, to deal with. And when the legislature overstepped its bounds Henry was careful in his response. When Thomas Adams of Henrico County was elected to the Council of State and the executive determined that this was unconstitutional because Adams was also clerk of the Henrico County Court, Henry informed the Speaker of the House of Delegates that they took this action with "very great Reluctance" because it might be considered "bold and presumptious."[10] Henry and his colleagues had every reason to tread carefully because criticism came quickly if it was perceived that they had acted improperly. Even such a simple matter as declaring a day of thanksgiving in response to the American victory at Saratoga was criticized. Edmund Pendleton wrote Richard Henry Lee that "I think . . . the Governor and Council (if they really have the Prerogative of such Appointments) were rather hasty in doing so" before being notified by Congress or "the General."[11] It was a legalistic age in which everyone seemed to read the laws and know his rights. Henry, for example, complained to the Speaker of the house, on being authorized to call out 600 militia to guard the Saratoga prisoners, that militia could not be relied on for such duty because they alleged that "the Law did not oblige them to perform it."[12]

Such a posture did not surprise the governor any more than having the House of Delegates require the executive to countermand orders for calling up the militia. But as time wore on he began to complain that the legislature seemed unable to deal with important matters and the executive powers were "too much cramped." "Can you credit it," he

[10] McIlwaine, ed., *Official Letters*, 1:38 and 51–52; Henry to George Wythe, Oct. 30 and Nov. 11, 1777, and to Benjamin Harrison, May 23 and 27, 1778, pp. 203, 280, 282–83.

[11] Pendleton to Lee, Nov. 8, 1778, Mays, ed., *Papers of Pendleton*, 1:233.

[12] Henry to Benjamin Harrison, Dec. 11, 1778, McIlwaine, ed., *Official Letters*, 1:333; see also pp. 338 and 347.

wrote Richard Henry Lee in June 1778, "no effort was made for supporting, or restoring public credit! I pressed warmly on some, but in vain. This is the reason we get no soldiers."[13]

Frustrations such as these and the heavy work load (it must be remembered that the governor and council, with a few clerks, were managing Virginia's war effort) caused him to comment that "I am ready to sink under my burden."[14] And functioning within the restraints placed on the executive made Henry and his colleagues very sensitive of their own prerogatives. When Brig. Gen. Edward Hand, the commander at Pittsburgh, informed the governor that he was going to call up western militia, Henry fired back a letter stating that except in cases of invasion and insurrection no militia could be called up except "by orders of the Executive" and when they were "embody'd" they were "under the sole Direction of the Governour." Hand knew, Henry told Col. William Fleming of the Botetourt County militia, that "he had not Authority to call out the Militia." Similarly when Lt. Col. Edward Carrington of the Continental Line told him what not to do concerning the creation of new Continental regiments, he exploded and called this "officious intermeddling." If officers, on "becoming Continental, may with impunity, forget that respect which is due their Country [Virginia] I must beg you will Judge of the consequences," he told the Virginia congressional delegation. Carrington was forced to apologize on threat of dismissal.[15]

But the governor survived three full terms and was able to give substantial direction to Virginia's war effort. Very early he began to forward suggestions to the assembly at the beginning of each legislative session. This device, when coupled with personal contact with legislators, had mixed but not un-

[13] Ibid., pp. 53–54; Henry to Richard Henry Lee, Dec. 18, 1777, and April 7 and June 18, 1778, pp. 219–20, 260–61, and 291–92.

[14] Henry to Richard Henry Lee, Apr. 7, 1778, ibid., pp. 260–61.

[15] Henry to Brig. Gen. Edward Hand, July 3 and 27, 1777, to the County Lieutenants of the Northwest, July 3, 1777, to the Virginia Delegates in Congress, Aug. 8, 1777, and to Col. William Fleming, Sept. 7, 1777, ibid., pp. 167–68, 170–71, 171–74, and 186.

important results.[16] More significantly, through the powers granted the executive, he and his colleagues were able to shape an overall strategy of defense and supply, and they inevitably set the pattern for much that was to follow. An examination of some of the major problems they faced and their response to them will be helpful in understanding the role and influence of the executive.

No problem was more important than supplying the Continental army with men. In the fall of 1776 Congress was calling on Virginia to provide fifteen of the eighty-eight battalions of which the Continental army was to be composed. Virginia then had nine battalions in service with an authorized strength of about six thousand soldiers. These battalions were not full, of course, and the governor and council were charged with seeing that their ranks were complete and that four thousand more men were recruited to make up the additional six battalions. The law provided that the commanding officers in the various counties appoint subordinates to recruit fixed quotas. Bounties in money and land were offered as inducements to enlisting. The governor and council had overall responsibility and could replace officers unsuccessful in enlisting recruits.[17]

Henry and his colleagues began by urging all county lieutenants to form volunteer companies to serve as long as the situation dictated. Plans were developed regarding the organization and deployment of the various regular battalions. The clergy "and every friend of this country" were urged to encourage enlistments. Advertisements were placed in newspapers, and orders and encouragement were repeatedly sent to the officers responsible for recruiting. While all this was going on, militia from the tidewater counties had to be called out because of the arrival of enemy ships in Hampton Roads. And in response to a request of Congress, measures were

[16] For example see ibid., pp. 148, 314; Henry to the Speaker of the House, May 13 and 21, 1778, pp. 271–72 and 277.

[17] Hening, ed., *Statutes*, 9:178, 179–84, and 192–98; McIlwaine, ed., *Official Letters*, 1:82–83; Edmund Pendleton to Richard Henry Lee, Dec. 28, 1776, Mays, ed., *Papers of Pendleton*, 1:204.

taken to recruit 200 men to garrison Fort Pitt and Fort Randolph in the Northwest. Additionally the commissary of stores was ordered to deliver clothes and equipment for the soldiers; field officers, who were also working to supply their troops, were authorized under a 1775 law to impress blankets if the prices charged were "exorbitant"; and money was allocated for these purposes.[18]

The executive pursued its goals energetically and efficiently, but the results were mixed. Recruiting proceeded slowly. In February the governor and council dropped the volunteer plan because it was interfering with regular enlistments. This did not solve the problem, and Henry complained that the executive did not have enough influence on the officers in the counties who were doing the recruiting. He said that "most people" felt that the executive had no authority over these officers and that in spite of all his efforts they were not exerting "themselves as they ought." He was also irritated that the assembly, in an act of misplaced generosity, had earlier authorized Georgia to recruit soldiers in the state to the detriment of Virginia's efforts. He guessed that only "two thirds of the continental troops" were enlisted and that the three battalions to be raised for the defense of the state were not "half full." By March he and the council despaired of filling the new battalions and were again considering raising volunteers from the "upper parts of the country" for six to eight months' service. To Gen. Adam Stephen, Henry wrote that "enlisting goes badly. Terrors of smallpox added to Lies of Deserters &c,&c, deter but too many. Indeed the obstacles & discouragements are great." Despite the governor's lament, the state was able to recruit two-thirds of the desired number of men from among a rural, ill-informed people.[19]

[18] Proclamation by the Governor of Virginia, Dec. 26, 1776, McIlwaine, ed., *Official Letters*, 1:85–86, 96–97, 97–98, 99, 100, 104–5, 105–6, 110, 113, and 134–35; Henry to Col. Charles Lewis, Feb. 21 and Mar. 5, 1777, pp. 111 and 124–25; McIlwaine, ed., *Journals of Council*, 1:369–70 and 376–77.

[19] McIlwaine, ed., *Journals of Council*, 1:122, 350, and 376; Henry to Richard Henry Lee, Mar. 20, 1777, to George Washington, Mar. 29, 1777,

But to the executive, with regular enlistments expiring in the fall, the results left something to be desired. In June 1777 the legislature took new measures. George Washington, who was in regular communication with the governor, suggested drafting men or allowing people to purchase substitutes, preferably the former. Henry forwarded these suggestions to the assembly, which authorized what might be called a partial draft to fill the six battalions. If assigned quotas in the various counties were not filled by August 10, a division of the county militia was to be made with each division required to provide one man. If this was not successful the militia field officers and justices of the peace were to pick men to be drafted. Edmund Pendleton called this the "only important Law" of the spring session.[20]

The "important" law did not suffice, and in its fall session the legislature, on the advice of the executive and General Washington, passed a law for drafting 2,000 men as well as raising 5,400 volunteers for six months' service. The draft law designated a quota for each county. All able-bodied, single men were eligible and on a specified day they were to report to the county courthouse. If the county's quota was 30 men, for example, thirty slips marked "Service" were placed in a hat with the remainder being marked "Clear." Those who drew "Service" slips were obligated to serve a year.[21]

The draft law was unpopular, and, as Edmund Pendleton

---

and to Gen. Adam Stephen, Mar. 31, 1777, McIlwaine, ed., *Official Letters*, 1:126, 130–31, and 133; Resolution Allowing Georgia Recruiting Officers to Seek Enlistments in Virginia, Dec. 18, 1776, Rutland, ed., *Papers of Mason*, 1:324–25.

[20] Pendleton to William Woodford, June 28, 1777, Mays, ed., *Papers of Pendleton*, 1:214–15; Hening, ed., *Statutes*, 9:275–80; McIlwaine, ed., *Official Letters*, 1:150, 165–66, and 205; George Washington to Henry, May 17, 1777, William Wirt Henry, *Patrick Henry: Life, Correspondence, and Speeches*, 3 vols. (New York, 1891), 3:70–72.

[21] Henry to Washington, Oct. 30 and Nov. 13, 1777, Henry, *Patrick Henry*, 3:111–12 and 117–20; Henry to George Wythe, Dec. 5, 1777, McIlwaine, ed., *Official Letters*, 1:210; An Act for Speedily Recruiting Virginia Regiments . . . , Rutland, ed., *Papers of Mason*, 1:362–75; Hening, ed., *Statutes*, 9:337–49.

commented, "generally execrated." By spring the draft had produced fewer than eight hundred men. Henry lamented this fact, which he said "no efforts of the executive have been sufficient to prevent," and predicted that "very few more . . . Drafts will ever be got into the Service." By that winter Virginia's leadership had returned to using "high bounties" to recruit for the Continental army and relying on a militia that no one had much faith in. Volunteer schemes had proved ineffective.[22]

Despite these difficulties, through the persistent efforts of its executive Virginia was regularly supplying troops to the "Grand Army," albeit in small numbers. Unfortunately these efforts, and the heavy taxation that accompanied them, were beginning to produce problems that would increase as the war went on. The draft law created so much "violent and riotous behaviour" in Loudoun County that the day set aside for drafting had to be postponed. The southwestern part of the state was a hotbed of disaffection, and the county courts, especially in Montgomery and Washington counties, were crowded with cases of persons charged with "maintaining the authority of the King of Great Britain" and even "levying war against the people of this State." Tories and whigs were equally unrestrained in their attacks on each other. A committee to investigate "disaffection" was sent to the new counties of Ohio, Monongalia, and Yohogania in the northwest part of the state; the citizens of Tangier Island were trading with the British; in Princess Anne County one militia captain refused to obey the governor's order to go to Portsmouth, another burned his commission—a prelude to insurrectionary activity in that area. Problems such as these were evidently not unexpected, for as early as May 1777 the governor and council were authorized to call out militia to oppose "insurrection." Henry and his colleagues clearly preferred not to use militia and relied where possible on legal

[22]Edmund Pendleton to William Woodford, Jan. 31 and Feb. 15, 1778, and to George Washington, Dec. 22, 1778, Mays, ed., *Papers of Pendleton*, 1:246–47, 250, and 276–77; Henry to the Speaker of the House, May 13, 1778, and to Henry Laurens, June 18, 1778, McIlwaine, ed., *Official Letters*, 1:271–72 and 289–90; McIlwaine, ed., *Journals of Council*, 2:120–21.

action through local officials—a policy that subsequent governors followed.[23]

In the area of offensive and defensive military operations, where the executive had a great deal of discretion, Henry and his colleagues were effective. They had a broad grasp of the military problem and did not, for example, need to be reminded that the British in the West, with their Indian allies, presented a serious threat. After a successful cooperative expedition with North and South Carolina against the Cherokee Indians in 1776,[24] the executive worked for peaceful relations with the native Americans through moderate behavior and treaties. The military was used only as a last resort. The attitude of the executive can be seen in the response of Governor Henry to the murder of Chief Cornstalk and other Shawnee Indians by Virginians at Fort Randolph in November 1777. The Indians were on the warpath, and in instructing Col. William Fleming, Henry stated that he was authorizing defensive operations only because he did not want to make things worse than they were. "I must tell you Sir," he said, "that I really blush for the occasion of this War with the Shawanese. I doubt not that you detest the vile assassins who have brought it on us at this critical Time when our whole Force was wanted in another Quarter. But why are they not brought to Justice? Shall this precedent establish the Right of involving Virginia in War wherever any one in the back Country shall please?" He went on to ask, "Where is this wretched Business to end?" Would the "Cherokees, the Delawares and every other Tribe . . . be set on us in this manner this Spring? . . . Is not this the work of Tories? No man

[23] Lewis Preston Summers, *History of Southwest Virginia, 1746–1786, Washington County, 1777–1780* (1903; reprint ed., Baltimore, 1966), pp. 272–74; Washington County Minute Book 1, 1777–84, Nov. 26, 1777, Mar. 18, 1778, June 16 and July 3, 1779, and Montgomery County Order Book 3, 1778–80, Apr. 8, 1778, May 5 and June 1, 1779, microfilm copies at Virginia State Library, Richmond; McIlwaine, ed., *Journals of Council*, 1:347 and 349, 2:93–94; Henry to the Speaker of the House, May 27, 1778, McIlwaine, ed., *Official Letters*, 1:282–83; Hening, ed., *Statutes*, 9:291–97 and 373–74.

[24] McIlwaine, ed., *Journals of Council*, 1:82, 103–4, 422–23, and 420–21; McIlwaine, ed., *Official Letters*, 1:12–13n.

but an Enemy to American Independence will do it, and thus oblige our People to be hunting after Indians in the Woods, instead of facing Gen[eral] Howe in the field." Although Henry's objective was to keep the peace if possible (even when military action was necessary, it bothered the governor),[25] he saw the strategic advantage of George Rogers Clark's proposed expedition against the British post of Kaskaskia, and after some initial hesitation authorized and fully supported it.[26]

Further, in all these military matters he recognized the importance of cooperation with other states, particularly those adjacent to Virginia. Early in his first term he wrote the president of the Committee of Safety in North Carolina that "we mean to act with vigor and upon a liberal plan. If your state will be distressed, ours will gladly contribute to its Relief if possible." He worked closely with both North Carolina and Maryland to develop defensive plans and later was to send Virginia militia to aid in the defense of Charleston.[27]

Unlike his successors Henry did not have to function, except briefly, with an enemy force in the state. On several occasions, especially in the early fall of 1777, it was feared that the British would invade Virginia; on these occasions the governor was prompt in calling up appropriate numbers of militia. In early May 1779 a British raiding party seized Norfolk, burned Suffolk, and pillaged much of the lower Virginia countryside. Again Henry responded promptly but it proved impossible to get militia into the field quickly enough to defend against such a raid. And despite the fact that over

[25] McIlwaine, ed., *Journals of Council*, 2:86–87; Henry to the Commissioners Appointed to Treat with the Cherokee Indians, June 3, 1777, and to Col. William Fleming, Sept. 7, 1777, and Feb. 19, 1778, McIlwaine, ed., *Official Letters*, 1:156–57, 186, and 243–45.

[26] McIlwaine, ed., *Journals of Council*, 2:56–57; Henry to George Rogers Clark, Jan. 2, 1777, McIlwaine, ed., *Official Letters*, 1:223–24; Meade, *Patrick Henry*, 2:172–76.

[27] Henry to the President of the Committee of Safety of North Carolina, Dec. 23, 1776, to Gov. Thomas Johnson, Mar. 21, 1777, and Apr. 10, 1778, and to Gov. Richard Caswell, May 16, 1778, McIlwaine, ed., *Official Letters*, 1:84–85, 121–22, 263–64, and 275; Lt. Gov. John Page to Richard Caswell, Sept. 26, 1777, pp. 192–93.

two thousand militia were mobilized in less than two weeks' time, the governor did not escape criticism. But as Henry commented, and Thomas Jefferson was to find out from bitter experience, "The extent of our shores hinders the possibility of defending all places." He might have added, as he knew, that militia were inadequate for the job they were supposed to do, but none of Virginia's wartime governors were able to solve this problem by keeping a permanent force on active duty.[28]

Finally, supplying the military with food, clothes, arms, and ammunition was crucial to the war effort, and here Henry and his council, who in this area had the necessary authority, did well. The business of acquiring and distributing necessary supplies was initially handled through a state agent and commissary of stores, and a commissary of provisions, both of whom were appointed by the executive. It appears that the commissary of provisions worked on a contract basis through the state agent and commissary of stores. Both of these offices were divided in 1777, the former into a commissary for issues and one for purchases and the latter into a state agent and a commissary of stores. The function of these offices was to obtain and disburse supplies under the general direction of the executive. The governor evidently gave the legislature annual estimates of what each year's expenses would be, and the legislature appropriated the necessary money against which the executive drew warrants.[29]

From the beginning the leadership in Virginia assumed that not only would they acquire necessaries from private citizens and companies through their appointed officials but the government would operate war industries, would buy and trade various commodities on the open market, and would transport these commodities in state-owned vessels. Before 1776 an arms-manufacturing firm was established at

[28] Henry to Richard Henry Lee, May 19, 1779, ibid., pp. 371–72; see also pp. 174–75, 176, 176–77, 177–79, 181, and 366–79; Edmund Pendleton to William Woodford, July 26, 1779, Mays, ed., *Papers of Pendleton*, 1:293.

[29] Hening, ed., *Statutes*, 9:50 and 178; McIlwaine, ed., *Journals of Council*, 1:62 and 494, 2:39–41; McIlwaine, ed., *Official Letters*, 1:205.

Fredericksburg and operated, under the direction of state-appointed commissioners, on a contract basis. This business was continued after Independence under executive direction, and in 1777 the governor and council contracted for a similar operation in Williamsburg. Toward the end of Henry's administration negotiations were begun with the French arms-manufacturing firm of Penet, Wendell, and Company to produce cannon and small arms near Richmond.[30] The executive also operated lead mines in the southwestern part of the state.

Trade with the West Indies, in both state and privately owned vessels, was initiated by the executive in the fall and winter of 1776–77. Agents were appointed to purchase tobacco and flour to be traded through state agents in various West Indian ports for salt, woolen and cotton cloth, sail duck, powder, arms, swords, blankets, and medicine. An agent was also appointed to purchase indigo in Charleston and trade it for needed articles in the West Indies. Similarly, trade with France was begun for salt and military supplies. These items were to be brought back in French ships to the West Indies and loaded into smaller vessels that could more easily slip into Virginia or North Carolina waters. Later William Lee was appointed an agent for the state in France and was authorized to borrow up to two million livres for the purchase of needed supplies. Negotiations were also opened with Spanish authorities in Cuba and New Orleans for loans and supplies, the latter to be shipped up the Mississippi to the mouth of the Ohio and from there overland to Virginia. The expedition of George Rogers Clark was seen by the governor and council as facilitating such trade by establishing a safe port at the mouth of the Ohio. The West Indian and French trade were especially successful.[31]

[30] Hening, ed., *Statutes*, 9:71–73 and 287–88; McIlwaine, ed., *Official Letters*, 1:31, 127, 156, 166, and 167; Richard Henry Lee to Henry, Feb. 10, 1779, pp. 358 and 358n.

[31] McIlwaine, ed., *Journals of Council*, 1:109–10, 157–59, 177, 349, and 398, 2: 29, 112, 177, and 222; McIlwaine, ed., *Official Letters*, 1:59, 61, 146, 212, 284, 286–87, 290–94, and 295; Henry to Richard Henry Lee, Mar. 20 and Nov. 10, 1777, and May 28, 1778, to the Governor of Cuba, Oct. 18, 1777, to Benjamin Franklin, Mar. 3, 1778, to William Lee, Apr. 10,

The executive also acted vigorously to obtain supplies, especially foodstuffs, within the state for both state and Continental troops—again with reasonable success. For example, in the winter of 1777–78, when it was learned of the desperate need of Washington's army for clothing and food, Henry and the council quickly appointed a "special agent" in the northwestern counties to purchase 10,000 pounds of beef and pork. Two thousand pounds of salt were seized on the Eastern Shore, and when the collection of supplies did not proceed expeditiously, Henry persuaded the former commissary to help. By May, in his own words, he was ready "to push some Pork up the Bay for the grand Army."[32]

The reason for the army's food shortage was, the governor felt, that the Continental deputy quartermaster general in Virginia was not doing his job. The "Executive," he told the Virginia delegates in Congress, "have been more than once called upon to make up for Deficiency's in that Department," the management of which, he said, "shocked" him. But "I forbear," he continued, "for Tis my business to exert all of my powers for the Common Good."[33]

Patrick Henry did labor effectively for the "Common Good." When his term was up in May 1779 there was little criticism. But the problems he had faced were to become more difficult and his successor was not to get off so easily. Henry knew that more difficult times were ahead. He was

---

1778, and to Henry Laurens, June 18 and July 4, 1778, pp. 126, 196, 202, 250, 262–63, 284, 290, and 294–95; Thomas Smith to Thomas Gray, July 12, 1778, p. 281; George Mason to Henry, Aug. 22, 1777, Rutland, ed., *Papers of Mason*, 1:350–51; Thomas Jefferson to Richard Henry Lee, June 5, 1779, Julian P. Boyd et al., ed., *The Papers of Thomas Jefferson*, 19 vols. to date (Princeton, 1950–), 2:194. See also 3:124–25.

[32] McIlwaine, ed., *Journals of Council*, 2:64–67, 113, 139, and 143; Francis Lightfoot Lee to Henry, Jan. 14, 1778, Henry to the Virginia Delegates in Congress, Jan. 20, 1778, and to Thomas Smith, May 20, 1778, McIlwaine, ed., *Official Letters*, 1:231–33 and 278. A somewhat different interpretation of this effort to supply the army can be found in Brant, *Madison*, pp. 317–19.

[33] Henry to the Virginia Delegates in Congress, Jan. 20, 1778, and to Richard Henry Lee, Apr. 7, 1778, McIlwaine, ed., *Official Letters*, 1:231–33 and 260–61.

especially discouraged by the lack of public support for the war effort. Early the next year he wrote Jefferson that he feared the "Body Politic" was "dangerously sick"; "tell me," he said, "do you remember any Instance, where Tyranny was destroyed and Freedom established on its Ruins among a people possessing so small a Share of virtue and public Spirit?" By then Jefferson, no doubt, agreed.[34]

Thomas Jefferson was chosen governor of Virginia on June 1, 1779, over his friends Thomas Nelson and John Page. The election was closely contested, and in the end he won by the small margin of 67–61. It was not a good time to assume office. The war dragged on irresolutely, the American army had done nothing for a year, inflation was rampant, and it was reported that the Virginia assembly "go very slowly, & entangle themselves at every step."[35]

Jefferson, despite a gloomy prospect, seems to have entered office confidently, and, other estimates to the contrary, he proved to be an extremely good governor.[36] Any careful study of his two years in office will reveal him to have been informed, practical, hardworking, tough, decisive, and infinitely patient. He was the master of detail but at the same time saw the state's and the country's problems in broad perspective. Like Henry, he was acutely aware of the limited authority of the executive and was sensitive to and respectful of the powerful role of the legislature. Yet on at least one occasion he acted before receiving legislative approval, and another time he issued an order to impress boats that was

[34] Henry to Jefferson, Feb. 15, 1780, Boyd, ed., *Papers of Jefferson*, 3:293–94; Honyman, Diary, Mar. 16, 1780.

[35] *Journal of the House of Delegates of the Commonwealth of Virginia; Begun . . . on . . . the third Day of May, in the Year . . . One Thousand Seven Hundred and Seventy-Nine* (Richmond, 1827), p. 29; J. J. Pringle to Arthur Lee, Aug. 18, 1779, Lee Papers, University of Virginia Library, Charlottesville; Honyman, Diary, June 1, 1779.

[36] For a negative interpretation of Jefferson's governorship see Fawn M. Brodie, *Thomas Jefferson: An Intimate History* (New York, 1974), ch. 10. See also Henry Lee, *Memoirs of the War in the Southern Department of the United States*, 3d ed. (New York, 1869), pp. 297–305 and 438. Baron von Steuben to Washington, Feb. 18, 1781, Boyd, ed., *Papers of Jefferson*, 4:652.

contrary to the decision of the council. He was not always the strict constructionist, yet he seems to have been generally effective in working with the legislature, and he never forgot, even in desperate periods, that both he and the military were functioning in a democratic society. For example, in April 1781 he patiently explained to an irritated Gen. Nathanael Greene, in connection with difficulties surrounding the impressment of horses, that "tedious as is the operation of reasoning with every individual on whom we are obliged to exercise disagreeable powers, yet free people think they have a right to explanation of circumstances which give rise to the necessity under which they suffer."[37]

The problems Jefferson faced were substantial. In an attempt to ease the executive workload the assembly in the spring of 1779 created a Board of Trade and a Board of War, elected by the legislature and responsible to the governor and council. These two bodies were to coordinate all of the varied activities concerning trade and the military, thereby lessening the executive's day-to-day involvement. Edmund Pendleton wondered why a Board of War had been created "as I think the Governor and Council have not so much to do," but he guessed that a Board of Trade would "be more useful." Neither body, as it turned out, served its purpose very well. Everything had to be cleared with the executive and the entire arrangement proved inefficient. The following year these boards were replaced by a commercial agent, a commissioner of the navy, and a commissioner of the war office who were appointed by and responsible to the governor and council. The legislature was beginning to loosen the reins a bit. No more administrative rearrangements occurred during Jefferson's tenure in office.[38] The legislature also pro-

[37]Jefferson to William Fleming, June 8, 1779, to Richard Henry Lee, June 5, 1779, to Nathanael Greene, Apr. 5, 1781, to Richard Claiborne, Feb. 16 and 17, 1781, to von Steuben, Feb. 16, 1781, to the Speaker of the House, Mar. 3, 1781, and to William Lewis, Mar. 4, 1781, Boyd, ed., *Papers of Jefferson*, 2:194, 288–89, and 298–99, 4:51–52, 57, 626, 633, and 635–36, 5:356.

[38]Hening, ed., *Statutes*, 10:15–16, 17–18, 123–24, and 291–92; Edmund Pendleton to William Woodford, Mays, ed., *Papers of Pendleton*, 1:290–92.

vided Jefferson and his colleagues with short-term authority similar to that they had granted the previous administration over such things as military operations, supply, and embargoes.[39] The council, recognizing that various kinds of business were being delayed when they were not present, gave the governor the authority to proceed without them in routine matters.[40]

The relations of the executive with the legislature continued to be crucial. Jefferson, like Henry, corresponded regularly with the assembly through the Speaker of the House of Delegates. He made recommendations and reports, offered suggestions, and forwarded information. Unlike Henry, he had been a legislative activist while serving in the assembly, but it is difficult to determine whether as governor he took more initiative with the legislature. He was in more frequent communication with the leadership in the House of Delegates and he appears to have worked well with them. The assembly, at least during his first administration, was said to be held in "low esteem" owing to its "Misconduct, Dri[n]king and Gameing," but again, unlike Henry, he was never openly critical of that body. And the assembly, even in that terrible winter and spring of 1781, does not appear to have been critical of him. There was some grumbling in the spring of 1780 that probably derived from the movement of the capital to Richmond and the dissolving of the Board of War and the Board of Trade, which Jefferson no doubt initiated. There may have been more legislative criticism, but there is no evidence of it until after he left office in June 1781.[41]

Certainly no one worked harder or had a better grasp of

[39] For example, see Hening, ed., *Statutes*, 10:105–7 and 214–15.

[40] Boyd, ed., *Papers of Jefferson*, 3:183–84.

[41] For example, see Jefferson to Benjamin Harrison, Oct. 2 and 30, Nov. 4, 22, 23, 24, and 25, and Dec. 11, 1779, May 30 and June 5, 8, 13, 14, and 16, 1780, ibid., pp. 109–11, 125, 125–30, 153–54, 197, 197–98, 199–200, 216, 403, 418, 423, 438, and 443–44; Archibald Cary to Jefferson, Dec. 18, 1779, pp. 230–31; Honyman, Diary, Apr. 15, 1780; James Innes to Mann Page, Oct. 27, 1779, to Jefferson, June 10, 1780, and Jefferson to Benjamin Harrison, Nov. 20, 1780, Boyd, ed., *Papers of Jefferson*, 3:121–23, 195–96, and 430–31; Edmund Pendleton to James Madison, Oct. 17, 1781, Mays, ed., *Papers of Pendleton*, 1:318.

what was going on than Jefferson. He was the master of it all, from planning an attack on Detroit to knowing how many yards of cloth were available for outer clothing. There are, for example, thirteen extant letters that he wrote on January 15, 1781. The council was absent and he dealt with supplying the Convention army, militia rotation, repairing the foundry burned by Benedict Arnold at Westham, appointing a deputy quartermaster general for Virginia, trade with Bermuda, and establishing better communications with the Lower Peninsula. He began the next day by ordering the construction of twenty "portable Boats" (he included plans) and by writing the governor of North Carolina the details of the British invasion. It was not all motion—he got things done. Horatio Gates, the American commander in the South, wrote him on July 20, 1780, requesting that attention be given to supplies and other items. Jefferson replied on August 4, indicating, among other things, that bridges were being repaired and that beef, cartouche boxes, axes, ammunition, and "spirits" were being sent. Nor was he indecisive. In the same letter he said that he had countermanded marching orders for Col. William Brent's infantry because it would bring on a "disagreeable dispute" over rank between his officers and those of Col. George Gibson's infantry; Brent had but thirty men and Jefferson was not going to be bothered with the situation. In addition he was tough. When the commissioner of the grain tax for the Northern Neck told him that he was not going to collect grain in Westmoreland and Northumberland counties because the "quantity" was small and the commissions "trifling," Jefferson told him that his charge "was an entire charge" not just those parts "as were beneficial. . . . You were to undertake or reject the whole." We "shall expect from you an account of the specific articles in all the counties put under your care." Later, when the British were seizing private citizens and releasing them only after they had signed a parole indicating that they would be hanged if they were subsequently "found in Arms," he was outraged. If the British persisted in this breach of the "Law of nations," it would be considered as "putting prisoners to Death in cold Blood," he told a Virginian who wanted to return home and be released from parole. "We are determined to retaliate by immediate execution of an equal number of British prisoners in our Hands." In denying the request for exchange by another private citizen seized illegally by the British, he stated that he was sorry, but the British could not be allowed to proceed in this manner for they "have conquered South Carolina by Paroles alone."[42]

But as hardworking, efficient, and tough as he was, there were some things he was not able to deal with satisfactorily. A common problem in all of the states was militia, for it had proved impossible to make that body an efficient fighting force. Additionally, in certain areas it took an interminable time to get anything accomplished. As early as February 1780 Jefferson was trying to get fortifications built at narrow spots on the major rivers, especially the James and the Potomac. A key place that needed fortifying was Hoods on the James River. By late fall some preliminary work had been accomplished, but the commissioner of the war office reported that labor and bricks were hard to obtain. Further, the engineer's overall plan had not been approved by the legislature. Approval came, but little more had been done when Arnold raided Richmond in early January. A month later an angry Baron von Steuben wrote Jefferson that "three weeks had elapsed Since the Enemy went down the River" and that there had been no further work on a job that at the most should have taken six weeks. Jefferson's reply is revealing. "The Executive," he stated, "have not by the laws of this State any power to call a freeman to labour even for the Public without his consent, nor a Slave without that of his Master." The work needed to be done and he and the council could furnish the "necessaries," but "they may possibly be disappointed in their expectations of engaging voluntary labourers, the only means in their power." The project would be pursued, and if they could not "accomplish it in a shorter, they will in a longer time." But despite continued efforts and

[42]For one day's activities see Boyd, ed., *Papers of Jefferson*, 4:369–78; Jefferson to James Maxwell and to Abner Nash, Jan. 16, 1781, to William Davies, Jan. 26, 1781, to Horatio Gates, Aug. 4, 1780, and to James Adam, Aug. 25, 1780, Brewer Godwin to Jefferson, Mar. 15, 1781, and Jefferson to Thomas Fletcher, Mar. 21, 1781, pp. 380, 381, and 453, 3:526–27 and 566–67, 5:148–49, 149–50, and 197–98.

some additional progress the fortifications at Hoods were never completed. In his last message to the legislature on May 10, 1781, he continued to press for river defenses. Acquiring workers was the problem because "a militia of Freemen cannot be easily induced to labour in Works of this Kind." The governor suggested an arrangement whereby slaves could be used, but by that time Lord Cornwallis was on the move and it was too late.[43]

Jefferson and the council brought no new solutions to the military manpower problem. Earlier he had applauded a more efficient recruiting plan for the regular army, belittled volunteer schemes, and suggested that Congress "commute a good part of the infantry required from us, for an equivalent force in horse" because this would open a "new fund of young men . . . whose indolence or education has unfitted them for footservice." In the end, during his administration, the same methods were relied upon that had been used previously. Bounties were offered in land and money ($12,000 and 300 acres of land for a regular soldier) for long-term enlistments. And both types of draft schemes, partial and regular, were resorted to as well as volunteer programs.[44]

Jefferson does appear to have been somewhat more successful in supplying the army with soldiers than Henry. But it must be remembered that as the tide of war turned south the pressure on Virginia for men and supplies increased. In the spring of 1780, out of an authorized strength of about

[43]Jefferson to George Muter, Feb. 18, 1780, Muter to Jefferson, Sept. 8, 1780, Jefferson to Benjamin Harrison, Nov. 30, 1780, von Steuben to Jefferson, Dec. 15, 1780, and Feb. 11, 1781, Jefferson to von Steuben, Feb. 12, 1781, and to John Allen, Feb. 16, 1781, John Allen to Jefferson, Mar. 12, 1781, Jefferson to William Call, Apr. 12, 1781, Call to Jefferson, Apr. 14, 1781, and Jefferson to the Speaker of the House, May 10, 1781, ibid., 3:301–2 and 616–17, 4:168–69, 209, 584, and 625, 5:126–28, 413, 441–42, and 626–28. Interestingly, the legislature did give Thomas Nelson the authority to impress slaves for labor on defense works and as late as July 27 work was continuing at Hoods. See John Senf to Thomas Nelson, July 27, 1781, Executive Papers, Virginia State Library, Richmond.

[44]Jefferson to Richard Henry Lee, June 5, 1778, Boyd, ed., *Papers of Jefferson*, 2:194; Hening, ed., *Statutes*, 10:23–27, 32–34, 214–15, 257–62, and 326–37.

ten thousand, the state had had roughly fifty-five hundred men on regular service. The enlistments of over seventeen hundred of these men expired that spring or in the fall. The governor wrote Washington as early as February expressing his concern with this situation. The problem, as he saw it, was the lack of money necessary to reenlist the soldiers and he vowed "to postpone . . . every other application of public money, and shall furnish for this every shilling possible." Heavier taxes were approved by the legislature in the fall of 1779 and the spring of 1780. To this were added two loan drives in February and May 1780, the second of which resulting from a request from Congress for $1,900,000. As a result, Jefferson seems to have gotten the necessary money to keep the regular forces at the 1780 levels. In addition draft laws were passed in the spring and fall of 1780 to help meet the increasing demand for troops in the southern army. These measures, along with the authority granted the governor and council to send militia out of the state, provided the means necessary for Virginia to respond adequately. Throughout his term Jefferson was able to keep a steady flow of soldiers going to the Carolinas and at the same time to get militia into the field for the defense of the state. Obviously he could often not provide the full number of men requested, but Virginia militia and regulars formed the backbone of the American army in the South, and the governor was never unable to send reinforcements.[45]

Jefferson always kept the larger perspective in mind, and

[45] For troop strength see Boyd, ed., *Papers of Jefferson*, 3: after p. 254; Jefferson to John Rutledge, Nov. 11, 1779, to Washington, Feb. 17 and June 11, 1780, to J. P. G. Muhlenberg, Apr. 12, 1780, to James Madison, July 26, 1780, to Horatio Gates, Sept. 13, 1780, to Benjamin Harrison, Nov. 24, 1780, to the County Lieutenants of Washington and certain other counties, Feb. 15, 1781, and to Baron von Steuben, Feb. 17, 1781, pp. 180–81, 296–97, 350–52, 432–34, 506–7, and 588, 4:150–51, 613–14, and 648; Hening, ed., *Statutes*, 10:165–72, 182–89, 257–62, and 327–37; Emory G. Evans, *Thomas Nelson of Yorktown: Revolutionary Virginian* (Williamsburg, 1975), pp. 84–87; Don Higginbotham, *The War of Independence* (New York, 1971), ch. 14; John R. Alden, *The South in the Revolution, 1763–1789* (Baton Rouge, 1957), chs. 14 and 16; Christopher Ward, *The War of the Revolution*, 2 vols. (New York, 1952), 2:722–844.

when the Virginia military situation eased he called for continued efforts to reinforce the southern army. After a British raiding force had left the state on November 22, 1780, he reminded the legislature that the Carolinas and Georgia were exhausted. "On this state . . . rests the weight of the opposition and it is infinitely important that our efforts be such as to keep the war from our own country." It was therefore "necessary to set every wheel in motion" to get supplies and troops flowing south again. Even after Arnold's invasion, with British troops still in the state, when Cornwallis began to move to meet Nathanael Greene at Guilford Courthouse, he was determined not to "permit the body of plunderers . . . to divert us," and he did not hesitate to reinforce the American general. On these occasions he was apt to rely, in part, on emotion-laden rhetoric. He told the county lieutenants that "Lord Cornwallis, maddened by losses at Cowpens and Georgetown, has burnt his own Waggons to enable him to move with facility, and is pressing towards the Virginia line." "I cannot believe you will rest a moment . . . until you see your men under march." To von Steuben he remarked that his information might not be accurate, "but as its truth is equally possible . . . I think it my duty" to call out every man "who has a firelock."[46]

Virginia never seemed to lack for necessary supplies of food, although on one occasion Jefferson did place an embargo on the exportation of grain, meat, and flour. The main problem was obtaining and transporting provisions. In the early summer of 1780 the legislature gave the governor and council the authority to appoint commissioners in every county to purchase and impress foodstuffs at fixed prices and, if necessary, to impress horses, wagons, drivers, and vessels and their crews for transporting this food. The executive used the law in a restrained but effective manner, and

[46]Jefferson to Benjamin Harrison, Nov. 24, 1780, to Abner Nash, Feb. 2, 1781, Nathanael Greene to Jefferson, Feb. 10, 1781, Jefferson to the County Lieutenants of Washington and certain other counties, Feb. 15, 1781, to von Steuben, Feb. 17, 1781, and to Greene, Feb. 18, 1781, Boyd, ed., *Papers of Jefferson*, 4:150–51, 502–3, 576, 613–14, 644–45, and 648.

though on occasion the southern army was short of provisions, such a condition was usually short lived.[47]

Keeping soldiers equipped and clothed was more difficult. Successful trade with France and the West Indies continued, but these sources could never adequately supply American needs, and it is probable that a large portion of the necessary clothing and equipment was produced in America. Jefferson and his colleagues expanded the manufacturing efforts begun under Patrick Henry. Arms of all sorts, canteens, cartouche boxes, axes, tents, camp kettles, coats, and shoes, among other things, were produced in Virginia in substantial numbers. One factory was turning out twenty axes a day, while another made ten to twelve pairs of shoes a day and fifty to sixty regimental coats a week. Jefferson seemed to think it routine to order 10,000 wooden canteens from a Virginia manufacturer. In his efficient and orderly way he was involved at every level, from planning the casting of cannon at Westham to instructing the commissioner of the war office about obtaining nails for the construction of warehouses. This kind of coordination and attention gave a stability to the Virginia war effort and made it possible for the state to use its substantial resources more effectively.[48]

Like Patrick Henry, Jefferson had a good grasp of the

[47] Hening, ed., *Statutes*, 9:530–32, 10:233–37; Proclamation of Embargo, Nov. 30, 1779, Jefferson to John Mathews, Sept. 12, 1780, to Horatio Gates, Aug. 14, Sept. 3 and 23, and Oct. 4, 1780, Instructions to Commissioners of the Provision Law, Sept. 2, 1780, Jefferson to Edward Carrington, Oct. 4, 1780, and to von Steuben, Dec. 21, 1780, Boyd, ed., *Papers of Jefferson*, 3:208–9, 584–85, 526–27, 588, and 658–59, 4:9–11, 3:609–10, 4:7–8 and 219–20.

[48] Higginbotham, *War of Independence*, pp. 303–9; Jefferson to Benjamin Harrison, Oct. 29, 1779, Agreement with De Francy, May 11, 1780, David Ross to Jefferson, Mar. 22, 1781, Contract between the State and Peter Penet, Wendel and Company, July 27, 1779, Jefferson to George Muter, May 27 and July 25, 1780, and Jan. 14, 1781, to Edward Stevens, Nov. 26, 1780, George Muter to Jefferson, Jan. 14, 1781, Jefferson to William Davies, Jan. 26 and Feb. 2, 1781, James Hunter to Jefferson, Feb. 20, 1781, and William Davies to Jefferson, Mar. 8, 1781, Boyd, ed., *Papers of Jefferson*, 3:124–25 and 372–73, 5:208–9, 3:49–50, 398–99, and 504–5, 4:159, 354, 453, 493–94, 500, and 666–67, 5:90–91.

overall military problem. And, like Henry, he lavished great attention on western operations and defenses, so much so that he was criticized for ignoring the eastern part of the state. He did not ignore the East, but he was convinced that the only practical defense of that area "was naval." Unfortunately the navy was in terrible shape when he came into office, and he said that the state would be better off if it burned the ships and started all over again. He was unable to do much to improve the navy, which in 1780 amounted to only fourteen vessels, most of them galleys, with a total of eighty-eight guns. Jefferson was also convinced, as mentioned earlier, that fortifications at narrow spots on the major rivers were essential for eastern defense, but he failed to get these completed.[49]

The West was farther removed but in some ways was easier to deal with. Jefferson continued Henry's policies of trying to keep peace with the Indians and of maintaining a regular force in the Northwest under George Rogers Clark. He had been one of those instrumental in sending Clark west and was as sensitive as his predecessor to the dangers of a two-front war. With the council, the governor developed detailed defensive plans, including the disposition of militia and regular forces and the location of forts. Early in his administration he began to bring to fruition earlier plans for an attack on Detroit. A powerful army in the South and an expected combination of the Indians and the British in the West made it essential, he told Clark, for Virginia to "aim a first strike" and put the enemy on the defensive. There must be a proper division of Virginia's forces "between these two objects" in the South and the West, he wrote to western county lieutenants. The Arnold invasion in January 1781 did not deter him. When the county lieutenant of Frederick County reported that there would be great difficulty in getting western militia to join Clark, Jefferson replied with "ex-

[49] Jefferson to Richard Henry Lee, July 17, 1779, Orders for Defense of the Western Frontier, and Notes and Plans for Western Defense, July 23, 1779, Jefferson to William Fleming, Aug. 7, 1779, and James Innes to Jefferson, June 10, 1780, Boyd, ed., *Papers of Jefferson*, 2:39–40, 3:51–52, 52–56, 62, and 430; for the Virginia navy see 3: after p. 254.

ceeding distress" at the prospect of the expedition being discontinued because "the Savages will spread on our whole Western frontier" and as a result western troops could not be used in the East. "We are all in one bottom," he said, "the Western end of which cannot swim while the Eastern sinks." "Trusting the zeal of your people which never failed us, I will . . . throw our safety on them" and "revoke the orders for their peremptory march as militia and depend on them sending a sufficient number of volunteers." By that time, February 16, 1781, conditions had deteriorated in Virginia and the Detroit expedition never materialized, but it is difficult to fault the logic of the governor's plan.[50]

It was in the West that the first manifestation of discontent with the war appeared. Henry had had to face disaffection. But during Jefferson's two administrations, as taxes became heavier, as the demands for men and supplies increased, and as the British moved closer and then invaded Virginia, the situation became serious. In virtually all cases the difficulties developed on the periphery of the state—on the western frontier, in the Northern Neck, on the Eastern Shore, and in the southeast. On the southwest frontier in the counties of Bedford, Henry, Montgomery, Pittsylvania, and Washington, where there was a heavy concentration of tories, there was real insurrection. There had been problems earlier, but actual fighting began in Washington and Montgomery counties in the spring and summer of 1779 and this flared into a major confrontation between loyal whigs and tories a year later. It was reported that late in July 1780 a large number of tories, encouraged to believe that British troops were coming to their aid, planned to seize the lead mines in Montgomery

[50] Jefferson to George Rogers Clark, Jan. 1 and 29, Mar. 19, Apr. 19, and Dec. 25, 1780, and Feb. 13, 1781, to Joseph Martin, Jan. 24, 1780, to John Todd, Jan. 26, 1780, to William Preston, June 15, 1780, to Western County Lieutenants, Dec. 24, 1780, and Feb. 16, 1781, and to William Preston et al., March 24, 1781, ibid., pp. 258, 273–77, 316–17, and 356–57, 4:233–38 and 597–98, 3:255–56, 271–72, and 447–49, 4:229–33 and 627–28, 5:263. Plans for the Detroit expedition continued into late May and early June. See George Rogers Clark to Jefferson, and William Harrison to Jefferson, May 23 and June 2, 1781, 6:11–12, 69.

County and then link up with and arm the Convention army in Charlottesville "and subdue the whole state." Spies tipped off the local militia and ultimately 400 were active in subduing the insurrection. How many tories were involved is difficult to determine, but in early August sixty were being held in local jails. William Preston reported later that "nearly one half" the Montgomery County militia was "disaffected." Jefferson said that this "dangerous fire" extended "from Montgomery County along our southern boundary to Pittsylvania and Eastward as far as the James River. Indeed some suspicions have been raised of its having crept as far as Culpeper." Hundreds had "actually enlisted to serve his Britannic Majesty," he claimed. Nothing so serious developed elsewhere, but in 1780–81 resistance and rioting over the draft and taxes occurred in ten other counties. Some of this activity is indicative of nothing more than weariness with the war. But this was not the case in the southwest or, for that matter, a year later in Hampshire County, where a riotous group "Got Liquor and Drink King Georges the thirds health and damnation to Congress." Ultimately over one hundred people were involved in this resistance to collecting provisions. Jefferson's advice in every instance was moderate. Use every legal means to bring the "ring leaders" to trial and try to avoid openly confronting "mutineers" for this might bring "open Rebellion or Bloodshed." The best way to deal with these situations, he suggested, was to wait until the resisters dispersed and then "go and take them out of Beds, singly and without Noise, or if they be not found the first time to go again and again so that they never be able to remain quiet at home." Militia were to be used if necessary and blank militia commissions were always sent along with copies of the relevant laws. The General Assembly was concerned enough about disloyalty that in July 1780 it required all its members to take an oath supporting the American cause. George Mason was subsequently to give some support to this concern when he commented, with respect to draft resistance, that he was sure that "principal men" in the counties where the difficulty occurred were "at the bottom of it." Although the strains of four years of war were beginning to show, it is significant that local authorities, unlike their counterparts in the Carolinas and Georgia, were ultimately able to control these explosive situations even if they were not always moderate in their handling of the problem. There is evidence to suggest that in some southwestern counties tories were hanged without a fair trial or with no trial at all.[51] But such activity seems to have been exceptional, and the fact that Virginia contained this disaffection testifies to the strength of its government and the political wisdom of its executive.

Before the fateful year 1781 Jefferson and his council had to respond to an invasion only once. There had been threats of invasion, and in these cases the executive had been very cautious about calling up the militia. In December 1779, when news of a possible invasion was received, Jefferson wrote the Speaker of the House of Delegates that the expense and difficulty connected with "a general call of the militia" and "the disgust it gives them . . . when they find no

[51] Hamilton J. Eckenrode, *The Revolution in Virginia* (1916; reprint ed., Hamden, Conn., 1964), ch. 9; Hening, ed., *Statutes*, 10: 195; Washington County Minute Book 1, 1777–84, June 16 and July 3, 1779, Aug. 15 and Nov. 22 and 23, 1780, and Montgomery County Order Book 3, May 5, June 1, Aug. 3, 4, 5, and Sept. 7, 1779, Nov. 8, 1780, and Apr. 4, 1781. The county court did not meet in Montgomery County from April 5 to November 7, 1780, and from May 2 to November 6, 1781. Jefferson to William Preston, Mar. 21, 1781, Preston to Jefferson, Aug. 8, 1780, Jefferson to James Wood, Oct. 5, 1780, to the Virginia Delegates in Congress, Oct. 27, 1780, John Taylor to Jefferson, Dec. 5, 1780, Thomas Gaskins to Jefferson, Feb. 23, 1781, James Callaway to Jefferson, and Daniel Morgan to Jefferson, Mar. 23, 1781, Garret Van Meter to Jefferson, Apr. 11 and 14, 1781, William Preston to Jefferson, Apr. 13, 1781, Jefferson to James Innes, May 2, 1781, George Moffet to Jefferson, May 5, 1781, Samuel McDowell to Jefferson, May 9, 1781, Commissioners for Collecting Taxes in Accomac County to Jefferson, May 15, 1781, Jefferson to James Callaway, Aug. 1, 1780, Jefferson to Garret Van Meter, Apr. 27, 1781, Affidavit of Benjamin Harrison's Oath as Speaker, July 7, 1780, and George Mason to Jefferson, Oct. 6, 1780, Boyd, ed., *Papers of Jefferson*, 3: 325 and 533–34, 4:14–15, 76–77, 180–81, 693, and 693n, 5:212–13, 218–19, 409–10, 455, 436–38, 593–94, 603–4, 621–22, and 651–54, 3:519–20, 482, and 482n, 5:565–66, 6:18–19; Hening, ed., *Statutes*, 10:195. Summers, *Southwest Virginia*, pp. 292–94. In Bedford County "when any of the inhabitants were suspected of wrong doing or treasonable conduct, they were dealt with according to what was termed Captain Lynch's Law" (ibid.).

enemy in place . . . induce us to refer to the decision of the general assembly." This attitude had developed as a result of invasion scares beginning in 1777. The governor and council did respond promptly when Gen. Alexander Leslie, with 2,500 troops, stopped for a month at Portsmouth on their way south. But in this instance it took three weeks to get militia in the field, an ominous warning for the future.[52]

In evaluating Thomas Jefferson's governorship, historians have more often than not focused on his last five months in office and especially on the few days in late December and early January 1781. The result is that, in the popular mind, he is considered not to have been a very good chief executive. Nothing could be further from the truth. It is true, of course, that the governor did not respond as quickly as he should have on December 31 to the news that a "fleet of 27 sail" had been sighted at the mouth of the James River. He sent Brig. Gen. Thomas Nelson, Jr., of the militia to the lower country to do what he could, and on January 1 he informed the legislature he was suspicious the fleet might be hostile and asked their advice. But it was not until January 2, with the British just below Jamestown, that he called out the militia. Invasion scares and raids during the past several years had made both the public and its leaders less alert than they should have been. But the demands on the state were now tremendous, and the governor did not want to take any action that would strain its resources unnecessarily. Further, it must be emphasized that even if Jefferson had called out the militia on December 31, it would not have helped the situation, for it took Benedict Arnold and his British troops less than a week to raid Richmond and fall back down the James River. Militia could not be gotten into the field that quickly and the fortifications at Hoods had not been completed. In this instance the militia responded more quickly than in October (over half of the 4,600 called were in the field within ten days), but

---

[52] Jefferson to Benjamin Harrison, Dec. 11, 1779, to Horatio Gates and to John Smith, Oct. 22, 1780, Steps to Be Taken to Repel General Leslie's Army, Oct. 22, 1780, Jefferson to Edward Stevens, Nov. 10, 1780, and Jefferson to D'Anmours, Nov. 30, 1780, Boyd, ed., *Papers of Jefferson*, 3:241, 4:57, 58, 59, 61–63, 111–12, and 168.

this did not ease the public's criticism of the executive. It was reported that "the Governor and Council are universally and heavily censored for their neglect and supineness on this occasion."[53]

Even if it is accepted that Thomas Jefferson did not act quickly enough in late December 1780, from January 2 until his retirement in June 1781, his efforts cannot be seriously faulted despite the fact that von Steuben, who had been left in command by Nathanael Greene to facilitate the southward movement of men and supplies, was constantly critical of Virginia's government. Greene himself was only slightly less disapproving. Neither of these soldiers, especially von Steuben, understood the workings of a democratic government, and Jefferson put up with a great deal from both of them. He was always cooperative and patient and never responded in kind. He appointed his friend John Walker to serve as von Steuben's aide in the hope that it would better enable the state to provide the general with what he needed. But this did not help, and von Steuben continued to complain of "bad management" and an "Executive power" that was "so confined that the Governor" could not get him "40 Negroes to work at Hoods." The situation was exacerbated when the governor and council blocked von Steuben's plan to march 2,000 militia to join Greene in North Carolina and stop any attempt by Cornwallis to join the other British army in Virginia. Von Steuben brought great pressure to bear, but Jefferson and the council felt it would weaken the state too much and determined that all they could do was to reinforce

[53] Jacob Wray to Thomas Nelson, Dec. 30, 1780, Brock Collection, Huntington Library, San Marino, Calif.; McIlwaine, ed., *Journals of Council*, 2:269; Jefferson to von Steuben, Dec. 31, 1780, to Benjamin Harrison, Jan. 1, 1781, to Thomas Nelson, Jan. 2, 1781, Diary and Notes of 1781 (1816 version), Jefferson to George Weedon, and to George Washington, Jan. 10, 1781, Boyd, ed., *Papers of Jefferson*, 4:254, 289, 297, 263, and 333–36; Honyman, Diary, Jan. 29, 1781. For a good defense of Jefferson's leadership in the winter and spring of 1781 see Peterson, *Thomas Jefferson*, ch. 4, esp. pp. 203–40; see also Dumas Malone, *Jefferson the Virginian* (Boston, 1948), ch. 24. For different views see Lee, *Memoirs*, pp. 297–305; Brodie, *Jefferson*, ch. 10; and Richard B. Morris, *Seven Who Shaped Our Destiny* (New York, 1973), pp. 147–49.

Greene with one-fourth of the militia from eleven southside and southwestern counties.[54]

Through it all the governor maintained his equilibrium. He continued to work incessantly to keep militia in the field and supplies flowing. Both tasks were difficult. He hated to impress, calling it "the most unpalateable of all substitutes" for money, and he probably did not use it as much as he should have. It was a constant struggle to get militia out and keep them in service. Gen. Edward Stevens told the governor that "militia won't do. Their greatest Study is to Rub through their Tower [tour] of Duty with whole Bones." As spring came and the planting season approached, they resisted more. The governor was sympathetic but firm. Everything was tried. One county lieutenant reported that they were trying to do the planting for those men who were "on duty." The fact was, Jefferson told the legislature, that the laws concerning militia duty and to which these men were subject while in the field were too weak. He "candidly" admitted to Lafayette that all he could do was "represent to the General Assembly that unless they can provide more effectually for the Execution of the Law it will be vain to call on militia." But he did continue to call them. Not a few militia responded, and supplies and provisions continued to be collected. And up to the time Banastre Tarleton almost surprised him and the legislature in Charlottesville in early June, Jefferson labored at his executive duties. Inevitably there was some confusion with the legislature and the public offices moving to Charlottesville. In this period three members of the council

[54] Von Steuben to Jefferson, Nov. 27, 1780, Jefferson to von Steuben, Dec. 1 and 4, 1780, and Jan. 9, 1781, to Sampson Mathews, Jan. 12, 1781, to von Steuben, Jan. 14, 1781, to John Walker, Jan. 18, 1781, von Steuben to Washington, Feb. 8, 1781, John Walker to Jefferson, Mar. 8, 1781, Jefferson to the Speaker of the House of Delegates, Mar. 9, 1781, von Steuben to Jefferson, Mar. 9, 1781, Jefferson to von Steuben, Mar. 10, 1781, Richard Henry Lee to Jefferson, Mar. 27, 1781, and George Weedon to Jefferson, Mar. 27, 1781, Boyd, ed., *Papers to Jefferson*, 4:163, 175, 178–79, 327–28, 343, 356–58, and 652n, 5:101–2, 105, 105n, 106–7, 119–20, 262, and 267; McIlwaine, ed., *Journals of Council*, 2:322. Richard Henry Lee and the state military board, including Gen. George Weedon and Lafayette, supported von Steuben's plan.

resigned and the governor, perhaps discouraged, wrote Washington asking that he personally return to aid Virginia and spoke of his "relinquishing" the governorship "to abler hands." Jefferson had considered resigning in the previous fall, but he had stuck to the job. Under the circumstances the conclusion must be that he did remarkably well.[55]

Thomas Nelson, Jr., was selected by the General Assembly meeting in Staunton as Jefferson's successor on June 12, 1781. A wealthy merchant-planter, he had served in the House of Burgesses, the House of Delegates, the Continental Congress, and, most recently, he had been commanding Virginia militia in the field. There had been talk of appointing a dictator but wiser heads prevailed and instead they resorted to what Jefferson was later to refer to approvingly as a "union of the civil and military powers." The selection of Nelson was generally approved, especially by the military. Von Steuben, who had written earlier urging Nelson to return to duty from his sickbed, telling him that "you are better acquainted with the Strength and weakness of this state and . . . have the Confidence of the People," was certainly pleased. General Greene was similarly approving, speaking of the happy union in Nelson of "both the Citizen and Soldier."[56]

[55] Jefferson to Washington, June 11, 1780, to Richard Claiborne, May 18, 1781, Edward Stevens to Jefferson, Feb. 8, 1781, William Davies to Jefferson, Mar. 18, 1781, Jefferson to James Callaway, April 16, 1781, James Barbour to Jefferson, May 2, 1781, Jefferson to Robert Lawson, May 4, 1781, to Sir John Peyton, and to Lafayette, May 14, 1781, David Ross to Jefferson, May 23, 1781, Jefferson to Ross, May 25, 1781, to the Speaker of the House, and to George Washington, May 28, 1781, to Lafayette, May 31, 1781, John Page to Jefferson, Sept. 22, Oct. 20, and Dec. 9, 1780, and George Mason to Jefferson, Oct. 6, 1780, Boyd, ed., *Papers of Jefferson*, 3:432–34, 5:667, 6:10–11, 4:561–62, 5:173–76, 464, 465, 587–88, 597–98, 605–6, and 645, 6:12–14, 17–18, and 24–25, 3:655–56, 4:18–19, 52–53, and 191–93.

[56] *Journal of the House of Delegates of the Commonwealth of Virginia; Begun . . . on . . . the Seventh Day of May, in the Year . . . One Thousand Seven Hundred and Eighty-One* (Richmond, 1828), p. 15; Honyman, Diary, June 11, 1781; Henry Young to William Davies, June 9, 1781, Boyd, ed., *Papers of Jefferson*, 6:84–85; von Steuben to Thomas Nelson, Mar. 10, 1781, von Steuben

The legislature, following Jefferson's advice, gave the new governor extensive powers. It authorized him, with the consent of the council, to call out the state militia in such numbers as he saw fit and to send them where their services were required; to impress food and supplies; to seize loyalists and banish them without jury trial; to redistribute the property of persons who opposed laws for calling up militia; to discontinue the state quartermaster department and put it in the hands of Continental officials; and to constitute courts with the same powers as the General Court of the state. Additional legislation provided the death penalty for desertion and empowered the governor and council to levy an embargo on exports from the state; to declare martial law within a twenty-mile radius of the enemy or American camps; and to strengthen militia regulations so that six months might be added to the service of those who failed to appear when originally summoned. Some of these laws, for example, the provisions concerning impressment and embargoes, were extensions of authority granted previous governors. But in these cases the authority was much broader. The executive could, for example, impress virtually everything "under such regulations as they shall devise," including "negroes as pioneers" and "all other necessaries as may be wanted for supplying the militia, or other troops." The laws regarding militia were new and, coupled with the remaining ones, gave the executive almost dictatorial powers. Any comparison of Jefferson's administration with Nelson's must take these powers into consideration.[57]

Nelson's and Jefferson's political views were similar, but there the similarity between them ended. Nelson was a man of direct action who was not immobilized by his concern for the public's rights and feelings. Also, during his brief, five-month administration it became evident that unfolding events might bring the long war to an end. Thus motivated,

---

Papers, New-York Historical Society, New York City. See also Evans, *Thomas Nelson*, ch. 6.

[57] Hening, ed., *Statutes*, 10:411, 413, 416, 419–21, 423, and 437; Jefferson to Lafayette, May 14, 1781, to House of Delegates, May 28, 1781, Boyd, ed., *Papers of Jefferson*, 5:645, 6:28–29.

Nelson's leadership took on a vigorous character; he did not hesitate to use the sweeping powers that had been granted, and in the end he exceeded those powers.[58]

Drastic action was required. The British army had been moving around the state almost at will. Large sums of money were needed, but no new taxes had been levied and perhaps could not be. Inflation was rampant, making Virginia currency almost worthless. With harvest time approaching, state militia began to disappear from the army of Lafayette, who was now in command in Virginia.

Nelson began to deal vigorously with all these problems. The legislature in the spring session had provided for the emission of $35,000,000 in paper money and Nelson spent about $15,000,000 of it while he was in office, mainly for the support of the army. But the real problem was to get suppliers to accept this currency. The governor and his council began immediately to impress goods and equipment. On occasion the threat of force had to be used because Virginia farmers were reluctant to exchange their produce for vouchers that stated the appraised price and were redeemable at a future date. Impressment caused great ill-feeling, but Nelson believed that "disagreeable" as it was, this method was necessary if "everything requisite" could not "be procured by other means."

Keeping the armies of Greene and Lafayette reinforced was similarly difficult. Each county's militia was divided into four groups and rotated in and out of service in a two-month tour of duty. Nobody wanted to serve in the Carolinas because they were inevitably away from home longer than those called for duty in the state. The executive uniformly enforced the provision in the militia law providing six months' additional duty for those evading army service. The law proved difficult to enforce in the West, where there was continued resistance to militia duty, but the governor and council dealt moderately with this problem and ultimately pardoned all dissidents. In dealing with all of these matters, Nelson was fortunate to have William Davies as the commis-

[58] This and subsequent details of Thomas Nelson's administration are taken from Evans, *Thomas Nelson*, ch. 6.

sioner of the war office.[59] Jefferson had appointed Davies, an extremely able man, in March. He had the responsibility, among other things, for coordinating and carrying out the supply function. All state quartermasters and commissaries, as well as the state clothier and the commercial agent, reported to this office, which Davies ran with admirable efficiency. Even Lafayette, who had complained of Virginia's niggardliness, was impressed with the results of the Nelson administration's increased exertions.

On August 1, 1781, Lord Cornwallis began to locate his army at Yorktown and to establish a defensible base. Governor Nelson sensed there was a possibility of a major action. Orders were dispatched rescinding the movement of militia to Greene, and the governor wrote the county lieutenants that "never was a Time when vigorous measures were more necessary, or when they promised greater advantages." He believed that a strong effort, of which the "state is very capable . . . will in all probability . . . put a happy period to the war."

By mid-August it was learned that it had been decided to move both Washington's and Rochambeau's armies to Virginia and to cooperate with a French fleet from the West Indies under Admiral de Grasse in an attack against Cornwallis. At this point Nelson became ill and for the last two weeks in August the administration of the government was handled ably by Lt. Gov. David Jameson and the council, as well as William Davies, who carried out the executive's plans for gathering supplies and calling up militia.

On September 2 Nelson was back in Richmond, where the government had again moved in July, just as de Grasse was unloading troops at Jamestown; he and the council immediately set plans in motion to supply the French troops. An embargo was placed on the exportation of beef, pork, bacon, peas, wheat, corn, and other grains. Two persons were put in charge of supplying the French army and fleet, and letters were sent to the governors of Maryland and North Carolina requesting flour, beef, and salt. Finally, Governor Nelson an-

---

[59] Jefferson to William Davies, Mar. 27, 1781, Boyd, ed., *Papers of Jefferson*, 5:204–5.

nounced that he was going to take command of a large body of militia that had been called out earlier.

Nelson's decision to lead the militia was quite controversial. Lieutenant Governor Jameson objected strongly, stating that without the governor in Richmond nothing could be accomplished and that he did not plan to stay there hearing the daily complaints of people when he was "without the power to do anything."

Nelson replied that the needs of the army that required "instant attention" were presented to him "on the Spot" and there would be no delay trying to meet these needs. Nothing should stand in the way of efforts to "give success to the present military operation, for if we fail . . . we shall have but the Shadow of a Government," but if "they succeed, the Hands of Government will be stronger."

Nelson took command of the state militia at Williamsburg on September 11 and began intense and systematic efforts to procure provisions for all troops, both French and American. He found that the French were seeking provisions on their own and paying for them in specie. This situation had to be controlled if there was going to be food for all. Nelson ordered that all provisions be centrally located and dispersed, on application, by himself or his representative. Officials in the counties were told to impress supplies if they could not be obtained otherwise and to use militia if there was resistance.

In these and similar steps Nelson acted without consent of the council and, as a result, unconstitutionally. He realized this but argued that the "trust my country had repos'd in me demands that I stretch my powers to their utmost extent regardless of the censures of the inconsiderate or any other evil that may result to myself for such a step." Adequately supplying a force that would ultimately number 20,000 allied troops required extreme effort, but by the middle of September Nelson was beginning to see positive results.

He became ill about this time, but he effectively carried on business through his secretary (a Nelson innovation) and his aide-de-camp. Successful efforts to acquire supplies continued; he had troublemaking loyalists arrested; and he did his best to keep undisciplined militia under control.

Nelson's problems became more severe when the full French and American armies began to land on September 21. The pressure for food was great, and the governor said he was now "under the necessity of taking from the people of this ravaged Part of the Country, what humanity strongly inclined me to spare them." Soon the situation eased when supplies from Maryland and the Eastern Shore began to arrive. By the time the siege of Yorktown began on October 9, the armies were being adequately supplied.

After the victory at Yorktown the pressure on the executive did not ease. French troops had to be fed and housed. The Virginia military establishment had to be maintained. Accounts had to be settled, cattle disposed of, and other supplies stored. Civil strife existed in the lower tidewater. Nelson worked on these and other problems until early November when he became ill again. He had been in poor health for several years and he eventually resigned the governorship on November 20. Benjamin Harrison was elected to replace him.

Soon thereafter Nelson's administration of the state began to be severely criticized. Edmund Pendleton, who could always be counted on for a critical comment, said that the governor had resigned because his "great popularity" had "suddenly changed into general execration" because of his impressment of food and his other policies which had "intercepted [French] specie that was about to flow amongst the people." The severest protest came from northern Virginia, where authorities had faced the greatest difficulty in collecting provisions, especially Prince William County. A petition of remonstrances from that county, written by George Mason, complained of Nelson's having acted "without advice of Council" in the impressment of provisions and condemned other measures such as the embargo on exports of corn, wheat, and other commodities. The result was a full discussion of Nelson's governorship in the House of Delegates, where it was reported "his conduct" was freely "arraigned."

Nelson defended himself successfully in Richmond on December 22. He evidently argued that "the initial situation of the army and the peculiar circumstances of the country, made vigorous exertions necessary." A bill was passed on December 27, legalizing the measures he took without the advice of the council and stating that he was "indemnified and exonerated from all penalties and damages."

When Thomas Nelson became governor he had at his disposal powers greater than those of any governor preceding him, and, except for a few days in June, he did not have the restraining influence of the legislature. A tremendous responsibility, which Nelson accepted, rested with the executive. A more politically minded person, such as Patrick Henry or Thomas Jefferson, would perhaps have shown more caution. But, with the council, Nelson exercised to its fullest extent the power that had been granted. When it appeared necessary, in the six weeks before Yorktown, he exceeded that authority without regard to the effect that it would have on his career. One could not consider his "own Interest," he said, "when it was necessary to make it subservient to the public good."

If the attempt to trap Cornwallis had failed, it would have been easy to condemn Nelson, and, as it was, his behavior did cause widespread criticism. But the conclusion can hardly be avoided that his effort to supply the army at Yorktown was a crucial element in the victory. He was the man for the time.

But Patrick Henry and Thomas Jefferson were also men for the time. Virginia was, in fact, blessed with outstanding governors during the Revolution. Henry, Jefferson, and Nelson were all very different, but they served Virginia and the emerging nation well. Their experience indicates that the executive branch in Virginia during the Revolution played a crucial role. Power rested in the assembly, but the regular extension of short-term authority by the legislature, the knowledge and understanding that came from keeping the machinery of government going on a daily basis, and the varying, but not insignificant, ability of the executive to influence the legislature, county officials, and the public gave the governor and the council more importance than has been assumed. Nevertheless it must be emphasized that the constitutional role of the executive was restricted, and both Henry and Jefferson were occasionally restive with their limited authority. Nelson in his brief term had more authority and did not have to deal with the legislature. But it is also safe to say that none of them believed that executive power should be substantially increased.[60] All three had served in the legislature and were to return there after serving as governor. They believed that the preponderance of power properly lay with the "peoples" representatives, and they were prepared to "pay the price" that such belief entailed. Jefferson was not complaining when he told Baron von Steuben that the executive could not "by the laws of this State . . . call a freeman to labour even for the Public without his consent." It might take longer under such circumstances to get fortifications constructed, but so be it. Nelson, of course, exceeded his authority, but while he believed that his actions could help bring the war to a quick conclusion, he did not favor a permanent expansion of executive authority.

Finally, the fact that the governors were as effective as they were resulted from the strength of the governmental establishment, grounded as it was in a century of experience. The structure of government, as it affected people's daily lives, had not changed radically with Independence. A county political elite, which showed up in the legislature and of which the governors were also a part, still ran things. This leadership did not go unchallenged, especially in southwest Virginia, but it understood the problems of government at all levels, was generally committed to the Revolution, and gave the state governmental stability even under the terrible pressures of the year 1781. Thus, to emphasize the weakness of the executive in Virginia during the years from 1776 to 1781 is to misperceive the situation in the context of the time.

[60] For example, see Peterson, *Jefferson*, p. 105.

MERRILL JENSEN

The Sovereign States

Their Antagonisms and Rivalries
and Some Consequences

WHEN THE AMERICAN colonies declared their independence
as sovereign states in 1776, they had much in common: a
common heritage of political ideas and institutions, a common language, and perhaps most importantly, a common
enemy, Great Britain. Patriot leaders in 1776 also asserted
publicly that all Americans, except for a few deluded, bribed,
would-be tyrants, were united for Independence. In effect,
they declared that people as varied as Boston artisans and
South Carolina rice planters were marching hand-in-hand
shouting "Give me Liberty or Give me Death." And since
then, from time to time, historians and others have said
much the same thing.

The Revolutionary leaders of 1776 were only doing what
revolutionary leaders in any age do, and must do, if they
hope to win. America's leaders knew that there was a wide
gap between their public professions and American reality.
They knew that there was bitter opposition to Independence
and that the mass of the people were probably indifferent.
They knew too that there were serious rivalries and fundamental differences among the states and among groups of
states that would be obstacles to winning Independence and
to creating a nation.

A young English clergyman who visited America in 1759
doubted that the colonies could ever unite in a "permanent
union," for, he said, "fire and water are not more heteroge-
neous than the different colonies in North America." He concluded that "such is the difference of character, of manners,
of religion, of interest of the different colonies" that "were

they left to themselves, there would soon be civil war, from one end of the continent to the other; while the Indians and Negroes would, with better reason, impatiently watch the opportunity of exterminating them all together."[1]

Nearly sixty years later, long after Independence had been won, John Adams said much the same. He wrote that

> the colonies had grown up under constitutions of government so different, there was so great a variety of religions, they were composed of so many different nations, their customs, manners, and habits had so little resemblance, and their intercourse had been so rare, and their knowledge of each other so imperfect, that to unite them in the same principles in theory and the same system of action, was certainly a very difficult enterprise. The complete accomplishment of it, in so short a time and by such simple means, was perhaps a singular example in the history of mankind. Thirteen clocks were made to strike together—a perfection of mechanism, which no artist had ever before effected.[2]

In fact most colonies had closer connections with Britain than with one another. Furthermore, an American tended to look upon his own colony as his "country" and upon the citizens of other colonies as "foreigners." It was no slip of the pen when John Adams called the Massachusetts delegation to the First Continental Congress "our embassy."[3]

After 1776 citizens were far more devoted to their own states than to that vague entity, the United States. In 1787 Gen. Henry Knox told a member of the Constitutional Convention that "the state systems are the accursed thing which will prevent our being a nation. The democracy might be managed . . . but the vile state governments are sources of pollution which will contaminate the American name for

[1] Andrew Burnaby, *Travels through the Middle Settlements in North America* (1775; reprint ed., Ithaca, 1960), pp. 113–14. Spelling, punctuation, and capitalization in all quotations have been brought into conformity with present-day practice.

[2] To Hezekiah Niles, Feb. 13, 1818, Charles Francis Adams, ed., *The Works of John Adams*, 10 vols. (Boston 1850–56), 10:283.

[3] To Abigail Adams, Sept. 18, 1774, Lyman H. Butterfield, ed., *Adams Family Correspondence*, 4 vols. to date (Cambridge, Mass., 1963–), 1:158.

ages—machines that must produce ill, but cannot produce good; smite them in the name of God and the people."[4]

The Constitutional Convention in 1787 did smite the states, but many citizens were not converted. Massachusetts congressman Fisher Ames complained in 1792 that there were factions in Congress who were trying to reduce the new government to a "state government." "The government is too far off to gain the affections of the people," he wrote. "We have paper enough blotted with theories of government. The habits of thinking are to be reformed. Instead of feeling as a nation, a state is our country. We look with indifference, often with hatred, fear, and aversion to the other states."[5]

An equally powerful force in shaping the future was loyalty to the sections of the new nation. Before 1776 Americans took it for granted that the colonies were divided into three distinct groups: the four New England, or "Eastern," the four Middle, and the five Southern, or "Staple" colonies. They agreed too that each group had differing political and social attitudes, and differing economic interests. And increasingly after 1776 American leaders described the division as being between the eight "commercial" states of the North and the five "agrarian" states of the South.

Geography, climate, and soil were fundamental in shaping those divisions. So too was time itself in an age when travel was largely dependent upon sailing ships and the winds and tides. When men used the terms *New England states* and *Eastern states* interchangeably, they did so because Boston was 600 miles east of Charleston, and they knew that if one sailed straight south one came ashore in eastern Santo Domingo. For that matter, if one sailed south from Philadelphia, the first land sighted would be the eastern tip of Cuba.

Americans of the Revolutionary generation seldom described the differences among themselves in admiring terms. Thus New Englanders were looked upon as religious bigots because Massachusetts had hanged Quakers in the seven-

[4] To Rufus King, July 15, 1787, Charles R. King, *The Life and Correspondence of Rufus King . . .* , 6 vols. (New York, 1894), 1:228.

[5] To George R. Minot, Feb. 16, 1792, Seth Ames, ed., *Works of Fisher Ames*, 2 vols. (Boston, 1854), 1:113.

teenth century. And after 1763 New Englanders were feared as wild-eyed democrats who wanted to spread their noxious practices throughout America. They were even suspected of being "Levellers," and calling a man a "Leveller" in the eighteenth century, when memories of the Puritan Revolution were still vivid, was like calling a man a "communist" in the twentieth century. But above all New Englanders had the reputation of being cheats in business.

That reputation was an old one by 1776. At the end of the seventeenth century an English visitor published a book in which he said that "the gravity and piety of their looks are of great service to these American Christians. It makes strangers that come amongst them give credit to their words." Then he added: "And it is a proverb with those who know them: Whosoever believes a New England Saint shall be sure to be cheated. And he that knows how to deal with their traders, may deal with the Devil and fear no craft."[6]

A half-century later New York manor lord Lewis Morris wrote in his will that his son Gouverneur, under no circumstances, should be sent to Yale for an education lest he "imbibe in his youth that low craft and cunning so incident to the people of that country, which is so interwoven in their constitutions that all their art cannot disguise it from the world, tho many of them, under the sanctified garb of religion, have endeavored to impose themselves on the world for honest men."[7]

Young Gouverneur Morris got a B.A. and M.A. at King's College in New York. Those who have read his diary of the French Revolution know that the title of his master's thesis was prophetic. The title was "Love." And those who know anything about his political career know that for "low craft and cunning" he was more than a match for any New Englander but that he never wore "the sanctified garb of religion."

Nor did all New Englanders for that matter. One example

[6][Edward Ward], *A Trip to New England* . . . (1699; reprint ed., Providence, 1905), p. 45.

[7]Max M. Mintz, *Gouverneur Morris and the American Revolution* (Norman, Okla., 1970), p. 15.

was Simeon Potter of Bristol, Rhode Island. He made money as a privateer during the Seven Years' War and then invested in the slave trade. Upon one occasion he instructed a captain: "Make your chief trade with the blacks and little or none with the white people if possible. . . . Water your rum as much as possible and sell as much by the short measure as you can."[8]

Events after 1763 intensified the distrust of New Englanders. Boston took the lead in adopting nonimportation to oppose the Townshend Acts of 1767. Shortly thereafter newspapers throughout the colonies began publishing accounts, provided by the new Board of Customs Commissioners in Boston, showing that Boston merchants were importing goods they had agreed not to import. When the Townshend Revenue Act was repealed in 1770 (except for the tax on tea) the New York merchants were the first to abandon nonimportation. They were roundly denounced, especially by Boston newspapers. One New York newspaper replied that Bostonians were hypocrites and that Boston was "the common sewer of America into which every beast that brought with it the unclean thing has disburthened itself."[9]

After 1770 most Americans agreed not to import taxed tea. New York and Pennsylvania merchants patriotically avoided the tax by smuggling, but some Boston merchants paid it, a fact reported in newspapers throughout America. John and Samuel Adams were much embarrassed at the First Continental Congress when they were asked to explain why their fellow delegate, John Hancock, had been paying the tea tax.[10]

The common people of New England did not fare much better than the merchants in the eyes of some outsiders. Shortly after he took command of the New England troops outside Boston in the summer of 1775, George Washington wrote to a relative in Virginia: "The people of this government have obtained a character which they by no means de-

[8] W. B. Weeden, *Economic and Social History of New England, 1620–1789,* 2 vols. (Boston, 1890), 2:465.

[9] *New York Gazette,* Aug. 27, 1770.

[10] Lyman H. Butterfield, ed., *Diary and Autobiography of John Adams,* 4 vols. (Cambridge, Mass., 1961), 2:135.

served; their officers, generally speaking, are the most indifferent kind of people I ever saw," and the common soldiers "are an exceeding dirty and nasty people."[11]

Those who attacked New Englanders displayed a certain myopia. The common people of New England might be "dirty and nasty" but probably no more so than those in the South, if accounts of tavern brawls are to be believed. In those brawls noses were bitten off, eyes gouged out, and ears torn off. New England was amply supplied with taverns, but I have not seen similar accounts about them. It should be said, however, that John Adams once remarked that taverns were places where bastards and legislators were begotten.

The business morality of New England merchants might be dubious, but so were the methods of land speculators in New York, the Middle States, and Virginia. Prominent men used their political positions to grab land illegally, and some of them were not averse to forgery and bribery. New England merchants ignored their nonimportation agreements, but so did the Virginians. They imported more goods after agreeing to nonimportation than they had before. George Washington, for example, ordered goods from England that he had signed an agreement not to buy. As for religious bigotry, Virginians jailed Baptist ministers right and left and, except for Presbyterians who had political clout, treated Dissenting churches more severely than Massachusetts did.

Philadelphians looked upon their city as the center of American civilization, but they should not have been so smug. While the Constitutional Convention was meeting in the summer of 1787, a Philadelphia newspaper reported: "We are sorry to hear that the poor woman who suffered so much some time ago, under the imputation of being a witch, has again been attacked by an ignorant and inhuman mob. On Tuesday last she was carried through several of the streets, and was hooted and pelted as she passed along. A gentleman who interfered in her favor was greatly insulted, while those who recited innumerable instances of her art,

[11]To Lund Washington, Aug. 20, 1775, John C. Fitzpatrick, ed., *The Writings of George Washington . . .* , 39 vols. (Washington, D.C., 1931–1944), 3:433.

were listened to with curiosity and attention."[12] A few days later another newspaper reported "that in consequence of the barbarous treatment lately suffered by the poor old woman, called a *witch*, she died on Wednesday last."[13]

One need not defend New Englanders. They were quite able to defend and speak for themselves as they demonstrated at the First Continental Congress in 1774. Most of the New England delegates were provincials as compared with the southern delegates, some of whom had traveled in Europe and had been educated in England. So far as I know, John Adams had never been outside Massachusetts, nor had Sam Adams ever been outside Boston except to cross the Charles River to attend Harvard.

They knew they had bad reputations, but that did not bother them, for they believed that New Englanders were superior to all other Americans, a belief confirmed by the trip to Philadelphia. The Massachusetts delegates met kindred spirits in New York, but they met others who were not. Philip Livingston talked of the "levelling spirit" of New Englanders, compared them to Goths and Vandals, and "mentioned" the hanging of the Quakers.

Afterwards John Adams noted in his diary that Livingston was "a great, rough, rapid mortal. There is no holding any conversation with him. He blusters away." Adams concluded that "there is very little good breeding to be found" and that he had not "seen one real gentleman, one well bred man" in New York, and that there was no agreeable conversation. "They talk very loud, very fast, and all together. If they ask you a question, before you can utter three words of your answer, they will break out upon you, again—and talk away."[14]

John Adams was impressed by Philadelphia at first, but Silas Deane of Connecticut was not. He had been unable to eat

[12] *Pennsylvania Packet*, July 16, 1787.

[13] *Freeman's Journal*, July 25, 1787.

[14] Aug. 22 and 23, Butterfield, ed., *Diary and Autobiography of John Adams*, 2:107 and 109.

for twenty-four hours before he got there, and when he did he declared that the meat, vegetables, and fruit were no good. Philadelphians, he reported, think that nothing is "right" but their city and province and "they look on me mad when I tell them, that I have seen more good pasture, clover, meadow, oxen, and cows in a circle of three miles in Connecticut than is here to be met with in thirty, but it is true, and every New England man in the company tells them the same."[15] The next year he wrote that he had gone to a fair where there was "a vast crowd of girls" but that he could not find "one handsome face."[16] For what it is worth, Deane was reporting to his third wife.

After John Adams had been in Philadelphia awhile, he recorded in his diary that the city did not measure up to Boston. "The Morals of our people are much better, their manners are more polite, and agreeable—they are purer English. Our language is better, our persons are handsomer, our spirit is greater, our laws are wiser, our religion is superior, our education is better."[17]

The New Englanders were canny political operators on stage and off. Sam Adams had spent years identifying the Church of England with the Roman Catholic Church, which he called "the Whore of Babylon." But on the first day of the Congress he got up, announced that he was no bigot, and then moved that a Church of England clergyman open the next day's session with a prayer. Two days later an admiring Pennsylvanian told the Adamses that it was a "masterly stroke of policy."[18]

The next year, after Lexington and Concord, Congress was asked to take charge of the thousands of New Englanders besieging the British in Boston. Most New England dele-

---

[15] To Mrs. Elizabeth Deane, Aug. 31–Sept. 5, Paul H. Smith, ed., *Letters of Delegates to Congress, 1774–1789*, 6 vols. to date (Washington, D.C., 1976–), 1:16.

[16] July 15, 1775, ibid., p. 626.

[17] Oct. 9, Butterfield, ed., *Diary and Autobiography of John Adams*, 2:150.

[18] Sept. 10, ibid., 2:131.

gates wanted a New England general. But John Adams knew that many people feared the imperial ambitions of New Englanders. Therefore he nominated, to the anguish of John Hancock, who expected the post, the only member of Congress wearing a uniform, a Virginia planter named George Washington.[19]

The appointment was another "masterly stroke of policy." But fundamental differences remained. That was demonstrated in the dispute between New Englanders and others over army pay. New Englanders believed that there should be little difference in the pay of officers and privates. Southerners argued that there should be great distinctions and Congress agreed. John Adams explained that "those ideas of equality, which are so agreeable to us natives of New England, are very disagreeable to many gentlemen in the other colonies."[20]

Some months later he reported back to Massachusetts that "the characters of gentlemen in the four New England colonies, differ as much from those in the others, as that of the common people differs, that is as much as several distinct nations almost. Gentlemen, men of sense, or any kind of education in the other colonies are much fewer in proportion than in New England. Gentlemen in the other colonies have large plantations of slaves, and the common people among them are very ignorant and very poor. These gentlemen are accustomed, habituated to higher notions of themselves and the distinction between them and the common people, than we are."[21]

Some Southerners did indeed have higher notions of themselves, as did a Virginia planter who opposed Independence and charged that New Englanders wanted Independence so they could "embrace their darling democracy."[22]

[19] Ibid., 3:321–23.

[20] To Elbridge Gerry, June 18, 1775, Smith, ed., *Letters of Delegates to Congress*, 1:504.

[21] To Joseph Hawley, Nov. 25, 1775, ibid., 2:385.

[22] Carter Braxton to Landon Carter, Apr. 14, 1776, ibid., 3:522.

They were horrified by what they looked upon as the democratic state governments proposed in John Adams's *Thoughts on Government*. Patrick Henry, who hoped that Virginia would adopt such a government, explained that "there is among most of our opulent families a strong bias to aristocracy." "Go on, my dear friend," he urged Adams, "to assail the strongholds of tyranny."[23]

John Adams was anything but a social or political radical, but he was a small farmer's son. He replied to Henry: "The dons, the bashaws, the grandees, the patricians, the sachems, the nabobs . . . sigh, and groan, and fret, and sometimes stamp, and foam, and curse, but all in vain. The decree is gone forth, and it cannot be recalled, that a more equal liberty than has prevailed in other parts of the earth, must be established in America."[24]

A few weeks later Edward Rutledge of South Carolina spoke for bashaws and grandees. He was a member of the committee to prepare Articles of Confederation, and he opposed the first draft which, he said, destroyed provincial distinctions. That meant, he said, that the colonies "must be subject to the government of the eastern provinces" and detested New Englanders. "The force of their arms I hold exceeding cheap, but I confess I dread their overruling influence in council. I dread their low cunning, and those levelling principles which men without character and without fortune in general possess, which are so captivating to the lower class of mankind."[25]

A year and a half later when the Articles of Confederation were laid before the South Carolina legislature, William Henry Drayton denounced the constitution for its imprecision and because it left hardly a shadow of sovereignty to the states. He said that because of differences in soil, climate, and crops, a Northern interest and a Southern interest were in-

[23] May 20, 1776, Adams, ed., *Works*, 4:201.

[24] June 3, ibid., 9:387.

[25] To John Jay, June 29, Edmund Cody Burnett, ed., *Letters of Members of the Continental Congress*, 8 vols. (Washington, D.C., 1921–36), 1:517–18.

evitable. The North would control Congress and the result would be that "the honor, interest, and sovereignty of the South are in effect delivered up to the care of the North."[26]

New Englanders were equally certain that the South would dominate a central government. As early as 1754, when the Massachusetts legislature overwhelmingly rejected the Albany Plan of Union, one reason given was "the great sway which the Southern colonies . . . would have in all the determinations of the Grand Council."[27]

In the spring of 1778, shortly after Drayton denounced the Articles before the South Carolina legislature, the little farming village of West Springfield, Massachusetts, met to consider the Articles which the legislature had laid before the towns of the state. The farmers stated their views in language much like Drayton's. They pointed to the "weakness of human nature and the growing thirst for power" and then declared that "it is freedom, and not a choice of the forms of servitude for which we contend." The powers granted to Congress by the Articles were too large and "the sovereignty and independence of particular states nearly annihilated." The farmers added that they were not jealous of the present Congress, but, they asked, "who knows but in some future corrupt times there may be a Congress which will form a design upon the liberties of the people, and will it be difficult to execute such a design when [Congress] have the absolute command of the navy, the army, and the purse?"[28]

Massachusetts leaders disagreed with small farmers about most things, but they did agree that the states should retain their sovereignty. The Reverend William Gordon spoke for many of them in 1782, the year after the Articles were ratified. He warned that "if America becomes an empire, the seat of government will be to the southward, and the Northern States be insignificant provinces. Empire will suit the

[26] Jan. 20, 1778, Hezekiah Niles, ed., *Principles and Acts of the Revolution in America*, rev. ed. (New York, 1876), pp. 357–64.

[27] A. B. Hart, ed., *Commonwealth History of Massachusetts*, 5 vols. (New York, 1927–30), 2:461.

[28] Instructions to the Town's Representatives in the Legislature, Feb. 16, 1778, Force Transcripts, 2, Library of Congress.

southern gentry; they are habituated to despotism by being the sovereigns of slaves, and it is only accident and interest that has made the body of them the temporary sons of liberty." New Englanders should therefore be "resolute in retaining the sovereignty of the several states."[29]

The leaders of Massachusetts did not change their minds until the winter of 1786–87, when they were frightened half out of their wits by the small-farmer uprising known as Shays's Rebellion. They went to the Constitutional Convention in 1787 where they agreed with the other delegates that the central government should have the power to protect the states "against domestic Violence." The delegates also agreed unanimously that the state legislatures should be stopped from yielding to the demands of tax- and debt-ridden farmers as many of the states had done since the war by issuing paper money and interfering with the collection of private debts.

But that is where agreement in the Convention ended. The most heated debates among the states were over issues rooted in the past. One concerned representation by population. According to the census of 1790 three states—Virginia, Pennsylvania, and Massachusetts—had nearly one-half the population of the United States, with Virginia alone having over 20 percent. Delegates from those three states demanded representation by population in the first Congress in 1774 and during the writing of the Articles of Confederation in 1776, but they were defeated both times. Ten years later some of the same men turned up in the Constitutional Convention and demanded representation by population in both houses of Congress while delegates from the small states, and those who insisted that the states must be represented as states, declared that the large states were plotting to govern the United States.

The dispute tied up the Convention much of the time from its first day until the 16th of July when the Convention finally voted that the states should have equal votes in the Senate. The delegates from the large states threatened to

[29] To John Adams, Sept. 7, 1782, "Letters of the Reverend William Gordon . . . ," Massachusetts Historical Society *Proceedings* 63 (1929–30): 469.

withdraw and create a government for themselves, but finally accepted the decision, although they predicted chaos and anarchy because of it.

The small states' delegates remained suspicious, and on the last working day of the Convention a proviso was added at the end of Article V, the amending article of the Constitution. The proviso reads that "no State, without its Consent, shall be deprived of its equal Suffrage in the Senate."

Therefore the Supreme Court's "one man, one vote" decision of 1964, which applies to every other level of government, cannot apply to the United States Senate. Today, whatever the merits of representation by population, such states as Nevada with a half million people have an equal voice in the Senate with California's twenty million. One wonders, if a constitutional convention were held today, would the large states resume the struggle they lost three times between 1774 and 1787?

Far too much attention has been paid to this so-called great compromise. Far more important was the struggle between the eight sovereign states of the North and the five sovereign states of the South over the regulation of trade, slavery, and the balance of power between the two sections in the government of the nation.

The dispute between the North and the South over slavery and the regulation of trade began during the writing of the Articles of Confederation in 1776. The first draft provided that common expenses should be shared among the states "in proportion to the number of inhabitants of every age, sex and quality, except Indians not paying taxes."

New Englanders argued that total population was the best index of wealth, but Southerners objected at once. Samuel Chase of Maryland moved that expenses be shared according to white population. Slaves were wealth and personal property, he said. If they were taxed, why not count them in apportioning representation, and why not tax the fisheries and navigation of Massachusetts? "The Eastern Colonies," he added, "have a great advantage in trade. This will give them a superiority." Edward Rutledge of South Carolina agreed: "The Eastern Colonies will become the carriers for the

Southern. They will obtain wealth for which they will not be taxed."

James Wilson of Pennsylvania infuriated the Southerners. He told them that "slaves occupy the place of freemen and eat their food," that they should free their slaves, and furthermore, that the importation of slaves should be discouraged. Thomas Lynch of South Carolina replied that if it was debated whether slaves were property, "there is an end to the Confederation." Since slaves were property they should not be taxed any more than land, sheep, cattle, and horses. Benjamin Franklin did not soothe feelings when he retorted that there was a difference between slaves and sheep: "Sheep will never make any insurrections."

Chase's motion to share expenses according to white population was defeated by a solid sectional vote: seven Northern states against and five states—Delaware, Virginia, Maryland, and the two Carolinas—for it. Chase then declared that Maryland would never confederate if slaves were counted, and the Congress deadlocked.[30]

The question was dropped for over a year. Then in October 1777 Congress voted that expenses should be shared according to the value of all lands granted to or surveyed for individuals. The delegates from the four New England states voted unanimously against the decision, which they believed exploited New England and allowed Southerners to escape paying taxes on their wealth in slaves.

At the end of the war Northerners again proposed that expenses be shared among the states according to population. This time two Southerners, James Madison of Virginia and John Rutledge of South Carolina, offered a compromise: that three-fifths of the slaves be counted. Congress agreed and in April 1783 proposed an amendment to the

---

[30] John Adams, Notes of Debates, July 30, 1776, Butterfield, ed., *Diary and Autobiography of John Adams*, 2:245–46, and Thomas Jefferson, Notes of Proceedings, Julian P. Boyd et al., ed., *The Papers of Thomas Jefferson*, 19 vols. to date (Princeton, 1950–), 1:320–23. For this and other matters concerning the writing of the Articles of Confederation, see Merrill Jensen, *The Articles of Confederation: An Interpretation of the Social-Constitutional History of the American Revolution, 1774–1781* (Madison, 1940).

Articles providing that expenses should be shared according to "the whole number of white and other free citizens and inhabitants, of every age, sex and condition, including those bound to servitude for a term of years, and three-fifths of all other persons." "Other persons" were, of course, Negro slaves.[31]

Eleven men who debated the amendment in 1783, including Alexander Hamilton, James Madison, John Rutledge, and James Wilson, were members of the Constitutional Convention four years later. James Wilson, who had attacked slavery in 1776 and opposed the formula in 1783, introduced the language of the amendment in the Convention for quite another purpose, and with explosive results.

The dispute between the North and the South over the regulation of commerce was explosive before the Convention met. The basic issue was simple. Southerners, whose exports were by far the most valuable in the nation, wanted competition among shipowners of all nations which would mean lower freight rates and higher profits for themselves. Northerners, and particularly New Englanders, wanted exports and imports confined to American ships—in other words, a monopoly.

George Mason, on the last working day of the Constitutional Convention in 1787, stated the view of many Southerners. He asserted that the power of Congress to regulate commerce by a simple majority vote "would enable a few rich merchants in Philadelphia, New York, and Boston to monopolize the staples of the Southern States and reduce their value perhaps fifty percent."[32]

The New England attitude was stated with equal simplicity by two delegates to the Massachusetts Convention in January 1788. One delegate declared that three-fourths of the exports of the Southern states were carried in British ships.

[31] Merrill Jensen, ed., *The Documentary History of the Ratification of the Constitution*, 3 vols. to date (Madison, 1976–), 1:64 and 148–50.

[32] James Madison, Notes of Debates, Sept. 15, 1787, Max Farrand, ed., *The Records of the Federal Convention of 1787*, 3 vols. (New Haven, 1911), 2:631. These and other references to the debates in the Constitutional Convention are from Madison's notes, unless otherwise indicated.

"This," he cried, "is money which belongs to the New England States." The next day another delegate said he supposed that, in the opportunity to secure the carrying trade, "the New England States have a treasure offered to them better than the mines of Peru."[33]

Some Northern delegates at the First Continental Congress in 1774 had argued that commerce must be regulated by a central government, but the Articles of Confederation did not give Congress the power. However, Congress was given the exclusive power of making treaties, including commercial treaties. When the Virginia legislature ratified the Articles in December 1777, the principal objection was that Congress might use the treaty power to grant a monopoly of the carrying trade to Northern merchants.[34]

After the war when the British closed their West Indies to American ships, Northern merchants and some Southerners demanded that Congress be given the power to retaliate. Congress responded in 1784 by requesting the states for temporary power to regulate commerce. Then in 1785 a congressional committee proposed an amendment to the Articles to give Congress permanent power to regulate interstate and foreign commerce. But Southern opposition helped kill the amendment in Congress.

Richard Henry Lee, then president of Congress, spoke for the majority of Southerners when he said that to give Congress the power "would be dangerous in the extreme to the five Southern or Staple States, whose want of ships and seamen would expose their freightage and their produce to a most pernicious and destructive monopoly." The South would be "at the mercy of our East and North. The spirit of commerce throughout the world," declared Lee, "is a spirit of avarice."[35]

[33] Jan. 21 and 22, 1788, *Debates and Proceedings in the Convention of the Commonwealth of Massachusetts* . . . (Boston, 1856), pp. 157–58 and 167.

[34] Thomas Jefferson to John Adams, Dec. 17, 1777, Boyd, ed., *Papers of Jefferson*, 2:120–21.

[35] To James Madison, Aug. 11, 1785, Robert A. Rutland et al., eds., *The Papers of James Madison*, 13 vols. to date (Chicago and Charlottesville, Va., 1962–), 8:340.

Frustrated Northerners began threatening to break up the Union and form a separate confederation, and such talk mounted until the eve of the Constitutional Convention. Meanwhile, Southern fears of Northern intentions were confirmed in the summer of 1786. John Jay, secretary for foreign affairs, requested Congress for permission to make a treaty with Spain that would surrender the United States claim of right to navigate the Mississippi River for twenty-five or more years in exchange for privileges for American merchants in Spanish ports. The Northern states voted solidly for the proposal and the five Southern states voted solidly against it. Southern opposition meant that such a treaty could never be ratified because the Articles required a two-thirds vote—the vote of nine states—to ratify treaties.

A far greater issue than commerce was involved in the proposed treaty with Spain. What was also at stake was the balance of power between the North and the South. Congress had accepted the Virginia cession of the Old Northwest in 1784 and had agreed that it should be divided into states. But settlement in the near future seemed unlikely because powerful Indian tribes threatened to exterminate settlers and the British retained their military posts in the area.

Meanwhile land-hungry Americans from all over the country were pouring across the mountains into the Southern backcountry. The migration began before the end of the Revolutionary War and was so rapid that by 1790 Kentucky had about 75,000 and Tennessee about 35,000 people, while settlers in backcountry Georgia increased that state's population from about 35,000 in 1776 to over 82,000 in 1790.

Settlers in Tennessee declared their independence from North Carolina in 1784 and established the state of Franklin. Virginia passed its first act for Kentucky statehood in 1785. Northerners and Southerners alike knew that the first new states would be Southern states, and they were fully aware what that would mean for the balance of power between the two sections. In fact, as early as the summer of 1783 a writer in a Maryland newspaper foreshadowed the dispute to come when he commented that "emigration from abroad prevails much more in the Southern States than in those to the eastward, especially to the back settlements; no one therefore can safely venture to predict which part of the Continent will be most potent or consequential a century hence, or how many additional states will by that time be formed." Four years later Pierce Butler of South Carolina rather smugly told the Constitutional Convention that "the people and strength of America are evidently bearing southwardly and southwestwardly."[36]

The disputes between the North and the South over slavery, the slave trade, the regulation of commerce, and western expansion embroiled the Constitutional Convention from the middle of July until the final session on September 17. They were far more bitter than those between the large and the small states and came far closer to breaking up the Convention.

James Wilson brought the issue of slavery into the Convention early in June. His purpose was to win Southern support for representation according to population in both houses of Congress, and in particular, the support of the South Carolinians who had argued ever since 1776 that representation should be based on wealth. Wilson quoted the 1783 amendment to the Articles of Confederation and then moved that "three-fifths of all other persons" be counted in apportioning representatives in the House. Southerners had no objections whatever to counting three-fifths of their slaves and only Elbridge Gerry of Massachusetts objected. The Convention adopted the motion nine states to two, and it became a part of the Constitution despite later attacks upon it.[37]

Trouble began a month later when a committee apportioned members in the House of Representatives among the states. A Massachusetts delegate at once denounced the "gross inequality" of the apportionment because it gave the four southernmost states more representatives than the four New England states, which, he said, had more people. A South Carolinian replied that the South insisted on some-

[36] "A True American," *Maryland Journal and Baltimore Advertiser*, July 29, 1783; July 13, 1787, Farrand, ed., *Records*, 1:605.

[37] June 11, 1787, Farrand, ed., *Records*, 1:201.

thing like equality, for if the South did not have it, and Congress had the power to regulate trade, Southerners would be nothing more than "overseers for the Northern States."[38]

Northerners and Southerners alike knew that the North would have a majority in the first House of Representatives, and the Southerners were convinced that the North would never give up that majority unless forced to do so. Therefore, Gov. Edmund Randolph of Virginia proposed that the Constitution itself require a regular census and reapportionment of the House after each census.

The Southerners, to a man, supported the required census. Northerners declared that the census would shackle the powers of Congress, but they soon abandoned that argument. Northerners had begun opposing the admission of new states by the end of 1785. Now they argued that if new states were admitted, they should never be given enough representatives to outvote the original thirteen. Finally they got to their real objection: The first new states would be Southern states and they would join with the older Southern states in an agrarian persecution of commerce.

The South Carolinians countered by demanding that all slaves be counted in apportioning representatives, whereupon James Wilson, who had proposed slave representation a month earlier, now said that he did not see upon what principle the representation of three-fifths of the slaves could be explained. Gouverneur Morris then asserted that he would never agree to encouraging the slave trade by allowing representation for slaves.[39]

A North Carolinian replied that if the North eliminated slave representation, the South would never "confederate" and that the business of the Convention was at an end.[40] Morris retorted that the South would never be satisfied until it got a majority in Congress and that would mean "such an oppression of commerce" that he would vote for the "vicious

[38] July 10, ibid., pp. 566–67.

[39] July 11, ibid., pp. 587–88.

[40] July 12, ibid., pp. 593.

principle of equality" in the Senate to protect the Northern states.[41]

The Southerners got enough help from Northerners to place in the Constitution the requirement for a census every ten years, followed by reapportionment of the House of Representatives. Furthermore, the Southerners blocked Northern attempts to insert in the Constitution a provision preventing the admission of new states on a basis of equality with the original thirteen.

The debate broke out with more heat than ever after the first draft of the Constitution was submitted on August 6. It was written by a five-man committee of which John Rutledge of South Carolina was chairman. It is clear that he, Edmund Randolph of Virginia, and Oliver Ellsworth of Connecticut, a born compromiser, had overridden the two spokesmen for Northern merchants, James Wilson of Pennsylvania and Nathaniel Gorham of Massachusetts.

The draft Constitution protected Southern interests in three ways. First, Congress could not levy export duties, and hence raise money from Southern exports such as tobacco. Second, Congress could not levy import duties upon "such persons" as the states might choose to import, and hence interfere with the slave trade. Third, Congress could not regulate trade except by a two-thirds vote of each house, thus giving the senators from the five Southern states the veto power.

Northerners were outraged. Nathaniel Gorham, a member of the committee, declared that "the Eastern States had no motive to Union but a commercial one" and that they did not need the help of the Southern states.[42] Gouverneur Morris compared the happiness and prosperity of the Middle states with the "misery and poverty which overspread the barren wastes of Virginia, Maryland, and other states having slaves." He asserted that if export taxes were forbidden, and if slaves were imported free of duty, Northern freemen would be exploited to pay the costs of the government. Fur-

[41] July 13, ibid., pp. 604.

[42] Aug. 22, ibid., 2:374.

thermore, the South would acquire more and more representatives based on slavery.[43]

Morris and other Northerners then attacked the slave trade and insisted that the new government should have the power to prohibit it. They were joined by two maverick Southerners. Luther Martin of Maryland declared that the trade was "inconsistent with the principles of the Revolution," while George Mason of Virginia denounced it as an "infernal traffic," and in an aside, "lamented that some of our Eastern brethren had from a lust of gain embarked in this nefarious traffic."[44]

John Rutledge replied that "religion and humanity had nothing to do with" the slave trade, for "interest alone is the governing principle with nations," and the three southernmost states would "never be such fools as to give up so important an interest." The true question, he said flatly, was whether the South would stay in the Union. General Pinckney, a fellow delegate from South Carolina, remarked that the reason Virginia opposed the slave trade was because it wanted a higher price for its surplus slaves, and agreed that if the slave trade was prohibited, it would exclude the South from the Union.[45]

The Convention was deadlocked, and even the most intransigent opponents realized it would collapse if the deadlock was not broken. Gouverneur Morris, who made more speeches than any other delegate to the Convention, who had talked on every side of almost every subject, and who had done more to antagonize the South than any other Northerner, now moved that a committee be appointed to work out what he called a "bargain among the Northern and Southern states."[46]

Delegates on both sides declared they would never bargain on this or that point, but two days later a committee reported a simple two-part deal between the New Englanders and the

[43] Aug. 8, ibid., pp. 221–23.

[44] Aug. 21 and 22, ibid., pp. 364 and 370.

[45] Aug. 21 and 22, ibid., pp. 364, 371, and 373.

[46] Aug. 22, ibid., p. 374.

Carolinians and Georgians. First, the migration or importation of "such persons" as the states chose to admit could not be prohibited until the year 1800, and a tax could be levied on their importation. Second, acts regulating commerce could be passed by simple majorities of both houses of Congress.

Delegates from various states objected loudly but the New England and the southernmost states pushed through the bargain after prohibiting Congress from interfering with the slave trade until after the year 1808, and providing that "such persons" could not be taxed more than ten dollars on importation, the only amount of money mentioned in the Constitution. All attempts to break the bargain failed as South Carolinians and New Englanders professed, however hypocritically, admiration for one another.

The Southerners, who had vivid memories of the proposed treaty with Spain the year before, and how they had blocked it, won a final concession. The Convention agreed that treaties must be ratified by the votes of two-thirds of the senators present. That decision, made almost incidentally near the end of the Convention, has had consequences no one at the time dreamed of.

The constitutional framework within which the United States functions today was thus shaped in part by the struggles among the sovereign states two centuries ago. The struggle between the large and the small states led to the constitutional guarantee that no state can be deprived of its equality in the Senate without its consent. In effect, therefore, that is the only part of the Constitution which cannot be amended since no small state would ever be likely to give up its equality in the Senate.

The struggle between the Northern and the Southern states led to the requirement of a census every ten years and the regular reapportionment of the House of Representatives, to the requirement that new states must be admitted to the Union on the basis of equality with the older states, to the requirement that treaties must be ratified by two-thirds of the senators present, and to the provision that trade can be regulated by simple majorities of both houses of Congress.

There was, however, one issue that transcended all others. The question of whether a "federal union of sovereign states" or a "national government" was best for the United States was the fundamental political and constitutional issue that divided Americans of the Revolutionary generation. For the most part men's answers were the result of their basic convictions about the nature of man and society, not of state and regional loyalties.

The Revolutionary leaders who controlled events in 1776 believed that each state should retain its sovereignty and independence, a belief expressed in the first constitution of the United States, the Articles of Confederation. Article 2 of the Articles declares that "each State retains its sovereignty, freedom and independence, and every power, jurisdiction, and right, which is not by this confederation expressly delegated to the United States, in Congress assembled."

But there were other leaders who from the beginning of the Revolution believed that the central government must have far more power than provided for by the Articles of Confederation, and such men constituted a majority of the Constitutional Convention in 1787. The Confederation Congress had called the Convention for the "sole and express purpose" of revising the Articles of Confederation, but on the second working day the Convention abandoned the Articles. After listening to a resolution declaring that "an union of the states, merely federal, will not accomplish the objects proposed by the Articles of Confederation," the delegates voted that "a national government ought to be established."[47]

The delegates soon divided on the issue of how "national" the new government should be. At one extreme was a small group of "nationalists" who wanted to abolish the states, or at the most, keep them as mere administrative districts subject to the absolute will of Congress. At the other extreme was a small group "federalists" who proposed amendments to the Articles to give Congress certain specific additional powers. In the middle were the delegates who insisted that the states were political realities that could not be ignored

[47] Journal of the Convention, May 30, Farrand, ed., *Records*, 1:30–31.

and that they must play a role in the future of the nation. As a result the Constitution contains a mixture of "national" and "federal" features. But in the end the extreme nationalists achieved their goal, the transfer of ultimate political and constitutional power from the sovereign states to a sovereign central government.

That goal was expressed in the "supreme law" clause of the Constitution (Article VI, paragraph 2), which reads: "This Constitution, and the Laws of the United States which shall be made in Pursuance thereof; and all Treaties made, or which shall be made, under the Authority of the United States, shall be the supreme Law of the Land; and the Judges in every State shall be bound thereby, any Thing in the Constitution or Laws of any State to the Contrary notwithstanding." Furthermore, "the Members of the several State Legislatures, and all executive and judicial Officers, both of the United States and of the several States, shall be bound by Oath or Affirmation, to support this Constitution."

Thus the Constitution provided for a "national" rather than a "federal" government. However, the supporters of the Constitution called themselves "Federalists" and labeled its opponents "Antifederalists." The labels have misled posterity, but they did not mislead newspaper writers and political leaders at the time. Thus after Samuel Adams read the Constitution for the first time, he wrote to his old friend Richard Henry Lee: "I confess, as I enter the building, I stumble at the threshold. I meet with a National Government instead of a Federal Union of Sovereign States."[48]

Americans have debated from that day to this whether the Constitution provides for a "national" or a "federal" government, and today there are those who still talk of a "new federalism" of returning power to the states. But such people's mouths are worked by ancient memories, not by present-day realities: "The realities of political and economic life in the twentieth century have created an all-powerful national government in fact. Hence under the 'constitution' as it exists in

---

[48] Dec. 3, 1787, Lee Papers, American Philosophical Society Library, Philadelphia.

practice, the central government has almost unlimited powers. And the only limitations on the exercise of ultimate power are more dependent upon the exigencies of politics and upon the self-restraint of those who govern than upon the restraints set forth in the Constitution of 1787."[49]

[49] Merrill Jensen, *The Making of the American Constitution* (New York, 1964), p. 151.

Contributors
Index

Contributors

EDWARD COUNTRYMAN is a Lecturer in the Joint School of Comparative American Studies at the University of Warwick, England, of which he was Acting Chairman in the spring of 1980. He has taught at the University of Canterbury, New Zealand, and, as a visitor, at the University of Cambridge. His publications include *A People in Revolution: The American Revolution and Political Society in New York, 1760–1790* (1981) and essays which have appeared in a number of journals and anthologies. His current research interests include radical thought in the Revolutionary period, comparative study of the American Revolution and the Spanish-American wars of independence, and the image of the Revolution in Hollywood films.

EMORY G. EVANS is Professor and Chair, Department of History, University of Maryland—College Park. He is the author of, among others, "Planter Indebtedness and the Coming of the Revolution in Virginia" (1962), "Private Indebtedness and the Revolution in Virginia, 1776–1796" (1971), and *Thomas Nelson of Yorktown: Revolutionary Virginian* (1975). Current projects include research on disaffection in Virginia during the Revolution and a long-term study of the Virginia elite in the eighteenth century.

MERRILL JENSEN was Professor of History at the University of Wisconsin, Madison. His publications were legion. His major books included *The Articles of Confederation: An Interpretation of the Social-Constitutional History of the American Revolution, 1774–1781* (1940), *The New Nation: A History of the United States during the Confederation, 1781–1789* (1950), and *The Founding of a Nation: A History of the American Revolution, 1763–1776* (1968). He edited several books, including a volume in the series English Historical Documents, *American Colonial Documents to 1776* (1955). In addition he served as director of two documentary publication projects: The Documentary History of the First Federal Elections and The Documentary History of the Ratification of the Constitution. Merrill Jensen died on January 30, 1980.

JACKSON TURNER MAIN received his Ph.D. from Wisconsin in 1949. He has taught at several institutions, notably Washington and Jefferson College, Whitman College, San Jose State University, the University of Maryland, and the State University of New York at Stony Brook, where he is currently a Professor. He has published six books including *The Antifederalists: Critics of the Constitution, 1781–1788* (1961), *Political Parties before the Constitution* (1973), and *The Sovereign States, 1775–1783* (1973). He is now concentrating on social history, particularly that of colonial Connecticut.

JEROME J. NADELHAFT is Associate Professor of History at the University of Maine, Orono; he received his Ph.D. from the University of Wisconsin in 1965. Professor Nadelhaft's major publications include "The Somersett Case and Slavery: Myth, Reality, and Repercussions" (1966), "Politics and the Judicial Tenure Fight in Colonial New Jersey" (1971), and *The Disorders of War: The Revolution in South Carolina, 1775–1790* (1981). "The Englishwoman's Sexual Civil War: Feminist Attitudes towards Men, Women, and Marriage, 1650–1740," is forthcoming. He is currently working on a study of America in the 1730s and 1740s.

EDWARD C. PAPENFUSE, Archivist of Maryland since 1975, is an American historian with primary interest in the seventeenth and eighteenth centuries. He has written extensively on archival matters (for example, see *An Inventory of Maryland State Papers*, 1977, and *A Guide to the Maryland Hall of Records: Local, Judicial, and Administrative Records on Microform*, 1978) and is managing editor of the blue book of Maryland state government, the biennial *Maryland Manual*. He is the author of a study of the economy and society of late eighteenth-century Annapolis, *In Pursuit of Profit: The Annapolis Merchants in the Era of the American Revolution, 1763–1805* (1975), coauthor of *A Biographical Dictionary of the Maryland Legislature, 1635–1789* (1978), and coauthor of a major revision of a WPA tour guide, *Maryland: A New Guide to the Old Line State* (1976). His atlas of *Historical Maryland Maps* will be published by The Johns Hopkins University Press in 1982. He is currently working on two books, the second volume of the *Biographical Dictionary* and a study of the English origins of Maryland, focusing on the granting of the Charter (1632) and the promotional efforts that led to colonization.

Contributors

STEPHEN E. PATTERSON is Professor of History at the University of
New Brunswick. His published work includes *Political Parties in
Revolutionary Massachusetts* and several articles. At present he is
engaged in writing a short history of the American Revolution
as well as in researching the political behavior of colonial and
early national elite groups. His article in this volume explores
some of the themes that he hopes to incorporate in a book ten-
tatively entitled "The Origins of American Conservatism."

RICHARD ALAN RYERSON was educated at Harvard College and at
The Johns Hopkins University, where he took his Ph.D. in history in 1972. He has published *The Revolution Is Now Begun: The
Radical Committees of Philadelphia, 1765–1776* (1978). He has held
postdoctoral fellowships at the University of Pennsylvania and,
in 1978–79, at Harvard University's Charles Warren Center,
where he wrote the essay in this collection. His current research
interests focus on eighteenth-century American politics both before and after the Revolution, particularly in Pennsylvania. He
is presently Associate Editor of The Papers of William Penn, at
the Historical Society of Pennsylvania, and is an active partici-
pant in the University of Pennsylvania's Philadelphia Center for
Early American Studies.

Index

INDEX

INDEX